INTELLECTUAL PROPERTY IN THE 21ST CENTURY

TARGETING WEBSITES DEDICATED TO STEALING AMERICAN INTELLECTUAL PROPERTY

INTELLECTUAL PROPERTY IN THE 21ST CENTURY

Additional books and e-books in this series can be found on Nova's website under the Series tab.

INTELLECTUAL PROPERTY IN THE 21ST CENTURY

TARGETING WEBSITES DEDICATED TO STEALING AMERICAN INTELLECTUAL PROPERTY

ANTHONY L. MOONEY

snova
New York

Library of Congress Cataloging-in-Publication Data

ISBN: 978-1-53613-705-7

Published by Nova Science Publishers, Inc. † New York

CONTENTS

PREFACE*

The problem of online infringement is real. It is substantial, and it causes a drain on our economy and it costs American jobs. Copyright piracy and the sale of counterfeit goods are reported to cost the American economy billions of dollars a year, thousands of lost jobs. This book includes the testimony of a range of witnesses that testify about how we can make some progress in the fight again online infringement and also the sale of counterfeit goods.

---

* This is an edited, reformatted, and augmented version of a Hearing before the Committee on the Judiciary United States Senate, One Hundred Twelfth Congress, First Session, Serial No. J-112-5, dated February 16, 2011.

In: Targeting Websites …
Editor: Anthony L. Mooney
ISBN: 978-1-53613-705-7

Chapter 1

STATEMENTS OF COMMITTEE MEMBERS

The Committee met, pursuant to notice, at 10:05 a.m., in room SD–226, Dirksen Senate Office Building, Hon. Patrick J. Leahy, Chairman of the Committee, presiding.

Present: Senators Leahy, Whitehouse, Klobuchar, Franken, Coons, Blumenthal, Grassley, Kyl, and Coburn

OPENING STATEMENT OF HON. PATRICK J. LEAHY, A U.S. SENATOR FROM THE STATE OF VERMONT

Chairman LEAHY. Good morning. I want to thank the witnesses who are here today to testify about how we can make some progress in the fight against online copyright infringement and also the sale of counterfeit goods. Last Congress, I introduced legislation, cosponsored by 12 other Senators on this Committee, to combat "rogue websites" that do nothing but traffic in infringing material. I thank those Senators who joined me, including Senator Hatch, who was the lead cosponsor and is a long-time leader on intellectual property issues, and, of course, our Ranking Member, Senator Grassley. I note that because sometimes you only read that members of opposite parties only work against each other, and this Committee has had a long record of working together in a bipartisan way on a whole number of issues, certainly in the high-tech area, but in the criminal area, fraud, oversight, and so on.

The legislation was then approved unanimously by the Senate Judiciary Committee, 19–0. Now, there are some concerns on both sides of the aisle which we will try to address. Some intellectual property owners argue that the legislation did not go far enough; others are concerned it may go too far. Senator Coburn asked me if we could hold this hearing to give all sides an opportunity to address this issue. At his request I have done that.

We work to address issues, but let us be clear. When we look at those issues, the problem of online infringement is real; it is substantial; and it causes a drain on our economy, it costs American jobs. Copyright piracy and the sale of counterfeit goods are reported to cost the American economy billions of dollars a year, thousands of lost jobs. A January study found that nearly 24 percent of all Internet traffic worldwide is infringing. It is a staggering number; it is growing. Certainly those of us on this Committee who have been in law enforcement—and there are several; I see Senator Blumenthal has just joined us. If you had somebody who was breaking into a warehouse and stealing a few hundred thousand dollars' worth of items, why, you would want to get after that. Well, you have these people stealing millions and billions of dollars. We ought to be just as incensed on that. So inaction is not an option. I think we have to pass online infringement legislation in this Congress before rogue websites harm more businesses and result in more lost jobs, because what they do is theft, pure and simple. They are no more than digital stores selling stolen and, in the case of counterfeits, often dangerous products. If they existed in the physical world, everybody would agree that you should shutter them and their proprietors arrested. And we cannot excuse the behavior because it happens on the Internet and the owners operate overseas. The Internet needs to be free and open, but not lawless.

Every one of the witnesses here today has an interest in an Internet marketplace that remains vibrant and continues to expand. I suspect no one here condones rogue websites. We have an interest in keeping Internet activity lawful. If we lose confidence that the products we are purchasing online are the real things rather than counterfeit, it hurts the entire Internet ecosystem.

I know some market participants have become more aggressive on their own initiative since we began consideration of a legislative approach to this problem last June. I commend them. After all, legislative action alone cannot possibly achieve the effects of self-policing in the private sector. MasterCard, for instance, has been working closely and productively with the intellectual property community to make sure they are not processing payments from sites that are trafficking in illegal goods. I know Visa has begun discussions with the IP community in that same way.

But voluntary conduct is not enough. Court orders are often necessary for appropriate action. AT&T first suggested in written comments an approach that allows law enforcement to seek a court order that could be used by AT&T and other Internet service providers to prevent rogue websites based overseas from reaching us. I applaud their leadership. That model not only became the basis of our legislation last year, but it is consistent with the work law enforcement has done recently.

So I am convinced we will pass legislation to target rogue websites this year. I want to hear from all sides. But I do refuse to accept that the problem is too difficult because people who want to steal will always find a way. That is like saying we should not prosecute drug crimes or child pornography because people will always find a way to do bad things anyway. As a former prosecutor, I find that line of argument unacceptable.

I have talked with Chairman Smith in the House. I intend to work closely with him and with other Members of the House who have been leaders on this issue. And I look forward to continuing to work with Senator Grassley and other members of this Committee. This issue is one of those like patent reform on which we can work in a truly bipartisan and bicameral basis. After all, as I said in a speech earlier this month, when you have the Chamber of Commerce and organized labor come together in support of legislation to address this problem, then so can Democrats and Republicans in both the House and Senate.

STATEMENT OF HON. CHUCK GRASSLEY, A U.S. SENATOR FROM THE STATE OF IOWA

Senator GRASSLEY. Before I go to my statement, I would follow up on three things. One, I may have to temporarily leave to go down the hall to help make a majority in the Finance Committee. And that reminds me. Since this involves intellectual property and trade and piracy, it is also issues that we deal with on trade issues down in the Finance Committee as well over the last several years. And the third one would be a commentary on your comment about this being a bipartisan issue. Very true, and stressing that, because people think that everything around here is very partisan. And I always remind my constituents that the reason they think everything is partisan around here is because controversy is what makes news, you know. And, consequently, when people get along, it is not very well noticed by the press.

I appreciate your holding this hearing on this very important subject. I agree that increased online theft of intellectual property has really become a rampant problem. There is a lot of interest in going after criminals who engage in pervasive piracy and counterfeiting online. That is because the impact of copyright piracy and sale of counterfeit goods imposes a huge cost on our American economy, which means lost jobs and lost sales and lost income. In fact, these detrimental impacts go far beyond the American economy. We recently had a report estimating that counterfeiting and piracy resulted in 2.5 million jobs lost in the G–20 economies, and that the global value of counterfeited and pirated goods exceeds $650 billion. Obviously, those are staggering numbers.

Piracy and counterfeiting also can present serious health and safety problems because we have counterfeit products such as ineffective pharmaceuticals, defective electrical products, tainted toothpaste, malfunctioning equipment, and sub-par materials, all posing dangers to the American consuming public. Addressing this problem would help protect consumers.

A large chunk of this piracy and counterfeiting is done online. That is because the internet reaches across the globe and is mostly anonymous. Moreover, part of the problem is that many Internet websites that engage in offering infringing content and counterfeit goods are actually foreign owned and operated. These websites appeal to American consumers because they reside at familiar top- level domains, such as .com or .net. These websites also appear to be legitimate because they have corporate advertising and credit card acceptance.

Today our testimony on the scope of intellectual property theft over the Internet and what efforts have been undertaken to combat this scourge, of course, is very needed information. I am interested in hearing whether the witnesses support or have concerns with the legislation that the Senate has proposed to address the problem. I am certain that everyone supports the underlying goals of S. 3804, the Combating Online Infringement and Counterfeiting Act, a bill that was introduced in the last Congress.

That said, a number of concerns have been raised about that bill, and it is appropriate for the Committee to look into those concerns to determine whether they are legitimate and should be addressed.

Certainly, we should act responsibly so that we do not harm consumers, innovation, or economic growth.

Thank you, Mr. Chairman.

Chairman LEAHY. Thank you.

Our first witness—and I should ask Senator Kyl, how long are you going to be able to stay with us?

Senator KYL. Mr. Chairman, I have got the same problem Senator Grassley does. We both are going to have to get over to the Finance Committee, and, therefore, I have the opportunity to introduce the witness, if I could be excused.

Chairman LEAHY. I am going to take the witnesses in the order they are here, but if you would like to introduce Ms. Jones out of order, why don't you just go now. Then you will be able to leave.

Senator KYL. I appreciate it. And I want to join Senator Grassley in thanking you for holding this hearing on an extremely important topic and to re-emphasize what he did about the bipartisan nature of this and, of course, my work in support of the Leahy bill on patent reform, which is just another example.

But I would like your permission to introduce a good friend of mine and a very important witness for us, and that is Christine Jones. She is the general counsel and corporate secretary for the Go Daddy Group of companies and is responsible for all of the legal affairs of that Go Daddy Group, including the two departments which deal with websites devoted to stealing intellectual property, which is the subject of the hearing today. She was the company's first lawyer and made it a priority to put Go Daddy on the leading edge of addressing bad actors on the Internet. She has helped to push through legislation aimed at protecting kids online, fighting the problem of illegal online drug sellers, and she has been a repeat visitor to the witness table here in Washington, having testified on numerous Internet-related issues in Congressional committees in recent years.

On a personal note, prior to joining Go Daddy, Christine worked as a commercial litigator and prosecutor and CPA. I first met her in 1997 when she first moved to Arizona. She has been very active in our community affairs, and I just also would add that one of the soft spots in my heart for Go Daddy is the fact that they are a big sponsor of car racing, which I am kind of a nut for, both Indy car racing and NASCAR racing. But obviously they do some incredibly important work in this problem of intellectual property, and I am delighted that Christine Jones will be here to testify today.

Thank you, Mr. Chairman.

Chairman LEAHY. Thank you. I will resist talking about the ad Go Daddy once had about appearing before a Senate Committee. [Laughter.]

Chairman LEAHY. This is not the one.

Senator COBURN. Mr. Chairman.

Chairman LEAHY. Yes?

Senator COBURN. Just to note I will have to go to the Finance Committee as well, so I am going to be here, and if I do not get a chance to question, I will submit questions.

Chairman LEAHY. Well, thank you very much. As I said before you came in, the reason we are having this hearing is at your request.

I wanted to give Senator Kyl, because I know he has to leave, that opportunity of introducing Ms. Jones because even privately he said some very nice things about you, too. So I wanted him to have the chance——

[Laughter.]

Chairman LEAHY. You know, it is not just what we say on the record, but if we say it in private, it is even better.

Tom Adams is chief executive officer of Rosetta Stone, a position he has held since joining the company in 2003. In his role as CEO, Mr. Adams was recognized in 2009 as the Ernst & Young Entrepreneur of the Year National Category Winner, and well deserved, I might say. As a native of Sweden, Mr. Adams is fluent in a number of languages, including Swedish, French, and English, and a working knowledge of Spanish. C'est bien.

Mr. Adams received his bachelor's degree from Bristol University in England, his master's from the international business school INSEAD.

Please go ahead, Mr. Adams. What I am going to do is I am going to have each witness testify, and then we will open it up for questions for all of you.

Go ahead, Mr. Adams. There should be a button that says "Talk."

In: Targeting Websites …
Editor: Anthony L. Mooney
ISBN: 978-1-53613-705-7

Chapter 2

WITNESSES

STATEMENT OF TOM ADAMS, PRESIDENT AND CHIEF EXECUTIVE OFFICER, ROSETTA STONE INC., ARLINGTON, VIRGINIA

Mr. ADAMS. Senator Leahy, Senator Grassley, and the rest of the Committee, thank you very much for holding this meeting today. My name is Tom Adams. I am CEO of Rosetta Stone, and our company, Rosetta Stone, has sort of grown up here in America. We have over 2,000 employees right now. We teach 30 languages. And over the past several years, we have frankly been under attack by pirates and counterfeiters that over time have appropriated our name and have used the ecosystem here in the United States to reach the U.S. consumer.

So I want to thank you for recognizing the harm that rogue websites cause the American consumer and businesses, too. American companies today are losing the battle against the counterfeiters. The amount of criminal activity is astounding. Our company has had over 1,000 websites created like these websites right here. None of these are legitimate website home pages of RosettaStone.com, although they look very similar. They have very similar URLs where they will, for example, call themselves RosettaStone-site.com, and so the entire purpose of these websites is to deceive the U.S. consumer.

While we welcome all aspects of the legislation contemplated, we are concerned that a key element of the ecosystem is not being addressed directly. Almost all these websites are first discovered—or the preponderance of discovery of these websites happens through search engines. So American consumers are looking for Rosetta Stone, let us say. They will type into the search box, and they will see on websites like Google and Yahoo! search results. Some of these search results are organic, and some are paid. And you can see here all the marked areas where these are fraudulent sites claiming to be selling Rosetta Stone. The URLs use the word “Rosetta” very often, and “Rosetta” is used in the header. And all of this is to confuse the consumer.

The consequences of this are that consumers end up with product that is faulty. It often does not work. They believe they have transacted with our company so they call our customer service. And so on a daily basis we get calls from customers who believe that Rosetta Stone is not a quality provider of software products, although we take great pride in the legitimate products that we sell through our own site. And so as a result, there is brand damage; there are consumers passing over their financial information to sites that they trust because they show “Rosetta Stone.” And all of this is happening, frankly, because of an ecosystem that is supporting this activity and which makes this activity profitable.

Many of the search engines say that it is very difficult for them to work against this problem, but we have seen a repeated number of times that they put on filters which do not have any pirates for a while. I would contend that that is the case today, but those pirates come back time after time.

The key issue is, of course, that there is a profit that is being made on these activities by payment processors or by search engines and so on. So there are many companies here in the ecosystem that make money from this illicit activity, and we simply must stop that, and we hope that this Committee is successful in moving the legislation forward.

I want to thank you all again for giving us the opportunity to appear at this hearing today. We are passionate about your issue, and we will do whatever we can to help support the very positive actions that you have taken so far.

[The prepared statement of Mr. Adams appears as a submission for the record.]

Chairman LEAHY. Thank you very much. I share your frustration. I am one who goes online often, and you want to make sure you are in the right place. But we will get further into that.

Our next witness is Scott Turow, a writer and an attorney. He is here today as President of the Authors Guild, the largest society of published authors in the United States. He has written eight best-selling books including "Presumed Innocent." He has been a partner in the Chicago office of—I am going to mispronounce this. Sonnenschein?

Mr. TUROW. Yes.

Chairman LEAHY.—Nath and Rosenthal since 1986. He has concentrated on white-collar criminal defense and pro bono matters. He was an Assistant U.S. Attorney in Chicago. He graduated from Amherst College and received his law degree from Harvard. We have known each other for years, and I believe it was Senator Durbin of this Committee who first introduced us.

Please go ahead, sir.

STATEMENT OF SCOTT TUROW, PRESIDENT, AUTHORS GUILD, NEW YORK, NEW YORK

Mr. TUROW. Thank you, Mr. Chairman.

First I want to express my gratitude that these hearings are being held. I do not believe it is hyperbolic to say that if piracy of intellectual property is allowed to go unchecked, it will either gravely damage or even destroy the creative community in the United States. And if I may, I would like to augment my written remarks with some personal observations.

I published a new novel——

Chairman LEAHY. And I should note that all the statements will be placed in the record in full, but please go ahead, sir.

Mr. TUROW. With gratitude, thank you, Mr. Chairman.

I published a new novel last May. I was lucky enough that it landed almost immediately on the various best-seller lists. And within the first week or two that it was available for sale, I had friends, four of them from different venues, some in publishing, some who had just been cruising the net, who informed me that there were pirated versions of my book available and, of course, at a fraction of the price at which legitimate venues were selling it. And what began then was, frankly, a game of whack-a-mole with my publisher sending take-down letters and new sites popping up where pirated copies of "Innocent" were on sale again.

You know, I came today with my iPad. I enjoy the benefits of the digital revolution, but it brings enormous peril particularly for authors. The sale of these devices, of course, is growing rapidly. The bigger that market gets, the larger the market is for the pirates. And my concern is not to protect the incomes of best-selling authors. My concern instead is for the sake of our literary culture.

At this point in time, because of the Internet and a number of other sources, American publishing is, frankly, wobbly. In 2008, which is the last year for which I have statistics, there were only two American publishing groups that reported a profit. And if the pirates destroy the remaining margin in the publishing industry, it will, frankly, collapse and with that will go the guidance of editors and, more significantly, the function that publishers actually play as the investment bankers or the venture capitalists, really, in our literary culture. They advance money to authors so authors can write books in the hope that those books will be profitable.

As you might expect, as the President of the Authors Guild, my concerns are even more so for our members. It is a hard world in which to get a book published. If piracy destroys the small margins that remain for publishers in books that are not going to be best sellers, those books will not be published at all. We will not hear new voices. Authors who are at the middle of their career will be stilled, and our cultural conversation will become stilted and impoverished.

The consequences are dire, with authors, frankly, headed in the same direction as our colleagues who are musicians, without the same options of performing to augment our incomes. As a result, I find myself with little patience for the third parties who enable the piracy of books and music and movies. And I would call to the Committee's attention. That I, too, was a Federal prosecutor. My career started in the late 1970s and ran into the 1980s. At that time we began to recognize that the selling of dangerous illegal drugs was becoming an international industry, that it could not be combated simply with on-street arrests, and that we had to follow the trail of money into the financial institutions where it was being deposited. And those financial institutions, of course, raised Cain. They said this was Government intrusion. They said that they could not afford the price of vigilance, that it would destroy their business. It did not. It was necessary, and the same kinds of steps are necessary now for those who profit by advertising, by collecting fees from payments for this form of intellectual piracy. There needs to be legislation, and as you said, Mr. Chairman, inaction really should not be an option for the Congress.

So I thank you for your attention to this very, very important issue.

[The prepared statement of Mr. Turow appears as a submission for the record.]

Chairman LEAHY. Thank you, and I appreciate the fact you brought up all the different things that might be on there, not only books but products. Somebody thinks they are getting a medication that controls a heart condition, for example, and they are getting a fake medication and they die.

Ms. Jones, you have already been introduced. I cannot do better than Senator Kyl has introducing you. Please go ahead.

Statement of Christine N. Jones, Executive Vice President, General Counsel and Corporate Secretary, the Go Daddy Group, Inc., Scottsdale, Arizona

Ms. JONES. Thank you, sir, and I really appreciate you letting Senator Kyl introduce me. That was very gracious. As with most Arizona citizens, I was very sad to learn of his impending retirement. He has done a lot of good for the community, and we really wish him the best in the future.

But I want to thank you, Chairman Leahy, and the members of the Committee, for the privilege of testifying today. We appreciate the efforts of the Committee and your staff, whom we have worked with closely——

Chairman LEAHY. If I might interrupt, Ms. Jones, it may not surprise you to know that I was at my home in Vermont when I heard the news, and I called Senator Kyl to tell him how much I was going to miss him on this Committee.

Ms. JONES. Yes, that is a mutual feeling.

But we appreciate what the Committee is doing. We have long taken it as a priority at Go Daddy to make the Internet a better and safer place, and so we are honored just to be a part of this conversation to try to move the ball forward on that.

For many years, we have taken an aggressive approach to assisting IP holders in their efforts to police and protect their marks, copyrights, designs, and other works on the Internet. We have established a series of standard operating procedures designed specifically to assist the IP community in the difficult task, sometimes very difficult task, of enforcing their intellectual property rights against the often elusive or, as Mr. Turow put it, whack-a-mole online infringers. In fact, we are arguably more willing to help IP holders than any of our fellow members of the Internet ecosystem, a position we take very seriously.

We do this because we are a large holder of intellectual property ourselves, and we understand the frustration of trying to keep up with the bad guys. And we do it because we appreciate the significant efforts of the

MPAA and organizations like them to protect their members. But mostly we do it because we believe it is the right thing to do. And at Go Daddy, we always try to do the right thing.

I would like to address some of what my colleagues have already discussed, but from the standpoint of the registrar and hosting provider, and to put the comments in perspective, let me point out we sit at the on ramp to the Internet. Every single website operator must have a domain name to function. So we end up in a unique position. We enable access to the Internet to a whole lot of people, more than 46 million as of today, to be exact. And while we understand the Internet is used for many, many really good things, we also know—we are not naive. We understand there is a whole host of bad stuff happening out there as well. We understand how easy it is for the bad guys to put up a website, copy a few books or some foreign language CDs, launch their online business, and start collecting money.

Because we do not wish for our service to be used to enable people to break the law, we have been very aggressive in taking action against some of these websites. And at the outset, to allay the fears of the EFF and the ACLU and some of the people who have opposed the legislation we are talking about today, let me make it clear, our position as a default is leave the website up. OK? We are in favor of the open exchange of ideas on the Internet. We like that. But we do not provide a platform for illegal activity, and that is what I want to talk about now.

We believe a hybrid approach to this problem is the best way to address it, and by that I mean we need a multi-stakeholder group, companies from the entire Internet ecosystem, to voluntarily cooperate in disabling their services, whatever the relevant service is, for infringing websites. It means we need targeted, narrowly tailored legislation to pick up the slack for the people or companies who cannot or will not cooperate, and it means preventing frivolous lawsuits, which we get from time to time, against the companies who voluntarily help IP holders by terminating those services. And there are a variety of ways to go about this once we get the framework in place.

At the end of 2010, for example, this Committee—no, that was the end of 2008. I am sorry. At the end of 2008, this Committee was instrumental in passing the Ryan Haight Online Pharmacy Consumer Protection Act, and we have used that very effectively in addition to our voluntary efforts to help end the rogue pharmacy contacts. And I would say that has been one of the most effective hybrid approaches we have had. We did a similar thing in the child pornography context where we got cooperation from all of the Internet ecosystem players, have legislation that is on point, work with the National Center for Missing and Exploited Children, and today it is much more difficult to find, buy, host, or register child pornography online. And so this kind of hybrid approach is what I would support and what I think is the best and most effective way to do it.

I am just going to jump to the end because I know I am short on time here, but I will just say we are happy to be part of this conversation, and we are happy that the Committee is really working hard to figure out how best to do it. And I do not think we can really make progress on this until we have the cooperation from all of what we call the Big Five players. That would be domain name registrars, hosting providers, payment card processors, Internet service providers, and online advertising providers, which, by the way, some people call "search engines." Without the cooperative efforts from all of these players, the criminals that Go Daddy works hard to take offline every day will come back almost certainly as customers of one of our more lax competitors. We do not like the whack-a-mole game any more than anybody else, and we want it to stop.

Thank you very much. I will be happy to take questions later. [The prepared statement of Ms. Jones appears as a submission for the record.]

Chairman LEAHY. Thank you very, very much.

Our next witness is Thomas Dailey. He is vice president and deputy general counsel for global internet strategy broadband programming for Verizon. He has the responsibility for the development and implementation of policies in areas such as anti-piracy, content regulation, and privacy. He has served as Verizon's chief Internet counsel since 1998. Prior to that, he was general counsel to Verizon's telephone business in Vermont. He received his bachelor's degree from Colby College and his law degree from Suffolk University Law School.

Mr. Dailey, it is good to see you again.

STATEMENT OF THOMAS M. DAILEY, VICE PRESIDENT AND DEPUTY GENERAL COUNSEL, VERIZON COMMUNICATIONS INC., ARLINGTON, VIRGINIA

Mr. DAILEY. Thank you very much, Chairman Leahy, Ranking Member Grassley, and members of the Senate Judiciary Committee. Thank you for the opportunity to testify today and to present Verizon's perspectives on the Combating Online Infringement and Counterfeits Act.

As we have heard from the other witnesses, online trafficking in counterfeit goods and infringing content is an important and legitimate concern for rights holders, and it is a concern that Verizon very much shares. This legislation, while offering a new approach to combating piracy, raises issues for a variety of different stakeholders who are concerned about the consequences of the bill beyond its impact on piracy, including its impact on global Internet policy interests. I am not here today to address these important issues, but I do urge the Committee to take in the views of other concerned stakeholders directly as you continue your review of the legislation.

The reason I am here today is that the Committee asked Verizon to comment on the legislation from the perspective of a service provider who would need to respond to a judicial order to restrict access to designated websites if the bill becomes law.

Before I get to our concerns with the legislation, let me first mention a few things that we think that the bill got right.

First, we appreciate the fact that the Committee has included in the legislation provisions that appropriately limit the bill's impact on Internet service providers, such as not requiring a service provider to modify its network or facilities to comply with a judicial order.

Second, we think the limitation that ISPs will be required to take action only pursuant to a judicial order issued in a lawsuit filed by the Department of Justice will help ensure COICA is narrowly invoked.

Third, the bill includes appropriate immunities for taking action in compliance with the law or arising from a judicial order issued under it.

And, finally, the bill recognizes that DNS-based restrictions are not 100 percent effective, and it protects service providers from liability based on actions taken by their subscribers to circumvent the restrictions that are put in place.

These provisions strike the proper balance between protecting a rights holder's property and allocating the burdens of that effort, and we thank the Committee for including them.

However, there are several changes to the legislation that we believe are necessary to ensure that the mechanisms described in the bill remain narrowly focused in their use and application and target only the worst of the worst Internet sites.

So the changes we propose—and I will just cut through them quickly because they are in my written testimony—are the following:

First, the bill should be clarified to ensure that service providers are required to take action only with respect to their U.S.-based DNS servers. Limiting the scope of a judicial order to DNS servers located here in the U.S. keeps the enforcement effort narrower, and it helps limit extraterritorial impact.

Second, the legislation should expressly forbid private rights of action and require that DNS restrictions be imposed only where they are the least burdensome form of remedy. This, too, will help keep the focus of the bill more targeted and narrow by ensuring only that the Justice Department can seek an order to restrict access to a website and that the DOJ must conclude that the website restriction is truly necessary in the circumstances.

Third, there are a number of operational perspectives that we believe should be put into the bill, particularly those around ensuring that ISPs are properly notified of what they need to do and, most importantly, that they are notified when a website that has been subject to a restriction is no longer subject to that restriction.

And, finally, we believe that service providers will incur costs in implementing these DNS restrictions, and to encourage the Government to keep the list of restricted websites short and to reimburse providers, we believe that the bill should place appropriate limits on the number of domain names that can be subject to restriction without cost reimbursement.

So, in closing, Verizon supports the efforts of Congress, the Department of Justice, and rights holders to combat the online theft of intellectual property. We believe that responsible members of the Internet ecosystem should work with Congress, law enforcement, and the courts to take efficient, effective, and judicially sanctioned steps to address this important problem. However, we also note that the new approaches to combating online privacy in the legislation raise complex issues and that Government—sanctioned website blocking represents a major shift in U.S. policy that requires careful consideration and input from a wide variety and group of stakeholders.

I hope this testimony is useful to the Committee, and I look forward to your questions.

The prepared statement of Mr. Dailey appears as a submission for the record.]

Chairman LEAHY. Thank you very much.

Our next witness is Denise Yee. She is senior trademark counsel for Visa. In her role at Visa, she heads the overall responsibility for managing Visa's trademark and domain name portfolios worldwide. She is also responsible for global enforcement of the Visa trademark worldwide and has played a significant role in developing Visa's anti-counterfeit and anti-piracy policies. She has been with Visa since 1999. She received her bachelor's degree from the University of California at San Diego and her law degree from Santa Clara University School of Law.

Ms. Yee, we are delighted to have you here.

Statement of Denise Yee, Senior Trademark Counsel, Visa, Inc., San Francisco, California

Ms. YEE. Chairman Leahy, Ranking Member Grassley, members of the Committee, my name is Denise Yee, and I am senior trademark counsel for Visa Inc. With me today is Martin Elliott, who is the senior business leader from P Payment System Risk. Visa welcomes the opportunity to provide its views on the targeting websites dedicated to stealing American intellectual property.

Visa fully appreciates the value of IP. The "VISA" trademark itself is one of our company's most valuable assets. We fight phishing scams and other infringements to the "VISA" trademark every day and expend millions of dollars doing so.

To promote growth in e-commerce, to protect the Visa brand, and because it is the right thing to do, we go beyond any legal requirements to prevent the use of our payment system for illegal e-commerce transactions. Our policy is unequivocal: Our system must not be used for illegal transactions. The integrity of the Visa brand is critical to the success of the system. The system works because of consumer confidence in its security and reliability. We are committed to ridding our system of merchants that engage in illegal transactions, including IP infringement.

Our payment network includes four parties: acquiring banks that sign up merchants, and issuing banks that sign up card holders. Visa has no direct relationship with either merchants or card holders; rather, we provide the network that enables these four parties to conduct transactions. Our rules state that the transaction entered into the Visa system must be both legal in the card holder's jurisdiction and the merchant's jurisdiction. In the context of IP, Visa enforces this rule through a simple approach. At no cost, the IP owner may report instances of online infringement to Visa. We then conduct a test transaction to identify the acquirer that signed up the merchant in the system. Visa instructs the acquirer to conduct an investigation into the alleged infringement and to report the conclusion of its investigation within 5 business days. Absent proof of legality, the acquirer must demand that its merchant comply with Visa rules or terminate the merchant. Also, we educate acquirers that they should not sign up merchants engaged in the sale of infringing content.

However, taking voluntary action against infringing merchants is not without risk. In 2006, Visa received a complaint that a Russian website called AllofMP3.com was allowing the unauthorized downloads of music, and Visa and its acquirer terminated the merchant from the system. That decision backfired, resulting in the merchant suing the acquirer. And even more surprising, the Russian courts found that AllofMP3 did not infringe under Russian copyright law and the acquirer breached its contract by terminating service. The court ordered us to resume processing transactions, which we allowed only between the west side and Russian customers.

There are other challenges to protecting third-party IP online. First, we are not well positioned to identify counterfeit or copyright-infringing content. IP owners are best situated to bring instances of infringement to our attention, but they rarely do. Second, where legality is not clear, we have no authority to decide what is lawful. We are then force into the precarious position of either agreeing with the IP owner or the merchant. Either decision could expose Visa to multiple lawsuits around the world. Third, when Visa is notified of an infringing merchant, Visa must work through the merchant's acquirer. These infringing merchants often cover their tracks by creating multiple shell companies under different names and entering into agreements with numerous acquirers under false pretenses.

Despite these challenges, Visa is committed to expelling bad merchants from our system, but we cannot permanently eliminate infringement from the Internet. The payment systems are only capable of limited enforcement to disrupt this activity. An effective long- term solution involves sustained international cooperation among law enforcement agencies and all e-commerce stakeholders, as my colleague from Go Daddy mentioned.

We appreciate the Committee's interest in exploring legal mechanisms to protect American IP, and Visa supports COICA's objectives. But imposing a regulatory framework on top of our existing voluntary procedures could have some unintended consequences. For example, extraterritorial application of U.S. law may invite retaliation by other countries' governments, or it may set an unrealistic expectation that payment systems can singlehandedly eliminate online infringement. It could also increase the likelihood that payment systems would be subject to conflicting legal obligations, such as AllofMP3.

Notwithstanding these concerns, Visa supports the objective of COICA: targeting and expelling websites dedicated to stealing American IP. Visa believes that its own voluntary procedures have the same objective and, thus, COICA and Visa's procedures should be viewed as complementary.

In conclusion, Visa supports legislation such as COICA and is committed to working with the Committee to help to American intellectual property and fight this global menace.

Thank you.

[The prepared statement of Ms. Yee appears as a submission for the record.]

Chairman LEAHY. Thank you. Let me ask one question of each of you and just answer this quickly because we will go into more detail.

Do you all agree that rogue websites that do nothing but traffic in infringing goods constitutes a problem for our Nation's economy and job growth that needs to be addressed? In other words, is it safe to say that none of you are here to defend rogue websites? Mr. Adams.

Mr. ADAMS. Absolutely not.

Chairman LEAHY. Mr. Turow.

Mr. TUROW. The faster we get rid of them, the better the United States will be.

Chairman LEAHY. Ms. Jones.

Ms. JONES. Yes, I would agree with that. We see a whole lot of them every day, and they definitely take away jobs from Americans.

Chairman LEAHY. Mr. Dailey.

Mr. DAILEY. I agree as well.

Chairman LEAHY. Ms. Yee.

Ms. YEE. I agree as well. We do not defend rogue websites.

Chairman LEAHY. Let me ask you this: We are trying to find solutions to this. Do any of you think that to date private sector solutions have been sufficient to stop these rogue sites? Mr. Adams.

Mr. ADAMS. Absolutely not, especially given the concentration of search around key engines like Yahoo! and Google.

Chairman LEAHY. Mr. Turow.

Mr. TUROW. Private actions have not provided any solution whatsoever, Mr. Chairman.

Chairman LEAHY. Ms. Jones.

Ms. JONES. I do not think so. I wish that everybody would do what Go Daddy does. Not to hurt myself by patting ourselves on the back too much, but I think we have got to keep in mind not everybody has the scale to do what we do, which is why the hybrid approach where you have to pick up the slack with the legislation I think is really important.

Chairman LEAHY. Mr. Dailey.

Mr. DAILEY. I think I am inclined to agree. I think that there are certainly existing mechanisms in the U.S. for dealing with U.S.- sited websites, and that is certainly—you know, there are a number of ways that we can go after those. We have seen some in the past, in the recent past, through some of the ICE efforts and others.

The issue I think comes to a head as a legal and policy matter when we are dealing with the non-domestic domains that are part of the subject of the statute.

Chairman LEAHY. Ms. Yee.

Ms. YEE. We have voluntary procedures to address issues relating to copyright infringement and counterfeit, but few rights holders have come forward.

That said, we do believe that with the objectives of COICA and we do believe that with collaboration among the private sector, we can combat counterfeit and copyright infringement on the Internet.

Chairman LEAHY. Well, let me ask each of you this: There will be legislation. If you were sitting in the room drafting that, what would you say is the most essential element in legislation to combat online infringement? Mr. Adams.

Mr. ADAMS. The No. 1 most important thing is to make it more difficult for these criminals to find a market here in the United States. That means that they cannot be allowed to buy advertising, and that means that they cannot be allowed to operate the way they do today on search engines.

Chairman LEAHY. Mr. Turow.

Mr. TUROW. I agree with what Mr. Adams said. Advertisers, payment processors, ISPs, anybody who is profiting from this, whether intentionally or not, once put on notice, needs to desist from aiding these illegal enterprises.

Chairman LEAHY. Ms. Jones.

Ms. JONES. I am not sure I can narrow it down to one, but I might be able to narrow it down to three.

Chairman LEAHY. Go ahead.

Ms. JONES. The most important thing is to have a hierarchical approach which targets the bad guys first and then works up the chain of custody, if you will, to use the former prosecutor analogy.

Second, provide a safe harbor for those of us who do the right thing against these lawsuits that Ms. Yee mentioned and the ones that we get from time to time, which cost a fortune to defend but have no merit whatsoever.

And then this might really raise the ire of some of my Internet colleagues, but I am just going to say it anyway. Have a consequence if they do not do the right thing.

Chairman LEAHY. That appeals to those of us, like Senator Klobuchar, who have been prosecutors.

Mr. Dailey.

Mr. DAILEY. To pick up on a couple of the statements that have been made so far, I think that the notion of all players in the ecosystem participating equally is something that Verizon has believed for a long time. And so I think that following the money is always a good place to go.

The safe harbor aspect, to the extent that a law is passed, I think is very important. Immunity from liability is very important because we do not want to be dealing with lawsuits that might follow from some of the activity that could be required under the law.

And then the final thing that I think is very important in the current draft of the bill, if it goes forward, is the requirement that there be a judicial order. I think that is a very important safeguard over the overbroad application.

So I think those would be the three things that I would suggest.

Chairman LEAHY. Ms. Yee.

Ms. YEE. We think that in order to curb counterfeit and copyright infringement, it is necessary for all of the stakeholders in the e-commerce environment to cooperate. It is a shared responsibility, so that we hope that all of the stakeholders in e-commerce are a part of the bill.

We are not opposed to legislation. We think it is important. And the essential part of the legislation—and I agree with my colleagues here, with Verizon and Go Daddy—is the safe harbor and to make sure that we are not penalized for trying to do the right thing.

Thank you.

Chairman LEAHY. I am going to yield to Senator Grassley, but I want to put in the record an op-ed that Mr. Turow had in the New York Times. It says that the ability of creators to make a living off their work is essential to culture in this country. Was it Oliver Wendell Holmes who said, "If music did not pay, it would be given up"? I think it is the same in this.

Chairman LEAHY. Senator Grassley, and then Senator Klobuchar.

Senator GRASSLEY. I was a cosponsor of last year's bill, and I think we will probably get to a point where we will have broad bipartisan support for a bill this year. But let me ask a question that we always ought to ask before we think a new law is the answer to every question.

Before we enact new legislation, it is important to determine whether there is an actual need for more laws. Some argue that statutes already on the books like the Digital Millennium Copyright Act or the PRO–IP Act are sufficient to fight criminal activity on rogue websites.

Number one, I want to know if you agree. Number two, do you believe that additional legislation like last year's bill is necessary? And, three, do you believe the Justice Department should have authority to bring legal action against rogue websites? And I am asking the questions of all of you, but try not to be repetitive, so maybe all of you do not need to answer. But I sure want your opinions, on either side. Go ahead.

Mr. ADAMS. So I will just start by saying that since most of these sites operate from overseas, current legislation does not help us in enforcing our intellectual property. And since current legislation does not really hold the ecosystem to account, we are unable to cutoff the actual merchants of this illicit product. And so either we have got to tackle the ecosystem here, or we have got to change the laws of China, Russia, and numerous other countries.

Mr. TUROW. I agree with Mr. Adams. The safe harbor provisions of the DMCA, while well intended, have not functioned well. Although I understand that my colleagues on this panel have tried to be good corporate citizens, that is not a universal truth, and not everybody is as vigilant. We need the help of legislation to make sure of that.

One of the suggestions that I make in my written testimony is that we require anybody who is going to get credit card payments to have a registered agent for service of process so that we do not have to deal with the intractable jurisdictional problems of trying to bring our legal system to bear against people whose sites are completely foreign. If they want to do business in the United States, then they should be amenable to process here.

Senator GRASSLEY. Anybody else have anything to add?

Ms. JONES. Just briefly, if I could, the DMCA has worked great for us, and so have other already enacted bits of legislation. I think in 2010 we took down around 36,000 domain names and websites under the Ryan Haight Act, for example, in the pharmacy context. We took down around 13,000 copyright and trademark infringements under DMCA or DMCA-like statutes. So that works great.

And with all due respect to Mr. Turow, those of us who do the right thing need the safe harbor, so let us not toy with that.

But should the DOJ have the right to bring an action? The answer is yes, and that gets back to my earlier answer, which is you have to have a consequence for the people who do not do the right thing.

Senator GRASSLEY. Did somebody else want to answer?

Mr. DAILEY. I was just going to echo Ms. Jones' remarks.

Senator GRASSLEY. OK.

Ms. YEE. I also agree with Ms. Jones' remarks.

Senator GRASSLEY. OK. The Department of Homeland Security, its immigration and customs people, has been successful at combating online infringement through the authorities provided under the PRO-IP Act and the Operation in Our Sites efforts. Do you believe that ICE has done a good job with its existing authority? Or could it do better? And if better, how? To any of you.

Mr. ADAMS. So we have worked quite a bit with ICE, and we think that they are doing a great job, but they need more resources. They need more help. And given that a lot of this activity is outside the United States, I think that they are not able to help quite as much as they would like.

Senator GRASSLEY. Does anybody else have anything to add to that?

Ms. JONES. We had experience with the take-down at the beginning of the year or the end of the previous year—I think there were 85 domain names that were seized, and then there were another nine that have first-run movies. And we cooperated and participated in that investigation and that worked well.

The focus on the top of the Christmas tree, if you will, is not our favorite way to approach. Again, we like going to the bad guy first, and I think this gets to Mr. Adams' point, which is a lot of the bad activity is offshore. You can disable the domain name, but you do not get to the root of the problem.

So what ICE is doing is great. It is a solution, but not the only solution.

Senator GRASSLEY. Would it be all right with you, Senator Klobuchar, if I ask one more question?

Senator KLOBUCHAR. Of course it would, Senator.

Senator GRASSLEY. Thank you.

What do you believe is the appropriate role for search engines to play in combating rogue sites?

Mr. ADAMS. Well, personally I think that if a domain or a counterparty is identified as one that on a serial basis is involved in criminal activity, search engines cannot be allowed to continue doing business with them. And as it stands, they repeatedly just take down the infringing ad but continue doing business with the counterparty. This must cease. There must be very serious consequences for a company like Google for that kind of behavior. We have sustained it over a number of years. It is really whack-a-mole, and it is impossible to discipline a company with that kind of market power, with a 70-percent share of search, and to get them to change their behavior. We need you to act now and legislate to protect IP owners like Rosetta Stone.

Mr. TUROW. I agree with that. With regard to the matter of a safe harbor, my own view would be that those who respond to this legislation and act consistently with it, of course, should be granted immunity. But I do not think, again, that the safe harbors that currently exist are sufficient to compel other people in the Internet ecology to be as vigilant as some of the people who are sitting at this table.

Ms. JONES. So it sounds like we are probably saying the same thing on that. But getting back to search, if I could just briefly— and we have gone around and around with the search providers on this, and not casting aspersions on anybody who operates in the Internet community, but you got to stop selling your product to the bad guys. Whether you are a search provider, whether you are a credit card processor, whether you are a domain name registrar, whatever you are, you have to stop the sale. But there is simply no reason why you should be able to search for any fake good or any replica good and have that search result return access to thousands upon thousands of websites that do this. There is no reason for that.

I do not run a search engine. I do not write that algorithm. I do not know what the issue is there, but we seem to get a lot of resistance from the search companies. And I am sorry they are not here today to answer that question, but we do not think you should be able to search for that and get a result so that you can go get fake Rosetta Stone from all of those websites that Mr. Adams displayed.

Senator GRASSLEY. I will yield, and, Mr. Chairman, I am going to have to submit questions for answer in writing.

[The questions of Senator Grassley appears under questions and answers.]

Chairman LEAHY. You mean you are going to leave me here on my own?

Senator GRASSLEY. Yes.

Chairman LEAHY. Kind of scary.

Senator KLOBUCHAR. No. I am here. I am here.

Chairman LEAHY. No, no. I was just talking about from their side of the aisle.

[Laughter.]

Chairman LEAHY. I would never forget you, Senator Klobuchar, a former prosecutor, a valued member of this Committee, and I yield to you.

Senator KLOBUCHAR. Well, thank you very much, Senator Leahy, and thank you, both of you, for your work in this very important area. As a daughter of an author and an author myself—OK, my book is for $7.99 on Amazon, "Uncovering the Dome."

[Laughter.]

Senator KLOBUCHAR. Sadly, I wrote a book in college. Unlike you, Mr. Turow, I wrote a book on the politics behind the building of the Metrodome, as in the one that just sunk. OK?

[Laughter.]

Senator KLOBUCHAR. But it did bring the value up a little. So I am very aware, mostly from my father's work, about the importance of protecting intellectual property, and I am very concerned as a former prosecutor, as Senator Leahy pointed out, about what is going on here, that we are basically losing a huge amount of money in our economy in an area where I think we can actually make a lot of money in our economy.

And I guess I would start with you, Mr. Adams. You mentioned the global sales of counterfeit goods via the Internet from illegitimate retailers reached $135 billion in 2010, and as a consequence of a global U.S.-based piracy of copyrighted materials, the U.S. economy lost $58 billion in total output in 2007. Do you know where those numbers came from? And could they be an underestimation given that we do not really know?

Mr. ADAMS. Those numbers are all from the Chamber of Commerce.

Senator KLOBUCHAR. Very good. I just think people have to start looking at it in this way as we look at every way that we can grow jobs and the economy that this is a major problem, and that is the way I look at it.

I guess my first question would be, as a fan and a sponsor of doing something here, would be one of the questions we get back with this legislation. Would these crooks just go to another website? You know, you shut one down and then they just go to another website. What is your answer to that?

Mr. ADAMS. I think that is exactly the problem. If you shut down one website now, within minutes there is a new one that appears. And so you have to tackle the problem in the ecosystem given that we cannot change the laws and the behaviors and the enforcements in countries like China, Russia, et cetera.

So what you have to do is deal with search engines, which, by the way, in other areas of intellectual property, like, for example, the YouTube site, they do a review before a video is posted, very often, because there were so many infringing videos. Why wouldn't we have a company like Google review a URL and just see is this legitimate? It is a very easy action. They do it for video. And here we are talking about not a video clip that someone would watch where, of course, it is an infringement on the intellectual property itself, but it is relatively harmless from a commerce perspective. Why wouldn't we stop the commerce by having the search engine review who they are doing business with? Instead, if you simply have a credit card and if you are based abroad, you can open an account immediately and start posting your ads and having them link these ads to illicit websites hosted on servers that are overseas, and you can do an enormous amount of transactions. Google does a manual review of the sites when you ask them to take them down. So it takes 3 days or so for them to take down an infringing site, but it takes the infringer minutes to set up a new site. We need to flip that. We need to have Google review a new counterparty and the domains that they are wanting to put in front of the customer to see if it is legit. And if it is legit, they can start advertising, and that would change the entire burden of policing this to them.

Senator KLOBUCHAR. Flipping the burden.

Mr. ADAMS. Which is where it should be, because we are not profiting at all from any of this activity, and yet we have to police it enormously because we do not want to have a harmed brand.

Senator KLOBUCHAR. Very good.

Mr. Dailey, just one of the concerns I know that Verizon has raised as we look at how we are going to combat this, what I consider crimes going on out there, and I will mention that Senator Cornyn and I have a bill to actually up the penalties for this. But my question of you, Mr. Dailey, is: I know one of the concerns is that Verizon customers would somehow be confused if a website was shut off, and I understand that the customer would see an error message instead of actually seeing the website. Well, from my understanding just from our staff, the error message would say something like “404 error” without any explanation to the customer regarding the court order. And my question is: Does Verizon have the technology and the capability to shape the wording of the error message to explain why the customer cannot get to the website and just update the technology to get at that concern?

Mr. DAILEY. Yes, and thank you, Senator. The technology does exist. It is not within our licenses, shall I put it that way. So it is a several million dollar effort to change the error message for the purpose that you have just described, but it is available, at least to us. I do not know about other ISPs who might be affected by the requirement.

Senator KLOBUCHAR. It just seems to me that there is a way to get around that.

Then the last thing I just have, and I will submit some questions for the record, of you, Ms. Jones, is: I am working on this legislation, as I mentioned, with Senator Cornyn that will keep our laws up to date with these new technologies. I have always believed that we need to be as sophisticated as the crooks that are breaking the laws, which is not happening right now. And currently, as you know, a person that streams pirated works for commercial gain can only be convicted of a misdemeanor regardless of the amount of content that is streamed. And then at the same time, if they sold $2,500 worth of DVDs, they could be convicted of a felony. And so we plan to introduce legislation that will make the penalties for streaming the same as it is for selling the DVDs on the street. And I just wondered if you thought that would be helpful.

Ms. JONES. Well, I can tell you, we have worked with the recording industry a lot on that exact issue, and the MPAA, for example, go after these websites that stream movies all the time, and I can tell you, there is more than $2,500 worth of product going out. We had one recently—I think it is OK to disclose this—where——

Senator KLOBUCHAR. Oh, everything is just between us.

[Laughter.]

Ms. JONES. I will not use any names. How about that? The customer——

Chairman LEAHY. Everybody else in the room, do not listen.

Ms. JONES. The customer had 32 dedicated servers. Now, to put that in perspective, that is a lot of data. OK? A lot of data. And the MPAA worked with Federal authorities. They came and seized the boxes, and I think the guy is now in jail. But they did not prosecute him for a felony for the streaming website. And I mean, come on, there were thousands upon thousands upon thousands of movies on that website. Clearly there was more than $2,500 worth of damage. So I think you are on to something there.

Senator KLOBUCHAR. OK, very good. I am out of time. I also wanted to thank you, Mr. Turow, for coming to Minneapolis for the legal aid dinner at one point. I was there and you came and gave of your time, so thank you for that. Thank you to all the witnesses.

Chairman LEAHY. Thank you very much.

Senator Whitehouse.

Senator WHITEHOUSE. Let me thank the Chairman for his focus on this issue. I contend that America is on the losing end of the largest transfer of wealth through theft and piracy in the history of mankind. Perhaps the Spanish kings who were having the treasures of the New World sunk and stolen in the galleons in the great treasure ships across the Atlantic were contenders for that role. But I think we take the prize, and we are doing virtually nothing about it. And it has many dimensions. It has the dimension of outright theft and fraudulent charges on credit. It has the dimension of industrial espionage, everything from entire fighter jet plans being exfiltrated to scientific processes. Often because there you are not stealing, you are copying, it can be a crime that is often unknown to the victim and, therefore, requires very energetic efforts to pursue it.

What we are talking about today is yet another element of it, and that is, public sales in violation of copyright and licensing agreements that are facilitated by legitimate members of our business community. And probably the most dangerous is the intrusion and insertion of potential attack mechanisms into critical private infrastructure, and they all have a common theme, which is our failure to adequately defend our interests in what is called "the wild, wild Web."

I was delighted to hear Ms. Yee describe this as a global menace, and I think everybody on the panel agrees with that description.

Ms. Jones indicated that efforts to voluntarily cooperate are important.

I think it is very important that the ISPs who provide the connections, that the search engines who provide the location, and that the payment providers who make it a profitable transaction for the criminals all work together to guide us in the best possible way. But I also worry that unless we act legislatively, there is an incentive to let everybody else go first—on the ISPs to let the payment people go first; on the payment folks to let the search engines go first; within the search engine, ISP, or payment communities to let the other card or the other engine or the other telecommunications company go first; and that as a result of those natural tendencies, we are simply not addressing what is particularly in our economy a really catastrophic loss of wealth to the American people.

And so I could not agree with you more about the importance of voluntarily cooperating, but please do not think that we are not going to be legislating in this area. You will do us great assistance and advantage by voluntarily cooperating in ways that guide that. But I really think we are well past the point where we can count on mere voluntary cooperation among all these different interests as being adequate to the task. There is simply too much being stolen right here as we speak.

I would be interested, Ms. Yee, to know if I went back to my computer and dialed in a—how long it would take me to find a website that Visa was attached to that was selling pirated product. I bet I could do it in less than 5 minutes.

And so I think it is really important that the scale of the effort that we engage in match the scale of the theft and piracy that America is suffering, and I guess I just would say that by way of encouragement to all of you to really take this seriously, because the legislation will be much more successful if it is worked out in really cooperative fashion. But we do have to see this as urgent. It is too important to our economy and to our National security not to see it as urgent, and I think the Chairman's leadership on this is particularly appropriate and important and particularly significant given his long and very distinguished career in the protection of civil liberties area. And so he has bona fides there that are unmatched, and his willingness to address this I think is very significant.

Chairman LEAHY. Thank you very much. I think as you listen to some of these comments, you realize there will be legislation, and we want your cooperation in doing the best possible. But this is a major, major issue. The transfer of wealth that Senator Whitehouse talked about is not overstated.

Senator Blumenthal.

Senator BLUMENTHAL. I want to join in thanking you, Mr. Chairman, for your leadership and the bipartisan commitment from Senator Grassley and others on the other side, and I want to associate myself with the remarks just made so compellingly by Senator Whitehouse in terms that I am sure would qualify for one of Mr. Turow's novels if——

[Laughter.]

Mr. TUROW. Eloquence far greater than I can muster.

Senator WHITEHOUSE. All right. Enough on that.

Senator FRANKEN. Yes, enough, enough.

[Laughter.]

Senator BLUMENTHAL. You can tell I am the junior Senator.

First of all, on that topic, I want to say that I found your op-ed piece in yesterday's New York Times a very succinct and cogent statement of why this is so important in historical terms, and I would like, with permission, Mr. Chairman, for it to be entered in the record.

Chairman LEAHY. Without objection.

Senator BLUMENTHAL. Thank you.

[The op-ed appears as a submission for the record.]

Senator BLUMENTHAL. You know, I approach this subject from the standpoint of an enforcer, having tried to hold accountable many of these enablers and facilitators in other contexts, not necessarily the intellectual property area but abuses concerning child predators and pornography. And I view it as imposing basic fairness and accountability, basic responsibility for the enabling or facilitating of the outright lawbreaking and theft of property that should be countenanced by no one. And so I welcome and support this measure, but with the perspective of enforcement.

I would like to ask perhaps Mr. Turow, as a former prosecutor and a litigator, will these measures really be effective in terms of stopping practically, immediately, these kinds of abuses? Are they enforceable? And will they be enforced to effectively stop them?

Mr. TUROW. Well, I certainly regard the legislation that was proposed in the last session called COICA as a great first step. Speaking from our perspective and from the perspective of a lawyer, I do believe there should be a private right of action so that there is some forum in which private parties can put the various members of the Internet community on notice that there is offending conduct taking place. Certainly in an era of budget deficits, it is unrealistic to expect the Government to dramatically increase enforcement efforts despite the fact that I have no doubt that the Justice Department is greatly interested in this problem.

And so if there is some form of private Attorney Generalship that is permitted, one that does not penalize the people who respond in good faith to the legislation so that they are immune from civil suits if they respond to the efforts of the orders that come down as a result of that private litigation, then I think we would be far better off that way.

Senator BLUMENTHAL. And, in fact, in many of our areas of enforcement, private rights of action incentivize the public enforcers to do their job better, don't they?

Mr. TUROW. That is, in fact, the structure that we have throughout our intellectual property laws. That is the way copyright is routinely enforced, the way patents are routinely enforced.

Senator BLUMENTHAL. Without putting any of you on the spot, as you know, the Department of Justice and the Department of Homeland Security have begun a more vigorous enforcement effort. I think it is called Operation in Our Sites. And I gather your feeling is that it has been insufficient to stem or stop this problem.

Ms. JONES. Can I talk to that for one second? It is not that it has been inefficient or insufficient, even. It is just these ICE agents are people, and they have to investigate these things just like any other crime. So what they have done has worked. We just need more of them and more voluntary cooperation so that we never have to get to the criminal prosecution in most of these cases.

And going back to what Senator Whitehouse said, if you get all of the players to cooperate, it really helps solve the problem of sort of the frogs jumping off the barrel overseas, because if you cannot buy this stuff with a credit card and you cannot search for it on a search engine and you cannot browse to it because the hosting provider or the ISP took the content away, it does not matter really where the source is coming from. It really helps to solve that problem.

But getting back to ICE, it is not that they are doing an insufficient job. They are really, really trying hard. They just need more people and more money and less infringers.

Mr. TUROW. And I would also add that, as you, Senator, are familiar with from firsthand experience, mounting a criminal prosecution where you need to gather evidence of intent as opposed to mere infringement is also a substantial burden on those who are doing a great and diligent job, but they are still trying to fulfill an evidentary standard that enhances the burdens on them.

Senator BLUMENTHAL. And the standard of proof, combined with the necessity for evidence of mens rea, or intent, is a very substantial burden. I agree.

Mr. DAILEY. Senator, if I could comment on the private right of action point in particular, I think it is precisely the discipline that an investigation brought by the Justice Department would bring to the process that is important, particularly when we are talking about blocking websites. And it is not just because it is a difficult process, it raises a number of policy issues. But I would also be concerned about the risks associated with private rights of action where there is less discipline, less rigor about what is being requested to be blocked, because if a court order comes in to us, we are going to have to follow it. And if you are overblocking consistently, that is going to be a recipe for disaster for the bill.

And so one of the themes in our testimony is that we should be looking—particularly when we are talking about orders to block access to website that we should be looking for ways to narrowly tailor those orders so that they are properly effective, because this is an enormously complicated issue. I will not bore the Committee with a discussion about second-level domains, third-level domains, and what we are actually targeting with these. But it is the type of thing that experts really need to consult with each other about.

We fully understand the scope of the problem. It is enormous, and we want to help. But we have to be careful here that we are not blocking more than what we really intend to do, which is bad as a general matter, but could also be bad for the law, and we do not want to see that happen either.

Chairman LEAHY. Thank you.

Senator BLUMENTHAL. My time is up, but if I may just say, Mr. Chairman, maybe we will have time for a second round.

Chairman LEAHY. We are. Senator Whitehouse has also requested time, and we will.

Senator Coburn, thank you for rejoining us. Like everybody else here, he has got about three different things going on at the same time.

Senator COBURN. Mr. Chairman, first of all, let me give you my personal thanks for having this hearing. I think it is an important area. I do not think the Bush administration did a good job on IP. I do not think this administration has done a good job in protecting intellectual property. And I think we need to be much more aggressive in it.

I am very sorry that there is not a search engine here represented because I think we need to hear from them. I think the fact Google refused and Yahoo! said they did not have anybody competent——

[Laughter.]

Senator COBURN.—bothers—and that is my word, not theirs. Chairman LEAHY. If the Senator would yield for a moment, you know they were invited.

Senator COBURN. I do. I know they were invited. But I think the fact that they are not here—and I think, Mr. Adams, it kind of goes to one of the things that you put forward. You showed American Airlines and AOL. Why do you think they do not have all the junk on the right side of the website when you go to Google? Do you think it is because their legal counsel has been rather aggressive on it? Or is it because they have so much more traffic than maybe Rosetta Stone? Or why is it that you do not see all that on their line but they see it on yours?

Mr. ADAMS. So our sense is that there are—you know, there is an arbitrary behavior, and it is very apparent. Rosetta Stone is not the most valuable brand in the world. There are many brands that are much more valuable and that do not see any competition. We have asked Google why they treat different companies different ways. They always tell us, "I cannot talk about that." So I cannot explain to you—-the account manager talking to our account manager cannot explain why.

I think that the fact that they are not here to sort of answer to their actions in this field of intellectual property is very disappointing. We very much want to partner with companies. We think this is a shared issue. We think that the ISPs, the payment processors, the search engines would all do much better in a world where this was not going on, and yet there is clearly a profit relationship right now between an illicit website and Google.

Senator COBURN. Because of the paid advertising.

Mr. ADAMS. Because they pay them for every single click. If you can imagine that there are a thousand websites that have been created, independent websites multi—levels deep that are replicas of the Rosetta Stone website, where they are selling ripped off software and they have payment processing on every single website, and each of those websites is doing business with an organization like Google, it is clear this is a massive issue, and they are very well aware of the size of——

Senator COBURN. So it is a revenue issue to them. Their balance—and we are putting words in their mouth, but that is fair to do if they are not here. The fact is that it is a revenue issue versus protecting intellectual property in this country.

Mr. ADAMS. That is correct. In our opinion, that is the tradeoff that they are making.

Senator COBURN. Well, I would just tell you, as Ranking Member on the Permanent Subcommittee on Investigations, I plan on sending a letter to Google. And with the authority that we have to subpoena, if they do not answer us, then I will seek my colleague and we will subpoena an answer to these questions since they refuse to come and testify.

Mr. Chairman, I want to thank you for having the hearing. I am going to submit some questions for the record to each of our guests, and I want to thank each of you all for your attentiveness to this issue.

[The questions of Senator Coburn appears under questions and answers.]

Senator COBURN. There is one other that maybe we can talk about before I go. What would happen to Go Daddy if last year's legislation would have been passed in terms of your costs?

Ms. JONES. Candidly, for us, not a whole lot would change because we have been voluntarily taking the actions mostly described in that legislation for a lot of years, almost 10 years now. What would happen to people who have smaller registrars and smaller hosting operations? I guess it would mean a couple more head count. It probably would cost them some money. Certainly every time we shut down a domain name or terminate a hosting account, it costs us revenue. So, yes, I mean, there is—

Senator COBURN. There is a cost.

Ms. JONES. There is a cost.

Senator COBURN. How about for Verizon?

Mr. DAILEY. Well, I think from Verizon's perspective, the answer is it sort of depends. We raised——

Senator COBURN. How aggressive we are with it.

Mr. DAILEY. Well, yes, there were a number of aspects of the bill that we commented on that, if narrowed, would make it administratively easier and, of course, affect costs. One of the big issues, as I mentioned a minute ago, in terms of structuring the type of domain name that is actually the target, if it is a second-level domain—Verizon.com, Verizon is the second-level domain there, .com is the top-level domain. If the order is to block Verizon.com that affects third-level domains, so e-mail.verizon.com. So it goes further down the stream. So it makes it a much bigger effort.

Senator COBURN. So it can be expensive.

Mr. DAILEY. It could.

Senator COBURN. How about with Visa?

Ms. YEE. Well, Visa today, you know, I just wanted to first mention that in six months Visa has received a total of 30 inquiries from IP rights holders, and so our voluntary procedures we provide at no cost. And so part of the problem really is to have the rights holders come forward, and we would like for them to try procedures first before they consider things like private right of action, as Mr. Turow suggested. But assuming that the legislation was passed as is, you know, we already have the voluntary procedures that are very consistent with what the legislation contemplates.

Senator COBURN. I wonder if you all might suggest to the Committee how we make that more effective in terms of them coming voluntarily to you to request those things, if you would submit that to the Committee. Knowing what is going on, how do we make it where they are more aware that you are in voluntary compliance if you are asked and except you are saying you are not getting asked very much. And so, you know, that is a void in what we were doing in terms of legislation. We do not need to legislate something that cannot be fixed if we increase information. So I am supportive of the concept. I know there were a lot of false rumors about our bill last year, and I fought back on those. But I think cost is an important aspect for us, and so I look forward to hearing the answers to the questions that I will submit for the record.

Thank you, Mr. Chairman.

Chairman LEAHY. Well, thank you very much, and thank you for your involvement, Senator Coburn.

Following Dr. Coburn, we have Senator Franken.

Senator FRANKEN. Thank you, Mr. Chairman. Thank you for your hard work on this very important issue, and also thanks to Ranking Member Grassley.

As many of you know, I am a copyright holder of intellectual property or, as Senator Whitehouse said to me coming in, in my case quasi-intellectual property.

[Laughter.]

Senator FRANKEN. And I resented that, but still would like to associate myself with his remarks, nevertheless.

Like Mr. Turow, I am well aware of how important it is that we protect the intellectual property of today's writers and artists and innovators. You know, this affects not just the writers and the producers and the movie stars and movies, but the people who work on the movies, the craftsmen and the technicians and the craft services people, because it changes the business model when this stuff is stolen.

Now, I have a longer statement on this that I would like to add to the record, if there is no objection, Mr. Chairman.

Senator BLUMENTHAL. I will not object.

Senator FRANKEN. Thank you.

[The prepared statement of Senator Franken appears as a submission for the record.]

Senator FRANKEN. You know, I also think it is essential that we move cautiously before we create a structure that will direct Internet service providers to block content at the domain level.

Let me start my questions with Ms. Yee. There are many people who believe that the best way to attack this problem is to follow the money and focus on rogue sites' means of financial support rather than targeting and blocking domain names. What do you think of this approach? I realize it would place more of a burden on companies like Visa and on advertising networks. But we have seen great success at shutting down child pornography sites with this approach, and I would think it would be even more effective for pirate sites, especially since these sites exist purely for financial reasons.

Have you looked at what percentage of pirated content you could stop with this approach?

Ms. YEE. Well, I want to answer your first question about our ability to interrupt this activity, and as I mentioned in my oral testimony, similar to domain name registration, nefarious merchants will find a way to get into the system. They will change their merchant account name. They will sign up with different acquirers. So once Visa takes swift action to terminate a merchant with the acquirer's assistance, the nefarious merchant will move on to another account name with a different acquirer under false pretenses.

So it is a whack-a-mole game for us, too. We honestly do not want it in our system; neither do the acquirers. Our policy is very specific.

Senator FRANKEN. Well, how is this different than on child pornography?

Ms. YEE. Well, I think our approach is very similar. You know, to the extent that we are made aware of the infringing activity by rights holders, we are, you know, happy to provide assistance to help terminate the merchant out of the system. At the end of the day, Visa does not want this type of activity in the system.

Senator FRANKEN. Mr. Adams, have you looked into this at Rosetta Stone? If we just shut down the advertising and payment processing functions of counterfeit goods sites, could we stop the vast majority of sales of counterfeit goods?

Mr. ADAMS. We believe that is true.

Senator FRANKEN. Thank you.

Mr. Dailey, I have heard that the process of blocking domain names will not work, that it will be incredibly easy to circumvent, and it will ultimately drive users to rely on unreliable foreign domain name services. I have heard that this could lead large numbers of users to abandon the current domestic DNS system and, therefore, threaten network stability and lead to more identity theft. Are you concerned about this? How easy do you think it will be to get around this process? And do you think there is a more effective tool to stop these pirates?

Mr. DAILEY. I think those are legitimate concerns. I think how widespread the problem becomes is something we just have to wait and see to see how many users actually go through the effort of reprogramming their computer to bypass their domestic ISP, such as Verizon's own DNS servers.

It is not terribly complicated to do, although I actually asked one of our folks to walk me through it yesterday, and I got bogged down in the process a couple of times. So I am not so sure that it is quite as easy——

Senator FRANKEN. That is reassuring.

Mr. DAILEY. Yes, but——

[Laughter.]

Senator FRANKEN. I think.

Mr. DAILEY. It certainly can happen, and that is one of the problems with DNS blocking, that it is certainly not 100 percent effective. I do not think that is really the bill's goal. The bill, as indicated, is really not designed to clamp down 100 percent, and I do not think that there are really very many 100-percent solutions in anything we try and do to regulate commerce on the Internet.

So I think that, yes, there are ways around it. If you start using a foreign DNS server that is also not secure, that has also been compromised so that you do not necessarily know where you are going on the Internet in terms of the results that are returned to your computer, yes, you certainly could increase phishing risk and privacy theft. How big a problem that really is is really hard to determine at this point.

Senator FRANKEN. Thank you. My time has expired. I guess we are going to do a second round.

I see, Mr. Turow, that the Screen Actors Guild, Directors Guild, the American Federation of TV and Radio Artists have all endorsed this legislation. I am a member of all three. I voted for this bill last year. I am glad that the Chairman has made some modifications. I am also interested in the architecture of the Internet to make sure that there is as much freedom on it—and, you know, I will be back for a second round, I guess.

Mr. Chairman?

Senator WHITEHOUSE. Everybody on the panel except perhaps Mr. Adams is a lawyer, correct?

Mr. ADAMS. That is certainly true in my case.

Senator WHITEHOUSE. OK, so we are four out of five. I am interested in Mr. Turow's notion of the private Attorney General aspect here, and it has certain historic resonance because, as long as you have got pirates out there, why not send privateers after them, which is what we in Rhode Island did years ago when we had pirates coming after our shipping. And so the notion of the private Attorney General is an interesting idea, but it raises the question of how effective our judicial branch has been in being an arbiter and forum for resolving these problems. And it strikes me that the judicial branch is sort of ready, willing, and able to do it, but it has not been used very much. The only case that I can think of that was exciting and interesting in this respect was Microsoft's lawsuit that went after—I want to say the domain providers that were connecting the botnets that were attacking Microsoft with their control nodes so that when the bad guys sent the signal to the control node to fire off the bots that they had out there, the signal went no place. They had been basically disabled from the net. And that was a wonderful countermeasure taken by Microsoft to counterattack, really, and it was done by going to court and getting an order from a United States district judge in California someplace, and the defendant, I think perfectly willingly once they had the case in front of them, complied and the attack on Microsoft was intercepted and shut down.

And it would seem to me that that ought to be happening more, and I would love to hear your opinions on why it is that we are— I mean, there are huge amounts of money at stake here, and why is it that you are not in the courts more often sorting through this with customers, with—I mean, it is not—there are theories that would tie you pretty closely to the criminal activity if they were stretched a bit. And certainly there are civil theories that could connect you to this. Why is it that this is not a more active Article III issue? Is it a lack of subject matter expertise? Is it a reluctance to go to the courts on the part of potential plaintiffs? Are there particular defenses and privileges that you have that keeps these things out of the court?

It just seems like that would be a very logical place to begin to develop a sort of common law in this area that could be much more flexible than what we do by statute here, and yet I see so little of it actually happening in practice.

Mr. TUROW. If I may answer, Senator, just from our perspective, there are two major issues, of course: one is the safe harbor in DMCA that allows people to say, "Not my fault," you know, the three monkeys routine, frankly. And the other, of course, is gaining personal jurisdiction over sites that are very often extraterritorial, which is why we think it would be wise to require a registered agent for anybody who is going to get a credit card payment to an overseas site.

Ms. JONES. Can I be heard on that just briefly?

Senator WHITEHOUSE. Yes, of course.

Ms. JONES. Since we do operate a massive percentage of the Internet's DNS around the world, the reason you do not see that issue in court more often is because all Microsoft has to do is pick up the phone and say, "Hey, Go Daddy, the Conficker virus is driving us crazy," and we say, "OK, we will fix it." And so do most of the other legitimate good corporate citizens. You do not have to go to court to get an order. We will just fix it for you, right? And this is the same thing that happens when there are other major massive attacks on people's systems, whether they come from in this country or outside the country. We just work on it, and we fix it for people, right? Do not go waste your money on a lawyer and file a lawsuit, for the love of God. Just pick up the phone and call us.

Senator WHITEHOUSE. Don't the studios whose content is all over the pirated sites pick up the phone and call you?

Ms. JONES. They do every single day. Thousands upon thousands upon thousands a year.

Senator WHITEHOUSE. So that does not work so well. Ms. JONES. And it works, right? The DMCA works in that context. We actually have a trademark policy that works in that context. You do not have to go to court and get a lawsuit in most of the cases. You only have to do that when there is a bad guy on the other end. And that is why—I think Mr. Turow and I are saying the same thing. Give the safe harbor to the good guys and give the consequence to the bad guys.

Senator WHITEHOUSE. My time has expired.

Chairman LEAHY. Thank you very much, and also thank you for all the behind-the-scenes work you have done on this, Senator Whitehouse.

Senator Coons, we are delighted to have you here, sir. Please go ahead.

Senator COONS. Thank you, Chairman Leahy, and thank you to the members of the panel. I serve, as most of us do, on two committees that are having simultaneous hearings, so I enjoyed reading your submitted testimony in advance and appreciate a chance to be with you today.

Counterfeiting and, in particular, online copyright infringement and the piracy of intellectual property is a very real and dramatically growing problem for us here and overseas, and it saps the creative energy and the resources that help sustain the sorts of innovations and service that you and your companies provide. But I also think, as we move forward in considering COICA, we have to balance America's historic role as a Nation that promotes free expression, and particularly given recent developments in Egypt and elsewhere, we have to make sure that we strike the right balance, that we continue to advance and promote democracy and free speech and strike the appropriate balance against infringing speech and outright theft, which are not things that we want to sustain.

Given that last exchange, if I could, Ms. Jones, I am just interested in how we might work in partnership with our counterparts abroad to help facilitate the efforts that are imagined under this bill and get your view on whether you think COICA, which allows the DOJ to compel third parties to take measures regarding sites registered abroad, either could help or hurt relations with counter-parties around the world that we need to engage. How might we effectively engage them and how might this challenge that relationship?

Ms. JONES. Counterparties means foreign governments?

Senator COONS. Foreign governments and, frankly, their comparable law enforcement entities.

Ms. JONES. We have been told repeatedly—and I think this is right—that the foreign governments with whom we are friendly, at least, are compelled and follow the example of the actions that are taken by the U.S. Government and U.S. law enforcement. And most of the countries that we have good relationships with will say, OK, the U.S. Government took this seriously, they made this a criminal action, their law enforcement are asking us for our cooperation, and to the extent that that action is illegal in this country, we are going to give it to them.

We routinely work with FBI—they have some clever name for it, but anyway, their local liaisons in foreign countries to help them investigate cases. It happens all the time. But to Ms. Yee's earlier point, you have to have the hook, OK? Because it is not enough for—let us use Great Britain, for example, to come and say, hey, Visa, hey, Go Daddy, can you help us out with this if what the person is doing is not illegal in their country.

Senator COONS. Right. Then my next question, in trying to strike that right balance between free speech protection and promotion of free speech and blocking outright piracy, how easy will it be for offending sites to effectively insulate themselves from domain name seizure if they, for example, Mr. Turow, take the pirated copies of your latest work and intermingle them with forwarded copies of the latest speech against the Government of Iran, you know, or other governments? How do we strike a balance that allows you to single out those sites that really are overwhelmingly dedicated to piracy from those that begin to insulate themselves from domain name seizure by mixing the two in a way that then makes it quite difficult to make the argument effectively overseas and at home? Any opinions on that, Mr. Turow?

Mr. TUROW. Well, first of all, I should say—and it will not come as any surprise—as president of the Authors Guild, the guild is obviously concerned about anything that borders on censorship, and we are clearly not advocating that and never would. We believe in due process before these sites are brought down.

You are completely right, Senator Coons, that this is a difficult enterprise, and there are all kinds of strategies to avoid whatever laws you craft. But I think that the point that has been raised here many times that a law that insists on coordinated activity by everybody in the Internet ecology is the best approach, so that, you know, the subtle alterations of websites can be addressed either through payment issues or by having the search engines be more vigilant about what they are allowing to be searched for in the first place.

Ms. JONES. Can I——

Senator COONS. My time has expired. I think with the Chairman's forbearance——

Ms. JONES. Can I just add to that real quick? As the company that probably responds to more of these than anybody else, our position is if there is any offending content, the whole website comes down. If you fix it, you take off the fake Rosetta Stone, you take off Mr. Turow's book, we will put it back up. OK? But it is either all of nothing, because we do not want that crap about, Are you 50/ 50? Are you 80/20? Are you really engaged in illegal activity? Are you really not? No. We want it to be black and white. Either you are or you are not. If you fix it, press on. But until you fix it, you are all gone.

Mr. DAILEY. May I comment on that as well?

Ms. JONES. I know he is going to hate that.

[Laughter.]

Mr. DAILEY. No, not necessarily. But it is good insofar as it goes in a notice and take-down environment. You pull down the site, and then it gets fixed, and then it gets put back up. The issue, I think, that the Committee is struggling with is what to do about non-domestic websites where we do not have a notice and take- down procedure necessarily. So that is a more complicated problem, and I think that the issue that you raised about websites restructuring their architecture, for example, to avoid a judicial order is a very real one, and that is part of the complexity that I was alluding to in my testimony earlier, that these are things that need to be, I think, discussed and figure out how do we work it, because we would like to see an effective mechanism to help the various copyright interests that are out there. We have no interest in seeing piracy continue, and we have done a lot of work at Verizon over the years with the content community to try and address the problem domestically.

But I just wanted to make that distinction between notice and take-down, which works, I think, reasonably well in the United States, different from, though, the issue that we are dealing with where we do not have that procedure abroad.

Senator COONS. Thank you. I just wanted to thank the Chairman in particular for this hearing and for his work on this. Global piracy is an enormously difficult thing that is draining billions of dollars of resources, and I want to thank the panel for the work that you represent today on behalf of your companies and you individually.

Thank you.

Chairman LEAHY. Thank you, and before I yield to Senator Blumenthal, I would note, as I did earlier, both Yahoo! and Google were invited to be here today. I wish they had come because a number of the answers you have given, each of you, it would have helped if they could have responded. But I would note to both those companies, there will be legislation, and it would have been helpful to have had their testimony here as we prepare for it, but we will have the legislation one way or the other.

Senator Blumenthal.

Senator BLUMENTHAL. Thank you, Mr. Chairman. And I join in your feeling that it would have been very helpful for them to be here and there will be legislation. And may I just say with all due respect to Mr. Dailey and Ms. Jones, taking down the website and then putting it back strikes me at least as an insufficient deterrent to this kind of conduct, almost part of the cost of doing business, which is why I think a private right of action, with damages, maybe treble damages, punitive damages, and an effective enforcement mechanism is absolutely necessary.

And to Mr. Dailey's point—I think it was your point—that there may be overuse or even abuse, that potential danger strikes me as no different in material respects than exists in many of our consumer protection laws where there are private rights of action and where it imposes costs that are in effect commensurate with the damage that is done.

I just want to say my view is—I know it may sound over simplistic—that we are dealing here with a situation that is comparable to the drug dealing kind of situation where the planes or the transport mechanisms that provide the vehicle that enable and facilitate the drugs to be imported or dealt in effect are knowingly going on with that activity without any real accountability. And if that were happening in the world of drug dealing, if planes or ships were knowingly transporting mules or the drugs directly, we would have a very different attitude toward them and should have a very different attitude toward the facilitators and enablers in this situation.

So I welcome your support for a private right of action, and my hope is that it will be in too big to fail.

Thank you, Mr. Chairman.

Chairman LEAHY. I thank the panel very much. I also thank all the Senators who have asked questions. We will keep the record open for one day for further questions. I will have a couple others that I will submit for the record.

[The questions of Chairman Leahy appears under questions and answers.]

Chairman LEAHY. Thank you for taking the time. It has been extremely helpful. This is a matter that we will have legislation. I appreciate the broad support from users, industry, authors, others.

We have at least two areas that everybody should have in their mind. You have websites that supply consumer goods. It can be everything from parts for your car to medication. If they are counterfeit, if they are such that can damage, people can die. I mean, that is not oversimplification. People can die from that. And that we should be concerned about.

But, also, if you are an author, you are a composer, you are a writer, you make a movie, if you have got something that is really not any good, well, you are not going to make money on it. But if you have got something you worked hard on and it is good, you ought to have the value of that and not have somebody who has simply stolen it, has a website, they get the value of it.

We had testimony once talking about the movie "Ray." Taylor Hackford, the producer of that movie on the life of Ray Charles, a great movie, one of my favorites, but he had spent years borrowing the money, trying to put this movie together. He put a lot of his own time and money and effort into it. He was so proud of the movie that he had a premier in

New York City. The next day he decided to walk up just to see the marquis with his name and the name of the movie on it. As he came around the corner, somebody offered to sell him a counterfeit copy. Now, at least he could go and say to the police, "The guy standing over there is doing it." But the same counterfeit copies are coming across the web.

Again, if people are going to make this effort, they ought to be rewarded. Mr. Turow, your comment about at least if you are a best-selling musician you can also do a concert. Authors cannot go out and do readings.

[Laughter.]

Chairman LEAHY. But even the people that have the music, it is great they can make money on their concerts, but they should not have to do that. And you have a lot of people who are writers of the music but are not the ones that are going to be seen in the concert.

So I think it is a very important issue. I do regret that the two companies invited here are not here, but we are going to push forward. Remember, this bill passed 19–0 in the Committee last year. We have bipartisan support. It will pass.

I thank everybody for being here, and we stand in recess.

[Whereupon, at 11:56 a.m., the Committee was adjourned.]

[Questions and answers and submissions for the record follow.]

In: Targeting Websites …
Editor: Anthony L. Mooney
ISBN: 978-1-53613-705-7

Chapter 3

QUESTIONS AND ANSWERS

SENATOR GRASSLEY'S WRITTEN QUESTIONS

For Judiciary Committee Hearing, "Targeting Websites Dedicated to Stealing American Intellectual Property,"
February 16, 2011

Questions for Tom Adams (Rosetta Stone)

1. Can you please explain how search engines can facilitate the business of rogue websites?

Answer:

"Rogue" websites, especially those based overseas, clearly understand that their success in perpetrating fraud on American consumers depends upon their ability to lure American consumers to their websites, and the most common and effect means of marketing their fraudulent sites is through paid advertisements on search engines such as Google. In the case of Rosetta Stone, Google misappropriates the value of the 'Rosetta Stone' trademark by selling the term 'Rosetta Stone' as a search engine "keyword" to counterfeiters who operate the "rogue" websites. When a consumer looking to purchase a Rosetta Stone product searches on Google for "Rosetta Stone", the resulting search results page will include not only links to Rosetta Stone's official website, but also paid advertisements linking to "rogue" websites. Google's search advertising market share of approximately 70% provides these foreign counterfeiters a convenient, low cost advertising platform to reach the majority of American consumers, without the threat of criminal prosecution. By selling the 'Rosetta Stone' term to such counterfeiters, Google instantly magnifies and proliferates the reach and potential impact of the "rogue" site on American consumers. These paid advertisements will typically offer to sell purportedly authentic Rosetta Stone products at steeply discounted prices, further diverting consumer interest from authentic Rosetta Stone websites, and when the consumer clicks on the link in the paid advertisement, the consumer is often directed to a website that is a "copy-cat" imitation of the official Rosetta Stone site. In this way, the counterfeiter is enabled by Google to easily and effectively reach the target of its fraud — the American consumer - and a Rosetta Stone product sale is diverted to the infringing website and the American consumer is deceived into providing his or her private credit and personal information, believing that he or she is buying an authentic Rosetta Stone product. Our customer care center has received complaints from a wide variety of "rogue" website victims who were misled by paid advertisements from search engines such as Google, including educators, law enforcement officers, business professionals, and retirees. Therefore, in order for any new legislation to be effective, it must include measures to prevent "rogue" websites from using search engines as their gateway to American consumers.

2. What do you believe is the appropriate role for search engines to play in combating rogue websites?

Answer:

Since the purveyors of counterfeit products rely heavily upon Internet search engines as their gateway to reach American consumers, we believe that the search engines such as Google should take proactive measures to block infringing websites from purchasing paid advertisements using the brand names of the pirated products as search engine keywords. It has been our experience that Google in particular has the ability, if and when it desires to do so, to filter out paid advertisements from pirate websites, thereby preventing them from bidding on the Rosetta Stone brand name as a keyword. Google also has the ability to “de-list” these infringing sites so that they do not appear in any of the search results of American consumers. The barrier to adopting these measures is not a lack of technology, but a lack of commitment on the part of Google to fighting piracy instead of profiting from it. Since last year’s legislation covered advertising networks, and “rogue” websites frequently rely on search engines for advertising, it would be a logical to expand the scope of the current legislation to include clear roles for the search engines in combating the proliferation and impact on US consumers of “rogue” websites.

3. What role should payment processors play in combating rogue websites?

Answer:

Payment processors should take reasonable steps to block payment transactions between U. S. consumers and the infringers who are attempting to sell them pirated copies of goods or services. They should adopt measures that would enable the brand owners of pirated products to expeditiously notify the payment processors that “rogue” websites are seeking to sell the pirated products to consumers and, upon receipt of such notification, block the “rogue” website and related website from using the services of the payment processors to transact sales with consumers.

4. Do you believe a private right of action should be included in any bill combating online infringement?

Answer:

The “rogue” website bill introduced last year puts the entire burden of seeking court action against “rogue” websites upon the Department of

Justice (DOJ). We are concerned, however, that the DOJ will not have the resources to investigate and bring about all the enforcement actions necessary to counteract the vast multitude of "rogue" websites, especially in light of the ability of the counterfeiters to put up clone copies of any "rogue" website which becomes the target of a DOJ enforcement action. Rosetta Stone alone has identified over 1000 rogue websites attempting to sell counterfeit copies of its products over the past 18 months. Therefore, the bill should allow the brand owners whose products and services are being counterfeited to have a right of action similar to that envisioned for the DOJ, so that brand owners and the DOJ are both empowered to combat these "rogue" websites, thereby maximizing the benefits to U.S consumers.

5. In 2008, the Ryan Haight Online Pharmacy Consumer Protection Act was signed into law. That law allows States to bring civil actions against websites that deliver or distribute controlled substances over the internet without a valid prescription. The law also allows courts to enjoin those websites from operating. Shouldn't the government have the same authority to combat websites that sell counterfeit goods that may pose a danger to consumers? Why or why not?

Answer:

We agree that the sale of counterfeit goods poses a danger to consumers because the pirated products may be of poor quality or even harmful. Consumers who purchase from "rogue" websites arc also exposed to the risks of identity theft, credit card fraud, software viruses and other malicious computer code. Moreover, the importation of pirated products causes substantial harm to the American economy and job growth. For these reasons, the analogy between the proposed legislation to combat "rogue" websites to the legislation on pharmacy products is very appropriate. Therefore, we agree that the government should have the similar authority to act against "rogue" websites that it has under the Ryan Haight law.

6. If the government already has the authority to domestically seize domain names of rogue websites, why shouldn't we authorize the government to take measures to combat these websites when they move outside our borders? Is it appropriate to ask corporate citizens to help us in the fight against counterfeiting and piracy?

Answer:

We agree that the government should have the authority to take measures to combat websites that are established outside the U.S. Under the existing take-down notice provisions of the Digital Millennium Copyright Act, we routinely send take down notices to the ISPs that host "rogue' websites. While the ISPs located in the United States have been generally responsive to our take down requests by removing or blocking the "rogue" websites, the ISPs located outside the U.S. have been mostly unresponsive. As a result, it has become common practice for the software pirates operating websites that are blocked by US-based ISPs as a result of our take down requests to re-create a cloned "rogue" website using an offshore ISP. Moreover, the government should have authority to act against "rogue" websites hosted on offshore ISP's because those offshore websites are more likely to harm American consumers by exposing them to poor quality products and to the risk of identity theft, credit card fraud and computer viruses and malware.

7. On November 29, 2010, ICE executed seizure orders against 82 domain names of websites engaged in the illegal sale and distribution of counterfeit goods and copyrighted works. Prior to Super Bowl 45, government authorities in New York seized several streaming websites that they accused of illegally showing live and pay-per-view sports events. Opponents of further legislative efforts argue that these actions were an overreach and that additional authority will lead to further abuse. What measures can be included in legislation to ensure DOJ does not overreach when exercising its authority?

Answer:

We do not agree with the assertion that the actions by ICE and other government authorities referred to in your question were an "overreach" of their authority. It is a criminal offense under existing law to copy, distribute and sell copyrighted goods and trademarked products. It should not matter what medium is used in order to conduct these illegal activities. Therefore, the mere fact that criminal offenders use the Internet as the medium for conducting their illegal transactions should not insulate them from enforcement actions by the government.

8. First Amendment constitutional concerns have been raised about last year's bill, do you agree? Do you believe the narrow definition of infringing websites, remedies directed at preventing only infringing content and the incorporation of the relevant Federal Rules of Civil Procedure alleviate concerns that the bill is overbroad?

Answer:

We do not believe that the illegal distribution and sale of counterfeit or pirated products and services should be sheltered from enforcement actions under the guise of the First Amendment merely because criminals choose to use the Internet as the medium in which to engage in those transactions. We agree that the provisions of last year's legislation strike a proper balance in ensuring that only infringing websites are subject to the enforcement actions envisioned in the bill.

9. The Federal Rules of Civil Procedure incorporated in last year's bill require advance notice for preliminary injunctions. For temporary restraining orders, they require a specific factual showing of immediate and irreparable damage and written certification explaining efforts made to give notice and the reason it is not required in a specific instance. Does the incorporation of these rules alleviate concerns that the bill does not protect process?

Answer:

We are in full agreement that the incorporation of Federal Rules of Civil Procedure in the bill alleviates the concern that the bill does not protect due process.

QUESTIONS OF SENATOR TOM COBURN, M.D.

"Targeting Websites Dedicated to Stealing American Intellectual Property" United States Senate Committee on the Judiciary.
February 16, 2011
Content Owners

Tom Adams, President and CEO, Rosetta Stone, Inc.

1. Do you believe there are any non-legislative ways to increase the fight against online piracy?

Answer:

Since the purveyors of counterfeit products rely heavily upon Internet search engines as their gateway to reach American consumers, we believe that the search engines such as Google should take proactive measures on a voluntary basis to block infringing websites from purchasing paid advertisements using the brand names of the pirated products as search engine keywords. It has been our experience that Google in particular has the ability, if and when it desires to do so, to filter out paid advertisements from pirate websites, thereby preventing them from bidding on the Rosetta Stone brand name as a keyword. Google also has the ability to "de-list" these infringing sites so that they do not appear in any of the search results of American consumers. The barrier to adopting these measures is not a lack of technology, but a lack of commitment on the part of Google to fighting piracy instead of profiting from it.

2. What methods does Rosetta Stone currently employ to enforce its trademarks and copyrights? Do you believe Rosetta Stone, as a rights holder, has an obligation to enforce those rights?

Answer:

Rosetta Stone believes that it has an obligation to enforce its trademarks and copyrights and believes that it is necessary for it to do so in order to protect the value of its substantial investments in research and product development as well as in marketing efforts to enhance its brand recognition. Because of the adverse impact of online piracy on our business, Rosetta Stone has committed substantial resources over the past several years to combat "rogue" websites and other sources of pirated copies of our products. We have created an enforcement department that has grown to six employees who, in conjunction with our Legal Department, are devoted full time to carry out a variety of programs to attempt to fight these illicit activities. Using sophisticated software programs, the enforcement team spends many hours each day scanning Internet search engines searching for "rogue" websites. This search effort is complicated by the fact that Google and other search engines enable their advertisers to `geo-target" their paid advertisements in any of myriad markets, so that the advertisements are shown only to the search engine users located in the targeted geographic locations. This functionality makes the possibility for a brand owner to adequately monitor and enforce its trademarks online impossible, since there is no way for a brand owner to adequately monitor all possible locations -- only the counterfeiter, and Google, are in a position to know everywhere the counterfeiter is marketing its fraudulent products to U.S. consumers.

When the enforcement team finds paid advertisements or organic search results that link to a 'rogue' website, they will send the search engine a take-down notice under the Digital Millennium Copyright Act (DMCA) in order to have the paid advertisement or organic links removed from the search engine results. We also send DMCA take down notices on a daily basis to the Internet Service Providers (ISPs) that host the "rogue" websites. However, this take-down process often results in a frustrating game of "whack-a-mole"; every time Rosetta Stone's enforcement team takes down a "rogue" website advertisement and/or the website itself, several other "rogue" websites resurface on offshore ISPs with new paid advertisements on the search engines.

The enforcement team also works extensively with the U.S. Customs and Border Protection (CBP) to train their customs agents to be able to identify and interdict the importation of counterfeit copies of our products into the U.S. The enforcement team also actively assists the Federal Bureau of Investigations (FBI), Immigration and Customs Enforcement (ICE) and other federal agencies as well as local law enforcement agencies in their investigations of criminal counterfeiting activities.

3. Do you use the current notice and takedown process under the Digital Millennium Copyright Act (DMCA)? If so, are search engines and others served with that notice responsive to your takedown requests?

Answer:

As stated in the previous answer, our enforcement department spends many man-hours on a daily basis scanning search engines thr "rogue" websites that sell counterfeit copies of our products. Then, the enforcement team sends DMCA notices on a daily basis to the search engines requesting that they take down the identified paid advertisements or organic links for "rogue" websites. In addition, we send daily DMCA take down notices to the ISPs that host these "rogue" sites. In fact, over the past 18 months we have identified and sent take down notices with respect to over 1000 rogue websites attempting to sell counterfeit copies of our products.

When the search engines receive our take down requests, they haven taken anywhere from one day to several weeks to remove the offending paid advertisement or organic link, but while the links remain up, unwitting consumers continue to be confused by the paid ads, and copyright infringers are able to purchase new paid advertisements from same search engines to replace the previous paid advertisements that are in the process of being taken down.

Regarding the ISPs' responsiveness, the ISPs located in the United States have been generally responsive to our take down requests by removing or blocking the "rogue" websites, but the ISPs located outside the U.S. have mostly been unresponsive. As a result, it has become common practice for the software pirates operating websites that are blocked by US-based ISPs as a result of our take down requests to re-establish a cloned "rogue" website with an offshore ISP. This results in the "whack-a-mole" process described in the previous answer whereby a new cloned "rogue" website reappears with a paid advertisement on a search engine almost immediately after our enforcement team gets the "rogue" site or its paid advertisement taken down.

4. Last year's legislation attempted to tackle online copyright infringement by asking registrars, ISPs, financial services providers and ad networks to suspend their respective services to the infringing site. Search engines, however, were not included in the legislation. Do you believe search engines should be asked to take some kind of action? Why or why not?

Answer:

Rosetta Stone strongly believes that Internet search engines must be included within the purview of the proposed legislation because the most common and effective way for "rogue" websites, especially those based overseas, to reach out to American consumers is through paid advertisements on search engines such as Google. In the case of Rosetta Stone, Google misappropriates the value of the `Rosetta Stone' trademark by selling the term 'Rosetta Stone' as a search engine "keyword" to counterfeiters who operate the "rogue" websites.

When a consumer looking to purchase a Rosetta Stone product searches on Google for "Rosetta Stone", the resulting search results page will include not only links to Rosetta Stone's official website, but also paid advertisements linking to "rogue" websites, Google's search advertising market share of approximately 70% provides these foreign counterfeiters a convenient, low cost advertising platform to reach the majority of

American consumers, without the threat of criminal prosecution. By selling the 'Rosetta Stone' term to such counterfeiters, Google instantly magnifies and proliferates the reach and potential impact of the "rogue" site on American consumers. These paid advertisements will typically offer to sell purportedly authentic Rosetta Stone products at steeply discounted prices, further diverting consumer interest from authentic Rosetta Stone websites, and when the consumer clicks on the link in the paid advertisement, the consumer is often directed to a website that is a "copy-cat" imitation of the official Rosetta Stone site. In this way, the counterfeiter is enabled by Google to easily and effectively reach the target of its fraud -- the American consumer - and a Rosetta Stone product sale is diverted to the infringing website and the American consumer is deceived into providing his or her private credit and personal information, believing that he or she is buying an authentic Rosetta Stone product. Since last year's legislation included advertising networks, and "rogue" websites frequently rely on search engines for advertising, it would be a logical to expand the scope of the current legislation to include search engines. This step would substantially enhance the effectiveness of legislation in combating the onslaught of counterfeit products being imported in the U.S. through rogue websites and the resulting adverse impact on U.S. jobs and the U.S economy.

Responses of Thomas M. Dailey

Vice President and Deputy General Counsel Verizon

1. Does Verizon currently block any type of material by taking action to prevent a customer from arriving at his desired website (ex. child pornography)?
   a. If yes, how is it different than what would be required under last year's proposed legislation?

Verizon Response:

Yes, with respect to its activities in the U.S., Verizon from time to time blocks access on a temporary basis to websites that are engaged in phishing, malware distribution or other network security-related activities. This is done to protect our network and our ability to provide services to our customers.

The difference between these network-security related activities and the proposed COICA requirements is not so much the specific technique itself—a domain name block is a valid and useful tool for temporarily addressing particular network security threats—but rather the fact that the scope and scale contemplated by COICA may require Verizon (and we assume other ISPs) to invest in different or additional technologies and/or to obtain new licenses to those technologies (which can be costly). In addition, the COICA processes around ongoing management of a dynamic list of blocked domain names are at this point undefined; the competitive and network impact of requiring fewer than all DNS providers to implement COICA blocks has yet to be examined; and the likelihood exists that some portion of U.S. consumers will be driven to offshore DNS providers, raising other complex issues related to security and network management.

The foregoing issues underscore the importance of ensuring that any blocking regime be narrowly tailored and used sparingly, that the legislation allow for cost recovery, and that the bill include language requiring the DoJ to develop appropriate procedures for implementing a blocking program in consultation with ISPs and other industry players.

2. What would the cost effect be on Verizon should legislation such as last year's bill be enacted? Do you believe the benefits outweigh the costs to Internet Service Providers (ISPs) in general?

Verizon Response:

The cost effect on Verizon, and we expect any ISP, of last year's legislation will vary depending on the number of DNS blocks ordered, the duration for which the blocks are in effect, and the narrowness of the domain names blocked (e.g., second level domains or resource records). Costs could be mitigated in part if the authority to bring suit were limited to the Department of Justice, DNS blocking were limited to situations where it is the least burdensome remedy available, and proper procedures were implemented to ensure judicial orders are narrowly tailored and blocks immediately removed once no longer justified. This said, potentially significant costs associated with blocking would remain, and Verizon believes that, as is currently done elsewhere in federal law, those costs should be shared by content owners above a certain threshold (depending on the size of the 1SP). While protecting the Internet from online actors who egregiously flaunt U.S. law carries a general benefit for all members of the Internet ecosystem, there is no specific benefit per se to ISPs. The "cost-benefit" analysis of COICA in terms of its impact on U.S. Internet policy is a closer question and one which requires further study and input from a broader segment of the Internet community, including the U.S. government.

3. Do you believe it would be effective for the bill to only focus on eliminating the counterfeit websites ability to host ads and process payments prior to using the DNS blocking mechanism (i.e. not involve ISPs)? Why?

Verizon believes that focusing on the hosting and financial infrastructure that supports rogue websites is the most effective way to combat online infringement, and that such targeted enforcement should he pursued before seeking any remedy that involves website blocking by a 1SP. Unlike ISPs, payment companies and ad networks may have a financial relationship with the rogue website. Cutting off the ability to monetize the website through ads or the ability to process payments for the sale of goods or content will eliminate the incentives for and ability of the websites to continue to operate. By targeting these aspects first, the bill would target the problem in the narrowest possible manner and avoid the over-breadth issues that may arise from ISP blocking.

4. The bill currently does not require search engines to block infringing websites from appearing in their search results. Do you believe search engines should be required to do so or otherwise act under any legislation? Why or why not?

Verizon Response:

Verizon's view on matters of Internet policy and regulation is that all participants in the Internet ecosystem should participate in efforts to further national interests where their involvement is reasonably necessary to achieving a public goal. If the DOJ blocklist is regularly updated and 1SP DNS servers are as a result updated as well, one would expect that the results returned to search engines should not include websites included in the blocklist. However, search engine companies have different processes for updating their DNS information and ensuring that caches are not out of date. Because DNS requests can get resolved in ways other than through ISP-operated DNS servers, we have recommended consulting more widely with other industry players — including search engine providers — in considering this legislation.

5. What type of relationship, if any, does Verizon have with rights holders to pursue enforcement of those rights under current law?

Verizon Response:

Verizon has been actively working with copyright holders to combat online infringement through efforts to notify Verizon customers of notice of alleged infringement submitted to Verizon by participating copyright holders. Under this program, Verizon informs affected customers that it has received notices of alleged copyright infringement from these rights holders. To protect customer's privacy, at no time does Verizon provide the name of the customer to the rights holder (absent receipt of a valid subpoena or other legal process). In addition, Verizon's customer portal provides educational information about copyright and infringement, FAQs regarding the notice forwarding program, and instructions on how to determine if peer-to-peer software as resident on a user's computer and ways to remove such software. We also provide instructions informing customers how to secure their wireless routers to help prevent third parties from accessing customer's internet connection.

SENATOR GRASSLEY'S WRITTEN QUESTIONS

For Judiciary Committee Hearing, "Targeting Websites Dedicated to Stealing American Intellectual Property,"
February 16, 2011

Responses of Thomas M. Dailey (Verizon)

1. What do you believe is the appropriate role for search engines to play in combating rogue websites?

Verizon Response:

Verizon's view on matters of Internet policy and regulation is that all participants in the Internet ecosystem should participate in efforts to further national interests where their involvement is reasonably necessary to achieving a public goal. When it comes to the role of search engines in combating Internet-based theft of intellectually property, the Committee should evaluate the extent to which their involvement would further the legislation's goals, balanced against the extent to which such participation would adversely impact their businesses or operations. This Committee and the search engine providers are in the best position to assess whether to include search engines within the scope of COICA.

2. What role should payment processors play in combating rogue websites?

Verizon Response:

As noted above, Verizon's general view is that all participants in the Internet ecosystem should participate in efforts to further national interests where their involvement is reasonably related to the issue at hand. In the case of combating Internet-based theft of intellectually property, payment processors clearly play a role in facilitating the sale and distribution of unlawful content to the extent they enable online merchants to receive payments for material sold on their websites. "Following the money" and cutting off the sources of funding of these rogue websites is the single most effective way to slow the unlawful distribution of trademarked and copyrighted material.

3. Do you believe a private right of action should be included in any bill combating online infringement?

Verizon Response:

No. For the reasons stated in my written testimony, Verizon strongly believes there should not be a private right of action under COICA. The website blocking proposed in the legislation is a major departure from U.S. policy on Internet blocking and it should be approached cautiously, if it is to be pursued at all. We have proposed a number of steps to help ensure that any ISP blocking requirements are narrowly tailored, including the establishment of procedures (in joint consultation between the Department of Justice, ISPs and others in the Internet community) to limit the number and duration of DNS blocks and properly to target the domain names to be blocked. While these procedures can be effective in limiting potential negative side-effects of the legislation when legal action is pursued by the DoJ, they will not be effective if private parties, motivated by their own financial and business interests, are allowed to pursue the blocks. The DoJ is far more likely than a private litigant to exercise discretion both in the number of cases it brings and the number and type of domain names it targets. The same cannot be said if private litigants are allowed to obtain a judicial blocking order. Moreover, administration of a process for notifying all ISPs and DNS service providers of the domains to be blocked (and when to unblock) is far better left to the DoJ than to private litigants. Finally, the blocking of third party, nondomestic websites is an extraordinary and unprecedented remedy that should not be entrusted to any entity with a direct pecuniary interest in the outcome of the litigation.

4. In 2008, the Ryan Haight Online Pharmacy Consumer Protection Act was signed into law. That law allows States to bring civil actions against websites that deliver or distribute controlled substances over the internet without a valid prescription. The law also allows courts to enjoin those websites from operating. Shouldn't the government have the same authority to combat websites that sell counterfeit goods that may pose a danger to consumers? Why or why not?

Verizon Response:

Verizon agrees that the government should have the authority to enjoin the operation of websites that traffic in unlawful trademark goods and copyright content, and remedies already exist under U.S. law to enjoin the operation of U.S. based websites that distribute such unlawful goods. The more difficult issue is how to address non-U.S. based websites. The questions COICA presents to U.S. policymakers in this regard are these: (1) how far should the U.S. should go in sanctioning Internet blocking of unlawful content resident on servers *outside* our borders; (2) how heavily should the government rely on the actions of private actors, like ISPs, to enforce the criminal and civil laws of the U.S.; and (3) is the financial and operational burden placed on such private actors justified and who should bear the cost of enforcing court orders to block access to websites deemed unlawful under COICA? These questions raise important Internet policy concerns, including the impact of a federally-sanctioned blocking scheme on global Internet freedoms and the free flow of online commerce.

5. If the government already has the authority to domestically seize domain names of rogue websites, why shouldn't we authorize the government to take measures to combat these websites when they

move outside our borders? Is it appropriate to ask corporate citizens to help us in the fight against counterfeiting and piracy?

Verizon Response:

The U.S. government's authority to act with respect to domestic websites is clear and well-established, but its authority to act regarding nondomestic websites is murkier and not only is likely to be the subject of significant debate but potentially could subject U.S. websites to retaliation by foreign governments. The issue is made all the more complex in light of the impact of website blocking on the free flow of information and commerce, and on issues of freedom of expression. As stated in my testimony, Verizon firmly believes that all responsible members of the Internet ecosystem can and should take steps to address the problem of online piracy, but the steps taken in furtherance of this legitimate goal should be cautiously taken and narrowly circumscribed to minimize the adverse impact of an Internet blocking scheme on the free flow of information and commerce across the globe.

6. On November 29, 2010, ICE executed seizure orders against 82 domain names of websites engaged in the illegal sale and distribution of counterfeit goods and copyrighted works. Prior to Super Bowl 45, government authorities in New York seized several streaming websites that they accused of illegally showing live and pay-per-view sports events. Opponents of further legislative efforts argue that these actions were an overreach and that additional authority will lead to further abuse. What measures can he included in legislation to ensure DO] does not overreach when exercising its authority?

Verizon Response:

Verizon believes that a number of steps can be taken to help ensure that the DoJ does not overreach when exercising its authority under COICA. First and foremost, the legislation should limit the authority to bring an enforcement action under COICA to the Dal. The DoJ is in the best position to independently investigate and narrowly tailor any judicial action to those rogue websites that should properly be targeted. Second, no private right of action should be allowed and the legislation should be amended to expressly state this limitation. Third, the DoJ should be required to work with ISPs and other members of the Internet community to determine the most effective ways to target the rogue websites — and only those domain names — that are unlawfully distributing trademark goods and copyrighted material, and to establish a set of procedures to ensure all ISPs are timely notified of their blocking obligations and, importantly, when the blocks should be removed. Finally, as outlined in my testimony, blocking should be used sparingly and only when it is the least burdensome remedy available and the rights holder community should provide reimbursement to ISPs for the costs ISPs incur in complying with blocking orders beyond established thresholds. These important steps will help ensure that overblocking does not occur and that the concerns raised over the ICE domain name seizures are not repeated.

7. First Amendment constitutional concerns have been raised about last year's bill. Do you agree? Do you believe the narrow definition of infringing websites, remedies directed at preventing only infringing content and the incorporation of the relevant Federal Rules of Civil Procedure alleviate concerns that the bill is overbroad?

Verizon Response:

Narrowing the definition of infringing websites, targeting remedies at only infringing content and incorporating relevant sections of the Federal Rules of Civil Procedure will help alleviate concerns regarding overbreadth, but they won't eliminate them. Verizon believes that additional safeguards are necessary to address further the constitutional concerns that have been raised regarding COICA. First, it is critically important that the blocking remedy be employed narrowly and, as stated in my testimony, only when it is the least burdensome way to achieve the stated goal of preventing the operation of a rogue website. Interfering with the financial operation of rogue websites will be a more effective means of combating unlawful websites and will be less likely to generate the constitutional concerns that accompany DNS blocking. The legislation should encourage the exhaustion of these financial remedies before turning to Internet blocking. Second, lawsuits should target onlythe "worst of the worst" rogue websites and judicial blocking orders should be narrowly tailored to focus on domain names that do not link to protected speech. Third, the additional precautions proposed in my testimony — no private right of action, implementation of proper procedures for notification to ISPs of the websites to be blocked and unblocked, and proper cost reimbursement — will further help alleviate the risk of an overblocking situation.

Finally, we recommend that the Committee avoid unnecessary extra-territorial concerns by changing the words "obtained in" to "targeted to" in Section 2(d)(2)(B)(iv). The use of the term "obtained", like the term "accessed", risks being seen as an endorsement of a line of foreign court decisions (such as *Dowlones v. Gutnick)* that have subjected U.S. news and e-commerce websites to defamation and parallel imports lawsuits simply because they were accessible in other countries. Replacing "obtained in" with "targeted to" would avoid raising this potential exposure for U.S. websites.

8. The Federal Rules of Civil Procedure incorporated in last year's bill require advance notice for preliminary injunctions. For temporary restraining orders, they require a specific factual showing of immediate and irreparable damage and written certification explaining efforts made to give notice and the reason it is not required in a specific instance. Does the incorporation of these rules alleviate concerns that the bill does not protect process?

Verizon Response:

Yes, we believe that reference to Federal Rule of Civil Procedure 65 regarding the standards for injunctive relief would be helpful. We also believe that it is important that the legislation establish a balanced and fair process, including robust notice procedures, particularly where *ex parte* proceedings are contemplated.

KLOBUCHAR QUESTIONS FOR THE RECORD

Responses of Mr. Thomas Dailey, Vice President and Deputy General Counsel, Verizon

1. Some experts have expressed concerns that COICA might "break the Internet" by causing more people to use alternative Domain Name System. or DNS, lookup services.
   a. How long have these alternative systems existed, and do you have any indication that their existence and current usage poses a threat to the Internet?

Verizon Response:

Alternative DNS services have been around for as long as the Internet. DNS is an open system and anyone can operate a DNS server for use by themselves and anyone else anywhere in the world. Historically and today, most DNS services arc commodities. It is only recently that entities like Google and Go Daddy have started to try to market differentiated DNS services based on claimed performance or security advantages. Verizon is not aware of any evidence that the existence or use of other equivalent DNS services — that is, services that all provide the same information in response to the same DNS query — threatens the Internet today.

This said, there are potential issues that could arise if there is a large-scale migration of U.S. Internet users to non-U.S. DNS services.

(1) Network Security Impact. If users leave their ISP's DNS service and migrate particularly to off-shore DNS providers, ISPs will start to lose visibility into DNS queries which can hamper network security efforts. For example, if an ISP can identify DNS queries

by hots (malware planted on a user's computer), the ISP can track and potentially thwart a botnet or denial of service attack. This ability would be diminished if customers no longer use their ISP's DNS. In addition, many ISPs employ techniques such as DNS cache-poisoning to help prevent their customers from inadvertently accessing malware and phishing websites. ISPs would lose the ability to help protect their customers from identify theft and other malicious activity for customers who do not use their own ISP's DNS.

(2) National Security Impact. If ISP consumers start using DNS services located outside the U.S., then all of the information generated by DNS query activity would be placed in the hands of foreign DNS providers and/or governments. This also starts to place a subtle operational capability in the hands of non-US companies or governments who could, if they chose to do so, determine which IP address is returned to a US consumer for a particular query. For example, if a computer asks France Telecom where www.whitchouse.gov is located on the Internet (which is what a DNS query does), France Telecom's DNS might not give the same answer as a US-based ISP might provide. This is the more benign case. A more serious situation arises if the foreign DNS provider is not a reputable ISP and instead of returning the correct IP address for www.bankothinerica.com the DNS provider sends the user to a site operated by a criminal organization by providing an IP address associated with the rogue site not the real one.

(3) Network Performance Issues. A number of commentators have alluded to impacts on Internet performance if U.S. consumers switch to foreign-based DNS providers. These concerns have some merit. As matter of simple physics, DNS queries will take longer if the answers to those queries are based in servers located overseas. Web pages often require multiple (sometimes dozens or more) of individual DNS look-ups to properly load all page content (e.g., images, text, advertisements and so forth), and use of overseas

DNS servers will slow this response time. In addition, some content distribution networks make assumptions about end-user location (e.g., East coast versus West coast) based on the IP address of the DNS server the person is using, and try to return geographically-proximate content to end users, which helps speed the delivery of content and provides shorter response times. These assumptions and models will need to change if U.S. consumers change their DNS usage patterns to using DNS services located off-shore.

2. Given that law enforcement would likely issue about 100 court orders per year, are you aware of any evidence that COCA enforcement might cause a massive changeover to alternative domain name systems?

Verizon Response:

The potential for a large-scale abdication of U.S. ISP-provided DNS services will depend on the number of domains actually subject to a blocking order (the fact that the DoJ may only obtain 100 court orders a year does not necessarily mean that only 100 domain names are blocked, since a single court order could involve tens or even hundreds of domain names). Moreover, the longer the blocking remedy is in place, the larger the pool of blocked domain names will become. As the pool grows, public reaction to the blocks may generate a disproportionate number of user defections. Just as importantly, however, the number of U.S. customers who change-over to a foreign-based DNS service also will depend on public perception of and reaction to this new tool in the hands of U.S. government. We simply do not know what the reaction among Internet users will be to government-mandated DNS blocking. Finally, we cannot predict what "work around" solutions people will develop in the future to circumvent the perceived threats posed by COICA. Some have speculated that such services will emerge overseas. If so, this could lead to the adverse consequences described above which would generally be bad for the Internet, even if it does not "break" it.

QUESTIONS OF SENATOR CHUCK GRASSLEY

"Targeting Websites Dedicated to Stealing American Intellectual Property"
United States Senate Committee on the Judiciary
February 16, 2011

Domain Name Registrar

Christine N. Jones
Executive Vice-President, General Counsel and Corporate Secretary.
The Go Daddy Group, Inc.

a. What do you believe is the appropriate role for search engines to play in combating rogue websites?

Search engines can, at a minimum, prevent paid and premium search results from resolving to websites containing infringing or counterfeit materials when they are properly notified of the existence of those websites.

b. What role should payment processors play in combating rogue websites?

Payment processors can disable the processing of payments on websites that they have been notified are selling infringing or counterfeit products. The involvement of payment processors in groups like the Financial Coalition Against Child Pornography (FCACP) has been invaluable in making it much harder for people to purchase child pornography. Similar actions to restrict the sale of infringing and counterfeit goods online would be extremely beneficial.

c. Do you believe a private right of action should be included in any bill combating online infringement?

No, we do not support the inclusion of a private right of action in a bill to combat online infringement. We believe that the existing mechanisms through which intellectual property owners may seek judicial redress and damages for online infringement and counterfeiting are sufficient to protect their private rights of action. We believe any proposed legislation should focus on establishing clear processes through which law enforcement can assist intellectual property owners to police and protect their rights online.

d. In 2008, the Ryan Haight Online Pharmacy Consumer Protection Act was signed into law. That law allows States to bring civil actions against websites that deliver or distribute controlled substances over the internet without a valid prescription. The law also allows courts to enjoin those websites from operating. Shouldn't the government have the same authority to combat websites that sell counterfeit goods that may pose a danger to consumers? Why or why not?

The government should certainly have the authority to combat websites that sell infringing or counterfeit goods, and we believe that existing law gives it such authority. However, we would support additional legislation that specifically allow s the States to bring civil actions against websites that offer counterfeit goods for sale, and that allows courts to enjoin them from operating. We would prefer that any such legislation differentiate between the various levels of unlawful activity that can be conducted through a website. In our view, the worst type of infringing activity occurs where counterfeit products pose an immediate danger to the public (medications, etc.). We believe that the strongest consequences should attach to this type of activity, versus, for example, the sale of bootleg DVDs or counterfeit tickets, which, while egregious, probably do not pose as serious and immediate a safety risk.

Any such legislation should clearly enunciate the standards and best practices to be followed by website hosting providers and domain name registrars and registries with respect to online infringements and counterfeits, and provide a safe harbor for the organizations that adhere to such standards.

e. If the government already has the authority to domestically seize domain names of rogue websites, why shouldn't we authorize the government to take measures to combat these websites when they move outside our borders? Is it appropriate to ask corporate citizens to help us in the fight against counterfeiting and piracy?

Go Daddy agrees that the government should have the ability to take measures to combat rogue websites operated outside of U.S. borders. We have also long felt that we and our fellow hosting providers and registrars have an opportunity and moral responsibility to help make the Internet a safer place. To that end we have always encouraged our fellow providers to adopt policies and procedures similar to the best practices we instituted years ago. It is absolutely appropriate to ask providers to help the government in this fight.

f. On November 29, 2010, [CE executed seizure orders against 82 domain names of websites engaged in the illegal sale and distribution of counterfeit goods and copyrighted works. Prior to Super Bowl 45, government authorities in New York seized several streaming websites that they accused of illegally showing live and pay-per-view sports events. Opponents of further legislative efforts argue that these actions were an overreach and that additional authority will lead to further abuse. What measures can be included in legislation to ensure DOJ does not overreach when exercising its authority?

Any proposed legislation needs to include clear and transparent standards for the identification of websites that are targeted under this effort.

In addition, where attempts to contact the website operator fail, takedown attempts and contacts with respect to content should be made through the website hosting provider, the domain name registrar, and the domain name registry, in that order. Domain name registries should rightfully be the last point of contact for website "content" issues. Involving hosting providers and registrars earlier in the process will prevent the confusion that occurred in the aftermath of the November 2010 ICE seizures. We would also advocate for the provision of some advance notice to the involved providers prior to the service of takedown orders.

g. First Amendment constitutional concerns have been raised about last year's bill. Do you agree? Do you believe the narrow definition of infringing websites, remedies directed at preventing only infringing content and the incorporation of the relevant Federal Rules of Civil Procedure alleviate concerns that the bill is overbroad?

Go Daddy is a strong believer in open expression and free speech on the Internet. We also believe that domain names, in and of themselves, do not violate intellectual property protections. It is the content on a particular website or sites that may be unlawful and should be the target of the proposed legislation. We would therefore like to see the legislation revisited and clarified with respect to the question of when and how a website will be determined to be "dedicated" to infringing activities.

h. The Federal Rules of Civil Procedure incorporated in last year's bill require advance notice for preliminary injunctions. For temporary restraining orders, they require a specific factual showing of immediate and irreparable damage and written certification explaining

> efforts made to give notice and the reason it is not required in a specific instance. Does the incorporation of these rules alleviate concerns that the bill does not protect process?

We appreciate the inclusion of the reference to the Federal Rules of Civil Procedure in the bill. However, we would like the final version of the bill to include a specific advance notice provision for domain names registrars and hosting providers, so that these entities can work to minimize the impact of domain name seizures on legitimate customers and can be prepared for media and public inquiries regarding government actions against domain names.

Some groups have raised technological concerns with the way last year's bill was drafted. Specifically, they are concerned with the DNS blocking requirement and the potential for collateral harm to the Internet ecosystem. They've indicated that the DNS blocking provision in last year's bill 1) would increase the risk of identity theft, spyware, malware, and other malicious activities; 2) would diminish the ability of network managers and cyber-security experts to monitor the network and protect U.S. internet users from cyberattacks; 3) would allow an offshore DNS provider to orchestrate a denial of service attack on U.S. internet websites; 4) would upset the work U.S. DNS providers have done to implement "DNS Security Extensions"; 5) would invite retaliation against U.S. internet companies by foreign governments; 6) would result in over-blocking of lawful content and other communications such as e-mail; and 7) would inject inefficiency into the internet infrastructure and slow down the internet for all users. Do you agree with each of these specific concerns? Please explain why each of these concerns has or does not have merit.

The widespread implementation of DNS filtering would absolutely result in a large number of Internet users attempting to circumvent such filtering. While the easiest and most common way to do this is to use a proxy site, undoubtedly some users will change their primary DNS resolver to an overseas provider.

(1) If more users begin using DNS servers that are not secured, they will be in a position of exposed risk to DNS poisoning and similar security concerns. Ironically, this increases the likelihood of their exposure to counterfeit websites.
(2) 'the DNS filter could also diminish the ability to monitor DNS servers, which is an important tool for domestic ISP and DNS providers. If a significant portion of a provider's customer base uses other DNS servers as a rule, the provider will be unable to effectively protect them.
(3) Denial of service attacks from foreign servers are a constant reality for any significant U.S. ISP. We do not believe that this threat will be significantly increased as a result of this legislation.
(4) The DNS filtering provision could adversely impact the work that U.S. DNS providers have done to implement DNS security extensions. We believe that the filtering provision would result in a shift towards overseas providers, which have not yet widely implemented DNSSEC authentication keys. Without such keys, providers have no way of verifying the validity of DNS record responses.
(5) In our view, DNS filters would potentially invite retaliation of U.S. companies by foreign governments, or, at a minimum, would result in widespread criticism of the system by free speech and free trade advocates. For example, the U.S. has long been a vocal critic of the Chinese government's well publicized filtering of Internet traffic for its citizens. The imposition of DNS filtering targeted towards foreign IPs could be perceived as hypocritical, at the very least.
(6) We agree that the proposed DNS filter, unless clearly and narrowly defined, could very likely result in the overblocking of lawful content and email. In our view, this is the most valid concern relating to the DNS filtering proposal. The "collateral damage" that could occur based upon the filtering of lawful sites is a stark reality.

(7) We agree that the DNS filtering proposal will lead to a significant adoption of foreign DNS servers, which will result in a drop of efficiency of lookups for those using the foreign servers. As a global hosting provider, we can attest that the proximity of the server certainly affects the speed of returning content results.

All these concerns, combined with the fact that DNS filtering is unlikely to actually stop anyone who wants to visit websites that contain infringing or counterfeit content, support our view that DNS filtering is an ineffective mechanism for combating the theft of intellectual property online.

Questions of Senator Amy Klobuchar

"Targeting Websites Dedicated to Stealing American Intellectual Property"
United States Senate Committee on the Judiciary
February 16, 2011

Domain Name Registrar

Christine N. Jones
Executive Vice-President, General Counsel and Corporate Secretary
The Go Daddy Group, Inc.

1. Ms. Jones, you have expressed the opinion that we should refine the definitions included in last year's COICA bill to ensure clarity in determining which sites are "dedicated" to infringing. One way to accomplish this would be to include various factors indicating a "dedication" to infringement which would assist the DOJ in their enforcement of COICA.
   a. Are there any factors you think would be relevant and appropriate to include in such a revised definition?

We would like the bill to include a requirement that the following factors be considered in determining whether a website is "dedicated" to infringing activities:

- Whether the infringing or counterfeit content is likely controlled by the website owner (as opposed to user-generated content that the owner may be unaware has been posted to the site).
- The amount of infringing/counterfeit content on the website.
- The amount, type and value of goods offered through the site.
- Whether there is an obvious attempt to pass counterfeit goods off as authentic goods.
- The number of days the site has been "live."
- The ability to contact the alleged infringer either through information provided on the website or through the WHO'S contact data.
- The response of the alleged infringer when requested to remove the infringing/counterfeit content.

2. You noted in your written testimony that previous COICA legislation conflicts with the current law under the DMCA to the extent that it authorizes the Attorney General to shut down domain names with user-generated content without first notifying the site operator.
    a. What steps, if any, could be taken to speed up DMCA notification processes to ensure that infringing content is quickly removed?

Go Daddy has found the DMCA to be an extremely effective mechanism in assisting intellectual property owners and hosting providers to "expeditiously" remove infringing content from websites (or to take down the entire website, when appropriate). We would support legislation that extends the current DMCA protections to content that constitutes trademark and trade name infringement. We would further support the inclusion of a specific timeline in which complaints must be reviewed and responded to by the hosting provider. Any such legislation should include specific notice and safe harbor provisions for providers that comply with its provisions.

3. Some experts have expressed concerns that COICA might "break the Internet" by causing more people to use alternative Domain Name System, or DNS, lookup services.
   a. How long have these alternative systems existed, and do you have any indication that their existence and current usage poses a threat to the Internet?

Alternate DNS providers, proxy sites, and similar work-arounds have been in existence for a long time — almost as long as the Internet itself. They are regularly used by people either wishing to avoid detection or otherwise trying to circumvent restrictions put in place by their service providers. ISPs are constantly combating these measures. It is true that as more filtering mechanisms are put in place, these existing, as well as new, circumvention measures will be more widely utilized.

   b. Given that law enforcement would likely issue about 100 court orders per year, are you aware of any evidence that COICA enforcement might cause a massive changeover to alternative domain name systems?

We do not believe that the number of orders issued under COICA will drive people to seek alternate DNS solutions. Rather, it will be the mere enactment of COICA, and the media attention given to any domain name seizures made under the new law, that will result in the proactive movement of potentially infringing users to alternative DNS systems.

Whether COICA is applied in only a handful of situations or in the thousands, individuals who intend to obtain downloaded copies of music, movies, etc., are likely to transfer their domain names before even one court order is issued. This would be an unfortunate, but somewhat probable, result of the legislation.

QUESTIONS OF SENATOR TOM COBURN, M.D.

"Targeting Websites Dedicated to Stealing American Intellectual Property"
United States Senate Committee on the Judiciary
February 16, 2011

Domain Name Registrar

Christine N. Jones
Executive Vice-President, General Counsel and Corporate Secretary
The Go Daddy Group, Inc.

1. Could you please explain the role of Go Daddy and other registrars in the current process Immigration and Customs Enforcement (ICE) uses to shut clown counterfeit websites?

Go Daddy and our fellow registrars are sometimes asked to remove active websites through domain name redirection. As a hosting provider, Go Daddy may also be asked to suspend hosting services for a website with infringing or counterfeit content. In other instances we are alerted to a claim of infringement or counterfeiting on a particular website only after a domain name has been redirected by the registry. Sometimes we are not notified at all.

a. Do you believe this process is effective?

No. This is one of the primary concerns we have about the current domain name seizure and website takedown process. The process should be consistently directed to the providers who are relevant to the situation.

We would like actions against infringing or counterfeit websites to be directed first to the website operator, then to the hosting provider, then to the registrar, then to the registry, in that order.

b. Do you believe last year's proposed legislation duplicates what ICE is already doing?

In our view, COICA is meant to provide additional direction to and support for ICE's (and other government agencies' and courts') existing processes.

c. Would your role be significantly different under last year's proposed legislation than it currently is with ICE? Why?

The legislation does not pose any significant change for Go Daddy as we have been taking action against websites with infringing and counterfeit content for many years. We feel it is Go Daddy's role to comply with seizure orders from ICE and DOJ by shutting down the requested websites. As we have an existing process to quickly comply with these orders, we see this mainly as causing an expansion of the quantity of issues / orders we implement.

The biggest change would be for domain name registries, which have historically not been involved in disputes involving website content. In addition, the legislation will impact smaller or less prepared registrars which may need to make major process changes and staffing additions in response to the new requirements.

2. Last year's proposed legislation will clearly not eliminate all counterfeit websites from existence, and that was not the intent. However, one of the goals is to prevent unassuming consumers from being taken advantage of by websites alleging to sell legitimate products.
   a. Do you think the legislation will be effective in protecting the average consumer? Why or why not?

The primary beneficiaries of this legislation are intellectual property owners. Although there can certainly be a direct safety-related benefit to the public in cases of counterfeit medications, etc., it seems inaccurate to imply that public safety is the primary aim of the legislation.

That being said, the takedown and replacement of websites selling counterfeit products with educational or warning landing pages can have an extremely positive effect on consumer education. The Internet security and anti-phishing communities have used a similar approach in recent years, with much success.

b. What, if any, potentially unintended consequences to registrars could result from enacting the legislation as it was reported by the Judiciary Committee last year?

Of the several possible unintended consequences that could flow from the current version of the legislation, one that is of particular concern is the method through which DOJ will determine what constitutes a website that is "primarily designed" to engage in infringing behavior. There are a large number of websites that display user-submitted content with a mix of legitimate and infringing material. If the line is drawn too liberally, legitimate content distribution will be hindered and public opinion and support for the measure will suffer.

3. The bill currently does not require search engines to block infringing material from appearing in their search results. Do you believe search engines should be required to do so? Why?

This is an area that is likely to meet stiff resistance from search providers. Many search providers claim that filtering or blocking is not possible or practical. From our perspective, there is already some blocking mechanism in place to prevent search results for things like "child pornography" from returning actual offending results. It seems reasonable that similar measures could be taken in the area of counterfeit drug sales or similar infringing activities.

4. What would the cost effect be on Go Daddy should legislation such as last year's bill be enacted? Do you believe the benefits outweigh the costs to registrars in general?

Although the proposed legislation will likely not impose a great cost on Go Daddy, it will certainly increase costs for many smaller registrars that will need to create or expand their mechanisms for responding to complaints and orders brought under the law. To the extent that the law results in the increased integrity of the Internet, however, the potential benefits to registrars are also very great.

5. What efforts, if any, does Go Daddy currently employ to block child pornography? Would last year's proposed legislation addressing websites selling counterfeit products require different action from Go Daddy than what it uses to combat online child pornography? Why or why not?

Go Daddy works directly with the National Center for Missing and Exploited Children to help identify, report, and act on reports of child pornography. With the National Center acting as the authoritative clearing house for information between providers and law enforcement, we have been very successful in helping to remove child pornography and related content from the Internet.

COICA is different in that it does not establish two-way communication between registrars and hosting providers and law enforcement. Under the proposed legislation, law enforcement groups (ICE, etc.) will be solely responsible for determining which content needs to be removed. The legislation would require Go Daddy to comply with government takedown requests and court orders, but it does not establish a reporting requirement for providers.

6. Your testimony states the numerous actions Go Daddy has already undertaken to cooperate with both U.S. and foreign law

enforcement, which has resulted in the disabling of websites offering counterfeit content.

a. Would enactment of last year's proposed legislation alter your ability to continue working with both domestic and foreign law enforcement as you have in the past?

No. We would continue to work directly with law enforcement in their investigations as we have in the past.

b. What additional benefits to your efforts to shutter these rogue websites would last year's proposed legislation provide, if any, either for domestic or foreign websites?

As we already willingly comply and assist in taking down websites as directed by law enforcement, the biggest potential benefits of the legislation to Go Daddy would be: (1) a clarification of the process through which law enforcement would work (i.e., the direction of instructions and orders to first the website operator, then the web host, then the registrar, then the registry); (2) a provision for advance notice to the web host and registrar where websites or domain names are found to be linked to infringe or counterfeit content; and (3) a safe harbor provision for companies that act in compliance with the law.

c. Is legislation necessary to enhance your work with law enforcement to take more counterfeit content offline either in the U.S. or abroad? Why or why not?

This legislation is not necessary to enhance the work Go Daddy has done in this area. This legislation would not be necessary at all if the Internet industry as a whole would implement procedures similar to ours to combat infringers and counterfeiters online. Unfortunately, not all hosting provides, registrars, registries, payment processors, and search providers have been willing to do that thus far.

7. What do you believe will be the technological effect on the internet of utilizing Domain Name System (DNS) blocking? Have you seen a large amount of Internet traffic move to foreign DNS as a result of ICE's recent actions to shut down counterfeit websites?

DNS filtering has never been a particularly effective way of preventing access to website. There are numerous ways to circumvent DNS filtering, including the transfer of a website's DNS to an overseas provider and the abundant availability of proxy sites. When weighed against the potential "chilling effect" arising from the large constituency of individuals who oppose any filtering of internet content, as well as the potential loss of hard-fought DNS security implementation by domestic DNS providers, DNS filtering becomes a very unappealing option.

Scott Turow Responses to Senator Coburn

1. Do you believe there are any non-legislative ways to increase the fight against online piracy?

Answer:

Yes, but without gaining legal jurisdiction over offshore entities that facilitate the trafficking of stolen books, music, and movies, these efforts will be woefully inadequate to the challenges we face. Copyright piracy is rampant online. It has largely undermined the recorded music industry and now threatens the book publishing industry. We need better legal tools to hold those who facilitate this piracy responsible.

2. What methods does the Authors Guild currently employ to enforce its trademarks and copyrights? Do you believe your members, as rights holders, have an obligation to enforce those rights?

Answer:

We regularly advise our members on DMCA procedures so they can compel online service providers to take down unauthorized copies of our members' books. While property owners may have some obligation to police their rights, it should not become — as it has for many— a full-time obligation. Our current law is in desperate need of repair.

3. How would the tools provided in last year's legislation benefit your members as compared to the current efforts by ICE to shut down counterfeit websites?

Answer:

Current efforts are limited to domestically based web domains. Authors and publishers need an effective means to bring fully offshore piracy operations to justice. In our view, this should include empowering authors to bring copyright infringement actions against certain classes of foreign online service providers using in personal jurisdiction, just as art author could against a U.S.-based online service provider.

4. Clearly, creativity and innovation were important to our Founding Fathers as protection of those rights appear in the text of the Constitution in Article I, Section 8. In addition, the First Amendment plays a role protecting the opinions expressed in the creative works of inventors and authors. Do you believe last year's proposed legislation also appropriately took those constitutional considerations into account? Why or why not?

Answer:

By incorporating the protections of the Federal Rules of Civil Procedure, last year's proposed legislation almost certainly passes constitutional master. To avoid any reasonable concerns, however, we believe that legislation should rely as little as possible on inner justification. Instead, we urge the Committee to provide a means for courts to exercise in personal jurisdiction over rogue websites.

Scott Turow Responses to Senator Grassley

1. What do you believe is the appropriate role for search engines to play in combating rogue websites?

Answer:

Far too many companies are profiting, in countless ways, from online piracy and counterfeiting. Until that ends, we cannot effectively address the problem of rogue websites. Search engines and all entities that regularly and predictably profit from online piracy and counterfeiting certainly must play a role in fighting rogue sites.

As things now stand, fighting piracy plays no visible role in the business of search engines. Small wonder. At the same time that search engines take cover under the DMCA's safe harbor protections, they are rewarded for turning a blind eye toward advertisers that plainly facilitate trafficking in stolen books, music and movies.

This simply cannot continue. Asking for voluntary cooperation is clearly not the answer. At this moment, search engines are profiting from companies that forthrightly market copyright infringement services even though the Senate Judiciary Committee, the House Judiciary Committee, and The White House are actively pursuing remedies for rampant online infringement.

To illustrate this point, I'd like to supplement my written testimony with a third case study.

CASE STUDY #3: MYPADMEDIA

Using Search Engine Advertising and Affiliate Networks to Market Copyright Infringement Services.

A search earlier this week for "ebooks" at Bing, Google, and Yahoo, yielded the following ads on the first page of results:

Bing:

Download eBooks!
Don't waste your hard earned dough on eBooks from other Websites
www.ibooks-r-us.com

Unlimited Ebooks Download
Books, Comics, Newspapers & More.
One-Time Fee, Full Access Forever.
www.thereadingsite.com

Yahoo:

Download Unlimited Ebooks
Download Unlimited Ebooks Today
Ebooks, Comics, Newspapers, & More
www.thenovetnetwork.com

Download eBooks!
Don't waste your hard earned dough on eBooks from other Websites
www.ibooks-r-us.com

Biggest eBook Database
Want to Read Thousands of Books
On your New Pad? You are a Click Away...
www.ePadLibrary.com

Google:

Unlimited eBooks Download
Special offer for NewYork residents
One time Fee — only $50/LifeTime
New York
Buy-ebooks.name/newyork

Each of these ads lead to websites that are apparently controlled by myPadMcdia, including, most frequently, the Novel Network, www.thenovelnctwork.com.

The Novel Network Home Page

Had any major search engine taken the time to set up a rudimentary system of occasionally reviewing the home pages of its advertisers, particularly those that use keywords tied to widely pirated goods, they would have found that the Novel Network boasts in large typeface at the top of its home page:

Thousands of Ebooks!
Download, read, and enjoy any eBook from our network!

The page lists six starred benefits of its service:

- The highest-quality eBook downloads on the net!
- Members have unlimited access, no restrictions!
- Unlimited free Novels, Comics, Newspapers & more!
- Free 24 hour Technical Support
- No monthly or 'Pay Per Download' fees
- Huge Media Selection — over 30,000+ titles available!

Above images of an iPhone, Kindle, iPad, and Nook, the home page promises "Unlimited eBooks for iPad, iPhone, Kindle, The Nook, PC, MAC."

The home page also displays a blue starburst proclaiming that the service "Includes Bestselling eBooks!"

The Novel Network's Answers to Frequently Asked Questions

A search engine employee instructed to conduct a modicum of diligence would then likely take a moment to click the "Learn More!" button, which leads to the frequently asked questions page. Here is a sample from that page:

What is The Novel Network?

The Novel Network is the internet's latest unlimited eBook downloading membership site. We allow our members to access thousands of eBooks, comic books, and newspapers and download them straight to their iPad, Kindle, Nook, or any other eBook reading device or Tablet you may own - without having to pay a cent for any of our downloads! ...

What Type of ebooks Can Members Get Access To?

Members can download thousands of eBooks in a range of genres, including bestsellers, classics, mystery, thriller, crime, romance, fantasy and children's books. These aren't books by authors you have never heard of Our network contains bestselling books which are being sold at your local bookstore or on sites like Amazon, Barnes & Noble, Borders and the iTunes iBookstore.

What about Comic Books?

The Novel Network allows members to download hundreds of superhero, action, manga, anime, and comedy comic books straight to their device! New, weekly releases from Marvel, DC, Image and Dark Horse are always being added to the member's area.

What Do You Mean By 'Unlimited' Downloads?

By unlimited, we mean UNLIMITED! You are free to download as many eBooks, newspapers, comic books and much more to your device, as many times as you like, and all content is yours to keep forever! ...

The same page displays a Nook e-reading device with the names of bestselling authors (Patricia Comwell, James Patterson, and Janet

Evanovich among them) on seven book spines. Shortly above a "Start Downloading Now!" button, we find:

So How Much Does This Cost?

To join The Novel Network, you simply pay the low, low price of 49.95 and you will get unlimited lifetime access to the member's area and the features it provides. There are no more hidden fees or costs per downloads. The Novel Network is amazing value for money when you consider how expensive individual eBooks are. Why pay $15 per eBook when you can get unlimited lifetime access to eBooks for only $49.95?

Throughout the site are buttons that take one to a secure payment page where one can pay $49.95 with MasterCard, Visa, or PayPal for a lifetime membership in the Novel Network.

After precisely two clicks (one on the Bing, Yahoo, or Google ad, the second on the frequently asked questions page), it's clear beyond any reasonable conjecture that the Novel Network either provides copyright infringement services or it defrauds purchasers into believing it sells those services. Either way, no search engine should be accepting advertising from myPadMedia. Yet they do so at this very moment.

Novel Network's "membership" business model for piracy services is not new. It's instantly recognizable to anyone with a passing familiarity with online trafficking in stolen hooks, music and movies. It is, chapter and verse, the business model for Pirate Bay. The Novel Network is a Pirate Bay clone.

So here's where we are: search engines companies, which by all accounts are among the most profitable online businesses, cannot find the motivation to do the most perfunctory of reviews of advertisers buying targeted search terms for a commonly pirated creative work: ebooks.[1] These companies are loaded with top computer engineering talent, yet they

[1] Other media fare no better. A search for "free music downloads" and "limewire" at Bing, Google and Yahoo brings up paid, first-page ads at each of the search engines for many sites purporting to offer versions of Limewirc's filesharing software. As a result of a copyright infringement lawsuit brought by music publishers, Limewire has been under a federal court order to stop distributing its software since October. The sites advertised at Bing, Google and Yahoo either actually offer the piracy software or are defrauding purchasers into believing they're offering the piracy software.

fail to deploy simple algorithms and procedures to detect advertisers that are Pirate Bay clones, and are either marketing piracy services or simply defrauding their customers.

But it's far worse than that.

Going Viral: Affiliate Networks + Search Engine Advertising

The Novel Network pays affiliates generously to help market its copyright infringement services. The affiliates page at its website hears the headline "Earn Hundreds of Thousands of Dollars with the Novel Network." This may be a bit of puffery, but it does offer 75% of the Novel Network's earnings per referred sale. "That means you get a massive $34 for each sale you send us!" To make earning those referral fees easy, The Novel Network provides banner ads and an embeddable YouTube video[2] that promises viewers unlimited e-books as it displays covers of "The Cat in the Hat," "The Catcher in the Rye," "The Wizard of Oz," and books from Stephen King and Stephenie Meyer.

The Novel Network encourages affiliates to use pay-per-click advertising at search engines and provide a list of 28 useful search-term phrases for those ads. Here's a sample (we've cut the list in half):

Feel free to use these keywords for PPC campaigns (like Google Adwords), article writing and blogging,

novel network review
download novels
ipad ebooks
ipad downloads
ipad textbooks
kindle ebooks
nook ebooks
c-reader books
kindle downloads

---

[2] http://www.youtube.com/wateh?v=11H8C7MARao&feature—player_embedded.

e-reader downloads
download children books
epub books
download books to kindle
download hooks to nook
free ebooks sites
net ebooks

Authors Guild staff found dozens of sites acting as Novel Network affiliates. A YouTube search for "the novel network" yielded 504 results, with the top ten, ranked by views, containing Novel Network affiliate links. Those ten videos had been viewed more than 25,000 times.

Enter Plimus of Silicon Valley

Prospective Novel Network affiliates are instructed to create an affiliate account at Plimus, one of the largest retailers of digital products online" where affiliates arc paid "by check, wire transfer, PayPay, and even prepaid Mastercards."

Plimus, according to its website, was founded in 2001 and is headquartered in Silicon Valley. (http://home.plimus.com/ccommerce/company/about-us). If one registers as a prospective affiliate and goes to the "marketplace" tab, one finds a list of online goods one can help sell, sorted by "Marketplace Score,- which "reflects a comparative item grading according to the level of affiliate revenues generated, current number of active affiliates promoting the item and its refund ratio. Rating runs from 1 (low) to 5 (high)."

The Novel Network ranks #9 out of 3,184 in Marketplace Score, with "Lots" of Active Affiliates. Its listing at Plimus couldn't be plainer:

The Novel Network
Seller: myPadMedia

> The Novel Network lets members download Unlimited eBooks, Comic Books and Newspapers straight to the iPad, iPhone, Kindle, Nook, or any other e-Reader! Fiction, Nonfiction, Bestsellers, Mystery, Thrillers, Romance, and more! Also works with PC & Mac.

The top twenty offerings, by Marketplace Score, in the Plimus affiliate marketplace include the following thirteen:

1. Download iPad Movies (Seller: AffiBank Network LTD)
2. Your iPad Downloads (Seller: AffiBank Network LTD)
4. Wii Games Download Services (Seller: AffiBank Network LTD)
5. MyDSiDownloads (Seller: "Self")
6. Unlimited PS3 Downloads (Seller: AffiBank Network LTD)
7. myPadMedia.com (Seller: myPadMedia)
9. The Novel Network (Seller: myPadMedia)
10. The Reading Site (Seller: myPadMedia)
12. cAudioLibrary (Seller: eGameDownloads)
13. YourPadCenter (Seller: Giga Publishing)
14. ePadLibrary (Seller: ePadLibrary)
19. All PSP Games (Seller: AffiBank Network LTD)
20. UnlimitedDSDownloads.com (Seller: Unlimitedds download. com)

A quick look at these top-ranked products promoted by Plimus discloses uncanny similarities to the offerings of Pirate Bay clone Novel Network. DownloadiPadMovies.com, for example, claims to provide unlimited free movies for iPads for a $129.95 lifetime fee, listing "The Green Hornet," "True Grit," and "Black Swan" among its current most popular downloads.

Plimus also provides e-commerce services for myPadMedia's Novel Network.

Putting it Together: NovelNetworkExposed.com

A person currently searching Yahoo for "net ebooks" (one of the search phrases recommended by the Novel Network for its affiliates) would find on the first page of search results ads for the Novel Network and ePad Library (Nos. 9 and I4 on the Plimus list). That person would also find an ad for:

Unlimited Ebook Downloads
Scam of The Century? Do Not Buy
Before You Read My Experiences.
NovelNetworkExposed.com

Novel Network Exposed, far from uncovering a seam, turns out to be an affiliate of the Novel Network. "Brian," the purported owner of the site, gives an exceedingly positive "review" of the site. If our search-engine user is intrigued enough by Brian's review to click on one of its many embedded links to the Novel Network, our user is taken momentarily through Plimus (to record the affiliate referral, no doubt) before being redirected to the Novel Network.

If that user then buys a "membership" in this Pirate Bay clone for $49,95 with a Visa card, the following companies and perhaps one individual profit:

1. myPadMedia, apparent owner of the Novel Network
2. "Brian," owner of Novel Network Exposed
3. Yahoo, which sold the ad to "Brian"
4. Plimus, which must take a transaction fee for its affiliate and e-commerce services
5. Visa, which takes a transaction fee for use of its services

If the Novel Network actually does teach its members how to infringe copyright, then each of these five parties has profited from facilitating the trafficking in stolen hooks. If it does not deliver on its promises, then they've all participated, knowingly or not, in a fraud.

Anyone caring to look could uncover this illegal activity in a matter of minutes. It seems that no one does, or bothers to act on the information if they do. Everyone, it appears, takes the money and the DMCA safe harbor, and looks the other way. We need to remove the profit from promoting the theft of books, music and movies. A big part of the profit is going to search engines, through advertising by sites that promote the theft of books, movies, and music, and their countless affiliates.

I will describe how to take the profit out of facilitating piracy, for search engines and others, in my answer to Question 3.

2. What role should payment processors play in combating rogue websites?

Answer:

The web of facilitation of piracy or fraud described in my answer to Question 1 is fueled by online payments at every step. Taking reasonable measures to assure that online payment processors are not used to reward plainly illegal behavior is critical to taking the profit out of trafficking in stolen books, music, and movies.

I will describe the role of payment processors in fighting online piracy in my next answer.

3. Do you believe a private right of action should be included in any bill combating online infringement?

Answer:

It is critical, above all, to remove two impediments to private causes of action. These impediments serve no useful governmental or commercial purpose and are exploited on a massive scale to facilitate nearly all online traffic in stolen books, music, and movies, allowing those who promote piracy to avoid all legal responsibility for their actions.

Impediment #1: Offshore, frequently anonymous enterprises have, through the Internet, become virtual participants in our domestic economy, yet they are beyond the reach of our laws.

Impediment #2: The MICA protects definable, distinct breeds of online services that exploit the act's safe harbors to facilitate trafficking in stolen books, music, and movies.

Removing these impediments would, overnight, clean up much of the metastasizing online networks that traffic in stolen creative works. We urge the Committee to allow our justice system to do its work by:

1. Providing our courts with in personal jurisdiction for copyright infringement actions against foreign, often anonymous enterprises that engage in activities that nearly always promote widespread trafficking in stolen books, music, and movies. A targeted list of online services should be required to register an agent for service of process for copyright infringement actions with the Copyright Office before online payment processors and ad service providers are authorized to do business with them. These high-risk online services include:
   (a) Services that offer (or purport to offer) online access to copyright protected works in digital form for a fee. These services include Pirate Bay clones, such as the Novel Network, and services that offer downloads and streams of copyright-protected creative works. They should not be able to receive online payments from the U.S., nor should they be able to host advertising from U.S.-based ad service providers, until they have subjected themselves to U.S. jurisdiction for copyright infringement actions.
   (b) Anonymous file-sharing services. The file-sharing services that are problematic are a narrow category. They uniformly allow anonymous uploading and downloading of works, storage of files in online "lockers," so they are hidden from

those visiting the service, and wide sharing of links that allow nearly anyone to download files. While there are legitimate uses for such services, they are so frequently subject to abuse that anyone operating such a service needs to take special care to assure that they do not become nests of online piracy. U.S. based enterprises running such services need to take care, or they are subject to lawsuits in our courts. Foreign enterprises, which have become a virtual part of our domestic economy, should also be legally responsible for their actions before they can accept online payments or online advertising from the U.S.

(c) Services that facilitate the anonymous downloading and streaming or copyright-protected creative works. A cottage industry of offshore service providers work to cloak and speed the transfer stolen creative works. They should be subject to our copyright laws before they are allowed to accept payments or advertising from the U.S.

2. Tighten up the DMCA's safe harbor for the high-risk online services described above to allow such service providers to be stripped of their safe harbor status and their ability to accept online payments and advertising after a reasonable notice period. If one of these high-risk online services receives a prescribed number of DMCA take-down notices that have been registered with the Copyright Office, then an author, publisher or other copyright holder whose work has been unlawfully used by the service provider should be empowered to serve notice, through the registered agent for service of process, that the service provider's DMCA safe harbor status is on probation. The high-risk online service provider would then have 30 days to challenge its probationary status and the validity of the requisite DMCA take-down notices. If the high-risk online service provider doesn't successfully challenge its probationary status and it again, after that 30-day period, receives the prescribed number of DMCA take-down notices, a copyright holder may serve notice that the service provider will automatically (I) lose its

DMCA safe harbor and (2) be barred from receiving online payments or hosting online advertising from the U.S. unless the service provider appears to challenge the validity of the new set of DMCA takedown notices within 30 days.

For this to work, online payment processors and ad service providers need to be obligated to abide by these rules. These obligations should allow payment processors and ad networks ample opportunity to remedy inadvertent errors. So, a third provision is needed:

3. Online payment processors and ad service providers should be subject to the loss of their DMCA safe harbor protections if they repeatedly process payments for high-risk online services that don't play by the rules. The Copyright Office should maintain a registry of such providers that have failed to register an agent for service of process for copyright actions or who have, through the procedure described above, been stripped of their privilege to receive online payments or host online ads. Payment processors and ad service providers should consult the registry before entering into transactions with high-risk online service providers, but they shouldn't be penalized for inadvertent, occasional transactions with such providers, and they should have ample opportunity to cure such errors.

Further recommendations are contained in my written testimony.

4. In 2008, the Ryan Haight Online Pharmacy Consumer Protection Act was signed into law. That law allows States to bring civil actions against websites that deliver or distribute controlled substances over the Internet without a valid prescription. The law also allows courts to enjoin those websites from operating. Shouldn't the government have the same authority to combat websites that sell counterfeit goods that may pose a danger to consumers? Why or why not?

Answer:

Yes it should. Protecting the public safety is a fundamental function of government.

5. If the government already has the authority to domestically seize domain names of rogue websites, why shouldn't we authorize the government to take measures to combat these websites when they move outside our borders? Is it appropriate to ask corporate citizens to help us in the fight against counterfeiting and piracy?

Answer:

We firmly believe that strong, effective actions are critical to fighting offshore piracy that undermines domestic copyright markets. Businesses are essential to that effort.

6. On November 29, 2010, ICE executed seizure orders against 82 domain names of websites engaged in the illegal sale and distribution of counterfeit goods and copyrighted works. Prior to Super Bowl 45, government authorities in New York seized several streaming websites that they accused of illegally showing live and pay-per-view sports events. Opponents of further legislation efforts argue that these actions were an overreach and that additional authority will lead to further abuse. What measures can be included in legislation to ensure DOJ does not overreach when exercising its authority?

Answer:

We believe the best answer is outlined in our written testimony and above: in personal jurisdiction with the notice and cure periods described answer all reasonable objections.

7. First Amendment constitutional concerns have been raised about last year's bill. Do you agree? Do you believe the narrow definition of infringing websites, remedies directed at preventing

only infringing content and the incorporation of the relevant Federal Rules of Civil Procedure alleviate concerns that the bill is overbroad?

Answer:

The First Amendment does not protect copyright violations, nor would it shield operations dedicated to infringing copyright or selling counterfeit goods. That said, I question the potential effectiveness of efforts to re-route the domain names of websites dedicated to piracy and believe that last year's proposed legislation does not go nearly far enough to protect markets in creative works.

8. The Federal Rules of Civil Procedure incorporated in last year's bill require advance notice for preliminary injunctions. For temporary restraining orders, they require a specific factual showing of immediate and irreparable damage and written certification explaining efforts made to give notice and the reason it is not required in a specific instance. Does the incorporation of these rules alleviate concerns that the bill does not protect process?

Answer:

The Federal Rules of Civil Procedure's requirements for preliminary injunctions and temporary restraining orders have repeatedly been found constitutional for actions brought against parties engaged in copyright infringement and counterfeiting in the real world. The virtual world is not entitled to a greater degree of due process protections.

Still, in personal justification is preferable, and we urge the Committee to fashion legislation that will make it routinely available for authors, artists, musicians, filmmakers and other copyright holders pursuing offshore traffickers in stolen books, music, and movies.

RESPONSES OF VISA INC. TO COMMITTEE MEMBERS' QUESTIONS

Denise Yee,
Senior Trademark Counsel

Senator Grassley's Questions

1. What do you believe is the appropriate role for search engines to play in combating rogue websites?

Visa believes that all legitimate participants in the Internet eco-system, including search engines, must play a role in reducing unlawful conduct online, including the distribution of counterfeit and copyright infringing material.

2. What role should payment processors play in combating rogue websites?

When a rogue website is brought to the attention of a payment system by law enforcement or a rights-holder, payment systems should cooperate to prevent the use of the payments systems for the purchase of infringing material online. To that end, Visa has worked with American Express, Discover, MasterCard and PayPal to develop "Best Practices to Address Copyright Infringement and the Sale of Counterfeit Products on the Internet" for the international Trademark Association (INTA) and developed "Best Practices to Address Copyright Infringement and the Sale of Counterfeit Products on the Internet," at the request of the Intellectual Property Enforcement Coordinator (IPEC), Victoria Espinel. And at the IPEC's recent request, an updated version of this best practices paper is being developed by the payment industry. These best practices are consistent with Visa's current policies and demonstrate the payment industry's commitment to work with intellectual property owners to prevent the distribution of counterfeit and infringing products on the Internet.

3. Could you elaborate on any actions Visa is taking on its own to fight online piracy and counterfeiting?

Visa voluntarily provides simple procedures for rights-holders to submit complaints concerning online merchants suspected of selling counterfeit and copyright infringing goods. These procedures can be found online at www.Visa.com/ReportBrandAbuse.

Upon receiving a documented complaint, Visa at its own expense will run a test transaction to identify the Acquirer (the bank who signed up the merchant to accept Visa card payments). Visa will direct the Acquirer to conduct an investigation into its merchant. Absent any written documentation disproving the infringement, Visa will demand that the Acquirer either force the merchant to stop engaging in unlawful sales or terminate the merchant account from the Visa system. Our procedures are discussed in more detail at pages 12-14 of our written testimony.

Additionally, Visa educates Acquirers worldwide that the sale of counterfeit and infringing goods is illegal and should not be allowed in the system. This past October, for example, Visa circulated a global communication to all Acquirers that specifically highlighted this issue.

4. How did Visa handle the 30 voluntary requests by IP owners?

When Visa received these inquiries, it first made sure that a test transaction was conducted so that it could verify that Visa cards were actually accepted as a form of payment at these websites. If the card was accepted, Visa could identify the merchant's Acquirer involved in the transaction. Visa then directed the Acquirer to investigate its merchant's activity. In most cases, the Acquirer determined that the merchant was engaged in infringing activity. The merchant was either required to stop selling infringing material or was terminated from the Visa system.

5. Were those requests legitimate?

Most of the requests were "legitimate" in that the complainants were legitimate rights-holders who identified merchants that accepted Visa cards as payment for infringing material. However, in some cases, the rogue website did not actually accept Visa cards even though it displayed our logo on their site. In other words, the website was also infringing Visa's trademark. In those cases, Visa sent a cease and desist letter to the merchant demanding that the Visa logo be removed.

6. How quickly does Visa process these kinds of requests?

Visa processes these requests expeditiously, paying careful attention to balance the demands of the rights-holders against due process for the merchant. Visa allows the merchant a fair opportunity to disprove the allegation of infringement with written documentation, if it has a viable defense. Visa has continually reviewed, refined and enhanced its procedures. Under its current anti-counterfeit and piracy policy, Visa requests the Acquirer's response within five business days of receiving the inquiry from Visa, including the Acquirer's investigation report into its merchant's business activities.

7. Do you believe a private right of action should be included in any bill combating online infringement?

Visa opposes the inclusion of a private right of action in legislation like the Combating Online Infringement and Counterfeits Act (COICA). Rights-holders already have a free, effective, and responsive avenue by which they may submit their complaints concerning rogue websites to the payment systems. Moreover, a private right of action could erode the prevailing secondary liability standard that applies to payment systems, Perfect 10 v. Visa International Service Association, 494 F.3d 788 (9th Cir. 2007). Courts could interpret such a private right of action as an indication that payments systems should be secondarily liable for copyright and trademark infringement, and this could result in the reversal of decades of judicial decisions defining the contours of secondary liability. Extending liability to payment systems for infringing acts of merchants would shift legal responsibility to parties far removed from the infringing activity. To protect themselves, Acquirers may become more reluctant to sign innocent, small business merchants, which may unduly hinder both domestic and international c-commerce.

8. In 2008, the Ryan Haight Online Pharmacy Consumer Protection Act was signed into law. That law allows States to bring civil actions against websites that deliver or distribute controlled substances over the internet without a valid prescription. The law also allows courts to enjoin those websites from operating. Shouldn't the government have the same authority to combat websites that sell counterfeit goods that may pose a danger to consumers? Why or why not?

Visa supports providing federal law enforcement agencies with necessary legal tools to combat websites that sell counterfeit goods that may pose a danger to consumers.

9. If the government already has the authority to domestically seize domain names of rogue websites, why shouldn't we authorize the government to take measures to combat these websites when they move outside our borders? Is it appropriate to ask corporate citizens to help us in the fight against counterfeiting and piracy?

It is completely appropriate for corporate citizens to assist rights-holders in the fight against counterfeiting and piracy, and for this reason Visa has voluntarily adopted and implemented its anti-piracy and counterfeit policy described above. With respect to authorizing the government to take measures to combat websites outside our borders, Visa is generally supportive of COICA as currently structured. However, as we noted in our written testimony, the extraterritorial application of U.S. law could have unintended consequences. For example, it may invite retaliation by other countries' governments. If U.S. law effectively makes payment systems instruments of intellectual property enforcement actions against foreign websites, foreign governments may well do the same in other countries where the payment systems operate. European countries, for example, believe that many U.S. merchants infringe European laws concerning geographical indicators. Under European law, only wineries in the Champagne region of France can call sparkling wine "champagne," and only cheese manufacturers in the Parma region of Italy can use the name "parmesan cheese." European countries could require payment systems to stop processing transactions for U.S. merchant websites that sell products that violate European laws concerning geographical indicators. Similarly, repressive governments could force payment systems to stop doing business with legitimate U.S. merchants that sell books critical of their regimes to residents of their countries.

10. On November 29, 2010, ICE executed seizure orders against 82 domain names of websites engaged in the illegal sale and distribution of counterfeit goods and copyrighted works. Prior to Super Bowl 45, government authorities in New York seized several streaming websites that they accused of illegally showing live and pay per-view sports events. Opponents of further legislative efforts argue that these actions were an overreach and that additional authority will lead to further abuse. What measures can be included in legislation to ensure DOJ does not overreach when exercising its authority?

Our understanding is that ICE employed the civil forfeiture procedures of title 18, under which the federal agency can obtain a seizure warrant in an *ex parte* proceeding in which it must only meet the probable cause standard. In contrast, COICA appears to provide for an adversarial proceeding after the website operator receives notice. Moreover, it seems that under COCIA, the Attorney General would have to meet a preponderance of the evidence standard.

11. First Amendment constitutional concerns have been raised about last year's bill. Do you agree? Do you believe the narrow definition of infringing websites, remedies directed at preventing only infringing content and the incorporation of the relevant Federal Rules of Civil Procedure alleviate concerns that the bill is overbroad?

The concerns about the overbreadth of the definition of Internet sites "dedicated to infringing activities" have validity. Under section 2(a)(1)(A) of COICA, a site meets this definition if it is subject to civil forfeiture under 18 U.S.C. § 2323. Section 2323 provides that any property used in any manner or part to commit or facilitate the commission of criminal copyright infringement is subject to forfeiture. (18 U.S.C. 2323 refers to 18 U.S.C. § 2319, which in turn refers to the criminal copyright provisions of 17 U.S.C. § 506(a).) Under 17 U.S.C. § 506(a)(1)(B), the reproduction or distribution of copies with a retail value of S1000 could constitute criminal copyright infringement. Virtually every c-commerce platform that enables third party sales (e.g., eBay) easily meets this $1000 threshold. All these platforms, therefore, could fall within the definition of a site dedicated to infringing activity.

12. The Federal Rules of Civil Procedure incorporated in last year's bill require advance notice for preliminary injunctions. For temporary restraining orders, they require a specific factual showing of immediate and irreparable damage and written certification explaining efforts made to give notice and the reason it is not required in a specific instance. Does the incorporation of these rules alleviate concerns that the bill does not protect process?

The incorporation of the Federal Rules of Civil Procedure into COICA means that COICA provides more procedural safeguards than the civil forfeiture procedures of 18 U.S.C. §§ 981 and 2323 employed by ICE.

Senator Klobuchar's Question

1. A key issue in your testimony was ensuring that Visa did not violate contractual obligations in other countries where infringing activities may be legal under local law. You also mentioned Visa implementing a "coding and blocking scheme" in the context of internet gambling sites to prevent American cardholders from using those sites.
   a. Would such a system be feasible in the copyright context to prevent Americans from using Visa's payment system to purchase counterfeit goods on these infringing sites?

The coding system used in the illegal gambling context cannot be applied in the IP context. Under Visa rules, every merchant must disclose the nature of its business to the Acquirer, and each merchant's business is categorized into a merchant code that generally defines their industry. For example, a merchant engaged in the sale of clothing has one merchant code, and merchant engaged in online gambling has another merchant code. Since online gambling is legal in many jurisdictions, merchants freely disclose to the Acquirers that they provide online gambling services, The Acquirers encode them as online gambling merchants, and their transactions with U.S. cardholders are blocked. In contrast, there is no code for counterfeit and copyright infringement, and no merchant would inform its Acquirer that it is engaged in counterfeiting and copyright infringement. Accordingly, a "coding and blocking" system will not work in the IP context.

   b. If so, would Visa be willing to work with other financial transaction processors to establish standards for such a system?

See previous answer.

Senator Coburn's Questions

1. Could you tell me a little about the process a website operator would use to set up a processing arrangement with Visa?

To join the Visa network, a merchant must file a merchant application with an Acquirer, a bank that is part of the Visa network, and the Acquirer must enter into a signed agreement with the merchant before that merchant can be a Visa accepting merchant. By signing up a merchant, an Acquirer is agreeing to underwrite that merchant's payment card transactions and is fully responsible for conducting an adequate due diligence review of the principals' business activity. This review typically includes background checks on the principals and a review the products, services and the conditions of sale. Because Acquirers are financially responsible for their merchants' transactions, they have a natural incentive to complete adequate review. Acquirers that fail to properly evaluate their merchants' activities may be subjected to considerable fraud losses and other operational risks.

a. It sounds like much of the process relies upon the website owner's bank (merchant bank) to determine whether the operator is selling legitimate products. How often does the merchant bank refuse to set up a processing arrangement with a website due to concerns with counterfeiting?

Because an Acquiring financial institution is responsible for soliciting merchants and determining whether they are allowed to join the network, we do not know how often Acquirers reject applications because of concerns with counterfeiting.

b. How often does Visa get involved in determining whether a processing arrangement should be granted?

Visa does not get involved in the process of determining whether an application should be granted. In the Visa system, Visa has no contractual relationship with the merchant. Visa has a contractual relationship with the Acquirer, and the Acquirer has the relationship with the merchant. However, our rules governing these relationships require the Acquirers to ensure their merchants do not submit illegal transactions into the payment system.

c. Does Visa impose any fines or other punishment on a merchant bank for submitting applications that are not thoroughly vetted?

Visa operates risk programs that include fines for Acquirers that violate our rules. Acquirers that submit illegal transactions are eligible to receive fines starting at 525,000 per incident which increase substantially if repeat violations occur.

2. Since the primary motivation for those operating websites truly dedicated to infringing activity is the ability to make a profit, do you believe it would be appropriate to first focus legislation on shutting down counterfeit sites' access to payment processors and ad networks before using the DNS to block access to a website? Why or why not?

Visa believes that all legitimate participants in the Internet eco-system must play a role in combating rogue websites. No one industry can successfully combat rogue websites alone. Because bad faith infringers have multiple identities, set up businesses under false pretenses, and hide in the shadows of the Internet, successful enforcement requires participation by all Internet players.

Moreover, many operators of websites dedicated to infringing activity do not seek profit. Rather, they make content available for free because they see themselves as part of a global community of fans. Indeed, some of these operators truly believe that they are helping artists by exposing them to new audiences. These free websites would be unaffected by legislation that addresses only payment systems and ad networks.

3. Do you have a process in place by which content owners can work with you to eliminate rogue websites' access to payment processing?

Yes, our voluntary system is discussed above in response to Senator Grassley's Question 3 and at pages 12-14 of our written testimony.

a. If so, how long have you had such a process?

We have had a process since 2007. Visa has continually reviewed, refined and enhanced its process since then.

b. Some in the content industry have stated they have existing relationships with Mastercard such that they can directly notify Mastercard of their concerns with certain websites. How often do the content owners notify Visa of the need to shut down processing from particular infringing websites?

Visa also has existing relationships with members of the content industry who can directly notify Visa of their concerns about suspect websites.

Visa has received a total of 30 inquiries from all rights-holders over a period six months.

c. Do you have a process different from Mastercard? Why or why not?

We do not know the details of Mastercard's process, and thus cannot comment on them. However, Mastercard and the other payment systems subscribe to the same "best practices" as Visa, described in response to Senator Grassley's Question 2.

4. What would the cost effect be on Visa should legislation such as last year's bill be enacted? Do you believe the benefits outweigh the costs to payment processors in general?

Because under our existing policy we have already committed to working with rights-holders to prevent the use of the Visa system for the purchase of infringing material, we do not anticipate a clear adverse cost effect from legislation such as COICA as it was structured last Congress.

However, as discussed at pages 16-18 of our written testimony, we think it is worth noting the possible unintended consequences of legislation such as COICA. Accordingly, the Committee should cautiously proceed in a manner that avoids those consequences.

5. What if any changes last year's legislation would you like to see occur? If those changes do occur, would you be supportive of legislation in this area?

At pages 19-20 of our written testimony, we propose two technical changes to COICA. First, to the extent a merchant provides written documentation disproving infringement outside of the U.S., a financial transaction provider should be permitted to authorize the continued use of its trademark on foreign sites in accordance with its Acquirers' contractual obligations. Second, similar to language provided for DNS server operators, a financial transaction provider should not be required to modify its systems to comply with an ordered issued under COICA. With these two technical amendments VISA would be supportive of COICA as structured in the last Congress.

However, our position on the legislation is likely to change if a private right of action is added or if DNS server operators are excluded.

In: Targeting Websites …
Editor: Anthony L. Mooney
ISBN: 978-1-53613-705-7

Chapter 4

SUBMISSIONS FOR THE RECORD

TESTIMONY OF TOM ADAMS CHIEF EXECUTIVE OFFICER

Rosetta Stone Inc.
Senate Judiciary Committee
Hearing on the "Combating Online Infringement and Counterfeits Act"
February 16, 2011

Chairman Leahy, Ranking Member Grassley, and honorable Members of the Committee. My name is Tom Adams, and I am President and CEO of Rosetta Stone Inc., a leading provider of technology-based, interactive solutions for language learning. Rosetta Stone provides interactive solutions that are acclaimed for the power to unlock the language-learning ability in everyone. Available in more than 30 languages, Rosetta Stone language-learning solutions are used by schools, our armed forces, government agencies, corporations, and millions of individuals in over 150 countries throughout the world. Rosetta Stone has grown from a family-owned business founded in the heart of the Shenandoah Valley in Harrisonburg, Virginia to approximately 2000 employees, most of whom are based in our headquarters in Arlington, Virginia, our main operational facilities in Harrisonburg, Virginia, and a research center in Boulder, Colorado. By investing heavily in research and development, with expenditures in this area exceeding well over $90 million over the past 8 years, we have continued to improve the effectiveness and sophistication of our innovative Language-learning technologies and solutions. In addition, we have expended many millions of dollars in marketing our products and in enhancing our brand recognition and reputation as a company, to the point where we have now achieved a public brand recognition exceeding 75% in the United States. As a result of these investments, we have been able to grow our revenue by a factor of 10, from roughly $25 million in 2004 to $252 million in 2009 and to become a publicly-traded company on the New York Stock Exchange in 2009.

I appreciate the opportunity to appear before you today and want to thank you and your colleagues for recognizing the harm that the proliferation of websites offering counterfeit products and services causes to American consumers and businesses and for prioritizing the enactment of legislation to address this serious problem. Intellectual property industries are a cornerstone of the U.S. economy, employing more than 19 million people and accounting for 60 percent of our exports. Rampant online counterfeiting and piracy presents a significant threat that our government must do more to address. The global sales of counterfeit goods via the Internet from illegitimate retailers reached $135 billion in 2010. As a consequence of global and U.S. based piracy of copyright products, the U.S. economy lost $58.0 billion in total output in 2007. This theft diminishes our ability to maintain and create jobs, and makes it far more difficult to attract the capital needed to invest in new products and services. Concomitantly, American consumers have been exposed to products that are often of poor quality and arc harmful while subjecting themselves to identity theft, software viruses or other malicious computer code.

At Rosetta Stone, we and our customers have experienced firsthand the harmful consequences of online counterfeiting. Because we offer a high value, premium product that has strong public recognition, we have been targeted by criminals seeking to profit from our heavy investment in our brand and our intellectual property by selling pirated copies of our software over the Internet. These pirates have created increasingly sophisticated websites that often copy pages of the Rosetta Stone website in order to lure consumers into purchasing pirated software at discounted prices. The "rogue" websites provide pirated software that is often inoperable or otherwise defective. In fact, our customer care department receives calls and messages on a daily basis from consumers in the United States who believe that they have purchased authentic Rosetta Stone products only to discover that they have received pirated copies from these "rogue" websites. Most of these pirates are based in China, Russia and other foreign countries, beyond the reach of U.S. law enforcement.

Having been adversely impacted over the past several years by this ongoing infringement of our intellectual property and the resulting diversion of sales to "rogue" websites, Rosetta Stone has devoted substantial resources to combat these websites, which steal our intellectual property, tarnish our brand and harm American consumers.

First, Rosetta Stone created an enforcement department to identify and combat the "rogue" websites and other sources of pirated copies of its products. This department, which has grown to six employees in our Harrisonburg office, has developed sophisticated software programs that scan Internet search engine results on a daily basis for "rogue" websites. When this team finds a "rogue" site which has purchased paid advertisements on a search engine such as Google or has a web link appearing in the search engine's natural search results, they will send the search engine a take-down notice under the Digital Millennium Copyright Act (DMCA) in order to have the paid advertisement or organic links removed from the search engine results.

The search engines can take anywhere from one day to a month to respond to our take down requests by removing the offending paid advertisement or organic link, but in the meantime, the copyright infringers have transacted with unwitting consumers and purchased new paid advertisements from search engines for new "rogue" websites to replace the previous paid advertisements that are in the process of being taken down.

Second, our Legal Department supports the efforts of our enforcement team by sending DMCA take down notices to the Internet Service Providers (1SP) that host the "rogue" websites. While we have found that the ISPs located in the United States have been generally responsive to our take down requests by removing or blocking the "rogue" websites, the ISPs located outside the U.S. have been unresponsive. As a result, it has become common practice for the software pirates operating websites that are blocked by US-based ISPs following our take down requests to re-establish a cloned "rogue" website with an offshore ISP. This take down process is like a maddening game of "whack-a-mole"; every time Rosetta Stone's enforcement team takes down a "rogue" website advertisement and/or the website itself, several other "rogue" website advertisements and/or "rogue" websites resurface with new paid advertisements on search engines and cloned websites utilizing offshore ISPs.

Third, our enforcement team has worked extensively with the U.S. Customs and Border Protection (CBP) to train customs agents to be aware of the existence of, and to be able to identify, counterfeit copies of our products that are being shipped into the country from foreign locations. The job of the customs agents is helped by the fact that all of our software products are manufactured in the United States, so any copies being imported into the country are immediately suspect. In 2010, CBP agents made 35 seizures containing over 400 counterfeit Rosetta Stone products. Since CBP can only inspect a very small percentage of goods entering the U.S., we believe that the inbound volume of pirated copies of our products is a dramatically larger number.

Finally, our enforcement team works actively with and supports the Federal Bureau of Investigations (FBI), Immigration and Customs Enforcement (10E) and the U.S. Postal Service (USPS) as well as state and local law enforcement agencies in their investigations building criminal cases against copyright infringers. We have also assisted the investigatory activities of the FBI Internet Crime Complaint Center and the U.S. Government's Intellectual Property Rights Center (IPR Center), which houses an interagency task force consisting of agents from the FBI, CBP, ICE and LISPS.

I would also like to take this opportunity to acknowledge the good work of [CE Director John Morton and his team. In an action named, "Operation in our Sites," ICE, in cooperation with the Department of

Justice (DoJ) and the IPR Center, has used the seizure authority under existing federal law to seize domains being used for piracy and/or counterfeiting. These actions took place in three phases and have seized about 100 domains thus far. Of course, the jurisdiction of ICE and all federal enforcement agencies is limited to the United States. That is why we need legislation — to address foreign "rogue" sites.

The magnitude of the problem we face from the sale of pirated copies of our products on the Internet cannot be understated. As a result of our enforcement team's daily monitoring efforts, we have detected and initiated take down actions against over"1000 "rogue" websites within the last 18 months. Of course, many of the sites are hosted on ISPs located overseas, so they are not threatened by our take down notices. Since we are unable to effectively pursue copyright infringers operating overseas, I want to express our strong endorsement of the Committee's efforts to empower the DoJ to take action against these foreign websites and specifically "to prevent and restrain the importation into the United States of goods and services offered by" the offending website.

We also appreciate that the proposed legislation recognizes that "rogue" websites rely upon the services provided by various service providers in order to be successful in the distributing counterfeit goods to U.S. consumers. Therefore, we are pleased that the bill empowers the DoJ to issue court orders to Internet service providers (ISPs), payment processors and online advertising networks requiring them to refrain from providing their services in support of the "rogue" sites. Specifically, these court orders would require (1) the ISPs to take reasonable steps to prevent the "rogue" site's domain name from resolving to its Internet protocol address, (ii) the payment processors to take reasonable steps to stop completing payment transactions between its U.S. customers and the Internet site using the blocked domain name, and (iii) the advertising networks to take reasonable measures to cease providing advertisements to the Internet site associated with the blocked domain name. Taken together, these steps would give the DoJ a potent weapon to disrupt the ability of the overseas criminals operating foreign "rogue" sites to complete sales transactions with American consumers. By blocking the resolution of the domain names with these "rogue" Internet sites, the offending internet sites will not be readily reachable by American consumers. Similarly, preventing advertising networks from carrying the advertisements of these internet sites will reduce their visibility to the American consumer. But even if the offending internet sites are still able to make themselves available to consumers, their inability to utilize payment processors to transact sales with consumers will go a long way in disrupting the flow of counterfeit goods and services into the United States.

We also urge the Committee to consider the fact that the most common way for "rogue" websites, especially those based overseas, to reach out to American consumers is by means of paid advertisements on search engines such as Google. By purchasing the brand name of the product being counterfeited as a search engine keyword, the infringing website can have a paid advertisement appear on the search engine results page whenever a consumer conducts a search using that brand name. Search engines such as Google misappropriate value created by Rosetta Stone and protected by its federal intellectual property rights by selling Rosetta Stone's trademarks as advertising "keywords" to counterfeiters who operate the "rogue" websites. When a consumer looking to purchase a Rosetta Stone product searches on Google for "Rosetta Stone", the resulting search results page will include not only links to Rosetta Stone's official website, but also paid ads linking to "rogue" websites. These paid advertisements will typically offer to sell purportedly authentic Rosetta Stone products at discounted prices, and when the consumer clicks on the link in the paid advertisement, the consumer is directed to websites that are often "copy-cat" imitations of the official Rosetta Stone site. In this way, the consumer is deceived into believing that he or she is buying an authentic Rosetta Stone product and a Rosetta Stone product sale is diverted to the infringing website. Our customer care center has received complaints from a wide variety of "rogue" website victims who were misled by paid advertisements from search engines such as Google including educators, law enforcement officers, business professionals, and retirees. The problem is exacerbated by Google's search advertising market share of approximately 70%, which provides foreign counterfeiters a convenient, low cost advertising platform to reach the majority of American consumers without the threat of criminal prosecution.

The key point is that without the ability to buy paid advertisements on search engines using the brand names of the pirated products, these infringing websites would not be able to easily reach American consumers, and likewise, it would be much less likely that American consumers would become aware of the existence of these websites. Therefore, it is critical that this legislation empowers the DoJ to prevent "rogue" websites from Using search engines as their gateway to American consumers. This step would substantially enhance the effectiveness of the legislation in combating the onslaught of counterfeit products being imported in the U.S. through rogue websites and the resulting adverse impact on U.S. jobs and the U.S economy.

The search engines may argue that this action would be an undue burden and difficult for them administer. However, in our experience, search engines such as Google have the ability, if they so desire to do so, to filter out paid advertisements from pirate websites, thereby preventing them from bidding on the Rosetta Stone brand name as a keyword. The barrier is not a lack of technology, but a lack of commitment to fighting piracy instead of profiting from it. We regret that Google declined an invitation to participate in today's hearing so that we could better understand why some companies receive stronger protection against "rogue" websites than others.

Finally, although the legislation introduced last year provides the DoJ with important new enforcement tools, we are concerned that the DoJ may not have the resources to investigate and bring about all the enforcement actions contemplated by the supporters of the legislation. As I mentioned previously, Rosetta Stone alone has identified over 1000 rogue websites attempting to sell counterfeit copies of its products over the past 18 months. An early draft of this legislation attempted to address that problem by authorizing the Justice Department to create and issue a list of websites where a preponderance of the evidence demonstrates that these sites are engaged in illegal conduct. This list would be analogous to the "notorious markets" list issued by the United States Trade Representative. Rosetta

Stone is supportive of this concept as long as it can be implemented in a manner consistent with principles of due process. In addition, we believe that the final bill should include provisions that allow, with certain limitations, the ability of rights holders to bring to the courts evidence that would allow the courts to determine if certain sites meet the bill's definition and order the remedies contained in the bill. We look forward to working with the Committee to ensure that the provision provides the proper balance for all the impacted parties. Finally, we believe that the effectiveness of this legislation would be strengthened by the addition of provisions to protect the rights of trafemark owners in a manner analogous to the protections afforded to copuright owners under the DMCA. Under this arrangement, a trademark owner would be able to notify as ISP or other services provider its trademank rights are being infringes by the contents of a website, and the service provider would be afforded immunity from liability if it acts epeditiously to remove the infringing website or web content. In this way trademark owners would be able to assert their rights under the Lanham Act through a notice process compared to provisions of the DMCA without the need for government intervention or expenditure of government resources.

Mr. Chairman, Rosette Stone recognizes that policy issues affecting online commerce, whether legitimate or not, are very difficult because we all want to enjoy the social and economic benefits of a robust Internet. However, the damage to American business and consumer via "rogue" websites cannot be ignored under the guise of Internet Freedom. We are committed to working with ISPs, payment processors, online advertisers and search engines to find non-legislative solutions to "rogue" websites, but in the absence of more aggressive action by these parties, we believe that federal legislation is essential to protecting American consumers and American jobs. We look forward to working with you to develop and enact legislation this year to ensure that job creation and growth remains here with American business rather than with foreign counterfeiting operations.

AMERICAN FEDERATION OF LABOR AND CONGRESS OF INDUSTRIAL ORGANIZATIONS

815 SIXTEENTH STREET, N.W.
WASHINGTON, D.C. 20006

RICHARD L. TRUMKA
PRESIDENT

ELIZABETH H. SHULER
SECRETARY-TREASURER

ARLENE HOLT BAKER
EXECUTIVE VICE PRESIDENT

LEGISLATIVE ALERT!

(202) 637-5057

February 15, 2011

The Honorable Patrick Leahy, Chairman
Committee on the Judiciary
United States Senate
Washington, D.C. 20510

Dear Chairman Leahy:

On behalf of the AFL-CIO, I want to thank you for holding a hearing on "Targeting Websites Dedicated to Stealing American Intellectual Property." This hearing demonstrates that, despite being unfairly attacked for introducing S.3804, the "Combating Online Infringement and Counterfeits Act" (COICA) in the last Congress, you remain appropriately focused on combating the torrent of digital theft that robs U.S. jobs while threatening the health and safety of U.S. citizens. American workers greatly appreciate the courage and leadership you have once again displayed.

This Congress must pass legislation to provide more effective tools against "rogue websites" operated by unscrupulous individuals who use the Internet as a platform to sell counterfeit and pirated goods. As you know, many of these rogue websites look legitimate and have become increasingly sophisticated in both design and operation. They deceive consumers into believing they are legitimate, threaten American jobs, and as we have seen with the recent instances of fake products such as toothpaste, pharmaceuticals and auto parts, represent a severe health and safety risk to U.S. citizens. This hearing will help Congress decide which additional tools would be most appropriate and effective for combating such "rogue websites."

The AFL-CIO will stand by you as you try to halt the destruction of American jobs by rogue websites. Last fall, more than a dozen unions and guilds, representing hundreds of thousands of workers in industries ranging from entertainment to firefighting, wrote you in support of S. 3804. I assure you that these unions and guilds were not outliers; the labor community as a whole understands that digital intellectual property (IP) theft affects not only jobs in the entertainment industry, where lost profits in music and motion picture production put tens of thousands of good-paying jobs at risk, but also jobs in manufacturing, such as pharmaceuticals, apparel, luxury goods, and auto parts. In all, counterfeiting and piracy of intellectual property has an impact on millions of American workers in IP-sensitive industries.

We thank you again for your efforts to fight for workers and their families, and to protect both their jobs and their safety. We look forward to continuing to work with you and your Senate colleagues to enact COICA.

Sincerely,

William Samuel, Director
Government Affairs Department

at&t

James W. Cicconi
Senior Executive Vice President
External and Legislative Affairs

AT&T Services, Inc
1120 Twentieth Street, NW
Suite 1000
Washington, DC 20036

T: 202.457.2233
F: 202.457.2244
james.cicconi@att.com
www.att.com

March 24, 2010

The Honorable Victoria Espinel
U.S. Intellectual Property Enforcement Coordinator
Office of Management and Budget
Executive Office of the President
The White House
Washington, DC 20500

RE: Request of IPEC for Public Comments Regarding the Joint Strategic Plan (Fed. Reg. Vol. 75, No. 35 -- FR Doc. 2010-3539)

Dear Ms. Espinel:

AT&T is aware of and truly sympathetic to the threat that the piracy of intellectual property through file sharing poses to the economic and creative well being of rights-holders. This threat compels an adequate and fair government deterrent to steer more casual users of unlawful content toward consumption of lawful content. Accordingly, in response to the February 23, 2010, request of the Intellectual Property Enforcement Coordinator,[1] AT&T Inc. ("AT&T") submits the following recommendations for improving the government's intellectual property enforcement efforts.

For well over the past decade, AT&T and other Internet Service Providers ("ISPs") have supported rights-holders' intellectual property enforcement efforts to reduce piracy under the Digital Millennium

---

1 Request for written submissions from the public, Coordination and Strategic Planning of the Federal Effort Against Intellectual Property Infringement Request of the Intellectual Property Enforcement Coordinator for Public Comments Regarding the Joint Strategic Plan, 75 Fed. Rog. 8137 (rel. February 23, 2010).

Copyright Act ("DMCA") through, among other means, forwarding notices of alleged infringement from rights-holders to its customers. In fact, AT&T has developed an Automatic Customer Notification Service to automate this process of forwarding notices of alleged copyright infringement. So manifest are the potential benefits of automated notice forwarding that AT&T believes it should be a standardized process so that rights-holders and ISPs alike do not have to navigate through myriad differing requirements. To that end, AT&T continues to work within the industry to establish standards and protocols for its program, including efforts to develop reporting specifications that would provide meaningful data on the effectiveness of the program.

While efforts like these have borne fruit, rights-holders nonetheless contend that significant factors impede a fully realized intellectual property rights enforcement regime. These include, on the one hand, the persistent misunderstanding of segments of the online community as to the propriety of unauthorized file-sharing and, on the other hand, the lack of resources and modern legal mechanisms to enable rights-holders and law enforcement agencies to investigate and prosecute civil or criminal violations of the copyright laws. These impediments are real and recalcitrant. Thus, it is not surprising that rights-holders would turn to whomever and wherever they possibly can to seek a solution, especially when the existing law enforcement structure seems overmatched by 21st-century digital-theft technologies.

AT&T believes that more can be done, and that the primary issue today is not that copyright laws are inadequate, but that the existing enforcement structure is antiquated, not built for today's digital environment. There is a vacuum not only in civil enforcement, due to the lack of an expeditious and proportionate remedy, but also in criminal enforcement, due to the lack of a formalized mechanism for federal law enforcement officials to foreclose major traffickers in illegal content. A new law enforcement structure that expeditiously, efficiently and fairly applies existing laws to new technologies, while ensuring due process and adequately and reasonably protecting the privacy of citizens, is in order. Making the existing laws more nimble, rather than adding yet another enforcement agent — especially non-state actors that do not have a statutory basis for such activities — is the right course of action for the future. Consequently, AT&T supports a mix of new civil and criminal enforcement procedures to remedy existing copyright enforcement shortcomings.

On the civil front, AT&T is sympathetic to the continued frustration of the rights-holder community. These frustrations, which seem rooted predominantly in the inadequacy of governmental processes, have unfortunately led some to propose that non-governmental entities should play the role normally, and more appropriately, played by government. For example, some rights-holders propose that, in addition to forwarding notices of alleged copyright infringement to our customers, ISPs should implement a "graduated response" process that would culminate in termination or suspension of the customer's Internet access service without a court order, and based solely on the receipt of multiple allegations of infringement. This industry segment has suggested that ISPs should not just facilitate enforcement of copyright laws by rights-holders or the government, but that ISPs themselves should take the primary role in evaluating the propriety of copyright infringement claims and defenses, stepping into the role of an enforcement agency to mete out punishment in the form of disconnection or some other penalty. While at AT&T we are willing to, and actively do, forward these notices to our customers today, we nonetheless believe that there are significant legal and policy issues associated with taking the next step of sanctioning our customers based solely on the receipt of multiple third party notices.

The most fundamental problem with the notion of graduated response is that private entities are not created or meant to conduct the law enforcement and judicial balancing act that would be required; they are not charged with sitting in judgment of facts; and they are not empowered to punish alleged criminals without a court order or other government sanction. Indeed, the liability implications of ISPs acting as a quasi-law-enforcement/judicial branch could be enormous. The government and the courts, not ISPs, are responsible for intellectual property enforcement, and only they can secure and balance the various property, privacy and due process rights that are at play and often in conflict in this realm.

Moreover, the practical effect on Internet users and households could be dramatic. Internet users are increasingly "cutting the cord" and using their home broadband service as their only household connection. They may be using a Voice over Internet Protocol service as their only source for voice communications, including access to emergency services, such as 911. Therefore, any solution where the end result is to take down or restrict the customer's broadband service would likely have a broad impact on a household's core communications needs. Indeed, it would seem counterintuitive to pursue a tactic that necessarily would result in cutting off potentially thousands of customers from the Internet at the same time the government has made clear that it considers broadband access an indispensable lifeline for all families and communities,[2] and is considering measures that could dramatically curtail a broadband provider's ability to manage and optimize its network.[3] This is especially true given that, in our experience, the automated notice-forwarding systems that ISPs have established are highly effective at deterring the offending behavior.

Indeed, while rights-holders are implementing measures to ensure the integrity and validity of their copyright infringement notices, there are instances in which such notices may be misdirected against non-infringing members of a household, against persons who have valid defenses, or against persons who are victims of unauthorized access to their home networks. Thus, a system where notices of infringement alone would justify termination of service necessarily would lead to situations where entire households are penalized based on faulty allegations or the actions of just one member of the household. It should give the government pause that a third-party allegation, alone, without any sanction by government or

---

[2] See, e.g., Federal Communications Commission, Connecting America: The National Broadband Plan (rel. March 16, 2010), p. XI ("Like electricity a century ago, broadband is a foundation for economic growth, job creation, global competitiveness and a better way of life. It is enabling entire new industries and unlocking vast new possibilities for existing ones. It is changing how we educate children, deliver health care, manage energy, ensure public safety, engage government, and access, organize and disseminate knowledge.")

[3] Notice of Proposed Rulemaking, Preserving the Open Internet, GN Docket No. 09-191, WD Docket No. 07-52, FCC No. 09.93 (rel. Oct. 22, 2009).

order by a court, could cause an entire family to be deprived of communications, access to financial or medical information, the ability to access government services, or even the ability of children to do their school work or interact with their teachers, Surely, such a system, and the public outrage it likely would provoke, would serve neither the interests of copyright holders nor foster respect for the rule of law we should seek in this area.

Given the myriad of negative and unanticipated impacts that are likely to result from any such graduated response scheme, it would seem counter-productive, at best, to try to fill an enforcement vacuum by requiring ISPs to perform the functions of police, judge, and jury. To be sure, AT&T grasps why some rights-holders might press for such measures given the inadequacy of the current enforcement regime, but these steps would only provide rights-holders a rush of short-term satisfaction. The notion of non-governmental players assuming, without legal authority, a governmental role simply would not endure.

We believe there is a better solution that properly balances the interests of rights-holders and end users and maintains the government's primary enforcement role. Specifically, AT&T proposes that the IPEC and the Joint Strategic Plan propose a streamlined and reasonable adjudication system for rights-holders to resolve civil infringement claims against end users. The U.S. Copyright Office initiated in 2006, but never completed, consideration of such a system, and IPEC could build on that work with its constituent agencies to initiate a streamlined and reasonable adjudication system for rights-holders to expeditiously and more easily resolve civil infringement claims against individual end users. ISPs would be a partner in this structure: forwarding notices of alleged copyright infringement from rights-holders or their agents to end users while still protecting the end user's identity from disclosure; providing rights-holders with regular reports on the number of end users who have received more than one notice from that rights-holder; appropriately categorizing the total number of notices received; and subsequently providing customer-identifying information to the streamlined claims adjudication body as part of the court-administered adjudication process. In this way, the rights-holder would be permitted an opportunity to present its infringement case and the end user would be given the opportunity to respond via standardized paper, telephonic or digital proceedings developed by the adjudicative body. Ultimately, we believe, this adjudication and resolution procedure would provide a meaningful deterrent by heightening end users' understanding that infringement activities are being monitored by the content industry and that there are material consequences associated with their actions.

Equally important to efforts focused on enhancing enforcement and deterrence on the civil side, there is a glaring need to fill a similar void on the criminal side. In this regard, AT&T proposes that the IPEC recommend in the Joint Strategic Plan an institutionalized process for identifying websites hosted in countries outside the U.S. that are not covered by the DMCA and that have been judged, following lawful process, to be engaged in trafficking in infringed copyrighted works. Just as law enforcement can close pawn shops that predominantly traffic in stolen goods, so too should law enforcement be empowered to shut down websites that predominantly traffic in digital stolen goods. Therefore, AT&T calls on the IPEC to explore the possibility of having the Department of Justice, independently or in combination with other federal agencies, create and maintain a list of international websites known to host and traffic in infringed copyrighted works, The Department of Justice would then be given the authority to require, after thorough investigation and governmental due process, that ISPs deny access to these websites. In this way, an updated enforcement regime could address not just the demand for digital stolen goods, but the supply of them as well.

AT&T is committed to continued lawful collaboration with rights-holders to end illegal copyright infringement through its networks. AT&T believes that intellectual property piracy can and should be prosecuted under the applicable civil and criminal statutes now in effect, and that ISPs can and should play the role of trusted ally in the intellectual property enforcement structure. But ISPs cannot and should not be the Internet's principle enforcer of the copyright laws. This is properly the role of government. In order to strengthen government's ability to pursue this task, a modem enforcement structure should be created that comprehensively addresses the problem. Therefore, AT&T respectfully requests that the coordinated civil and criminal proposals suggested above be considered by the IPEC for inclusion in the Joint Strategic Plan.

Sincerely,

February 11, 2011

Chairman Patrick Leahy
Ranking Member Chuck Grassley
Senator Orrin Hatch
Senate Judiciary Committee
United States Senate
224 Dirksen Senate Office Building
Washington, DC 20510

Re: *COICA*

Dear Chairman Leahy, Ranking Member Grassley and Senator Hatch,

I write with regard to the Combating Online Infringement and Counterfeits Act ("COICA"), which this Committee unanimously approved on November 18, 2010.[4] I represent the Directors Guild of America, the American Federation of Television and Radio Artists, the Screen Actors Guild, the International Alliance of Theatrical and Stage Employees, and the Motion Picture Association. I write to you at their request to offer my view that COICA is consistent with the First Amendment and to set forth the basis for that conclusion.

---

[4] Throughout this letter, I refer to the final version of the bill passed by the Judiciary Committee in the 111th Congress, S. 3804 (Reported in Senate), in anticipation of the Senate considering the bill during the 112th Congress.

In this letter, I will summarize the provisions of the statute briefly and then turn to its constitutionality under the First Amendment. I think it useful, however, to begin with some observations about copyright law and the First Amendment in the age of the Internet.

I start with what should not be controversial. The Internet is one of the greatest tools of freedom in the history of the world. That is why, as Secretary of State Clinton observed last month, there is an "urgent need" to protect freedom of expression on the Internet throughout the world. At the same time, however, she pointed out that "all societies recognize that freedom of expression has its limits," observing specifically that those who use the Internet to "distribute stolen intellectual property cannot divorce their online actions from their real world identities" and that our ability to "safeguard billions of dollars in intellectual property [is] at stake if we cannot rely on the security of our information networks."

It is no answer to this challenge to treat loose metaphors—the Internet as "the Wild West," for example—as substitutes for serious legal analysis. It is one thing to say that the Internet must be free; it is something else to say that it must be lawless. Even the Wild West had sheriffs, and even those who use the Internet must obey duly adopted laws.

It is thus no surprise that libel law applies to material that appears on the Internet. *Milum v. Banks,* 642 S.E.2d 892 (Ga. Ct. App. 2007) (holding that defendant published libelous statements by posting them on his website) *cert. denied* (June 4, 2007). Or that libel precedents regarding printing information on paper are given comparable meaning as to information posted online. *Nationwide Bi-Weekly Administration, Inc. v. Belo Corp.,* 512 F.3d 137 (5th Cir. 2007) (holding that the "single publication rule" for the statute of limitations in libel suits applies to Internet publication). Or that principles of privacy law are applied to personal information posted online with the same animating principles that apply in more traditional media. *Yath v. Fairview Clinics, N.P.,* 767 N.W.2d 34 (Minn. Ct. Ap. 2009) (holding that posting information from a patient's medical file on a social networking website constitutes the "publicity" element of invasion of privacy); *Benz v. Washington Newspaper Publishing Co.,* 2006 WL 2844896 (D.D.C. Sept. 29, 2006) (holding that false information posted on independent websites provided reasonable claim for defamation, invasion of privacy and false light against private party defendant, in addition to claims regarding publication of related information by a newspaper).

Copyright law is no different. It is not disputable that "fall existing copyright protections are applicable to the Internet." Edward H. Rosenthal, *JD. Salinger and Other Reflections on Fair Use,* 1003 PLI/Pat 35, 42 (2010). *See Video Pipeline, Inc. v. Buena Vista Home Entertainment, Inc.,* 342 F.3d 191 (3d Cir. 2003) (upholding preliminary injunction against website compiling video clips of copyrighted movies for commercial use); *UMG Recordings, Inc. v. Stewart,* 461 F. Supp. 2d 837 (S.D. III. 2006) (finding *prima facie* case of liability in support of default judgment against Internet user who downloaded, reproduced and distributed copyrighted audio recordings online). The seizure provisions of copyright laws are applied to seize and stop the use of online property to facilitate infringement, such as domain names, just as offline property can be seized to stop its use to facilitate infringement. United States v. The Following Domain Names: TVShack.net et al., 2010 WL 2666284 (S.D.N.Y. June 29, 2010) (treating domain names hosting infringing videos as forfeitable property under 18 U.S.C. §§ 2323(a) and ordering their seizure, locking domain names at registry level, replacing registrar information to identify the government as the domain names' owner, and compelling the registry to route traffic to the domain names to a government IP address notifying the public that the domain name was seized).

Copyright law has existed throughout our Nation's history. The Constitution itself authorizes Congress to adopt copyright legislation (Art. I, Sec. 8, Clause 8) and the first such legislation was enacted in 1790, a year before the First Amendment was approved by Congress. Ch. 15, 1 Stat. 124 (1790) (repealed). From the start, injunctions were one form of relief accorded to victims of copyright infringement. (Courts applied the 1790 Act, and its later amendments, to grant injunctions "according to principles of equity." Act of Feb. 3, 1831, eh. 16, 4 Stat. at 438 (1831) (repealed 1870) (cited in Kristina Rosette, *"Back to the Future: How Federal Courts Create a Federal Common Law Copyright Through*

Permanent Injunctions Protecting Future Works," 2 J. Intell. Prop. L. 325, 340 (1994)). However, since injunctions in non-copyright cases have frequently been held to be unconstitutional prior restraints on speech, *Vear v. Minnesota,* 283 U.S. 697 (1931); *New York Times Co. v. United States,* 403 U.S. 713 (1971), and for other reasons, the subject has arisen as to the application, if any, of the First Amendment to copyright principles. *See generally,* Melville B. Nimmer & David Nimmer, Nimmer on Copyright § 19E (2010).

The issue of whether and, if so, how certain elements of the Copyright Act should be read to accommodate various First Amendment interests remains open. The law could hardly be clearer, however, that injunctions are a longstanding, constitutionally sanctioned way to remedy and prevent copyright violations. Indeed, that premise was explicit in the critical concurring opinion in the Supreme Court's most famous prior restraint case, assessing publication of the Pentagon Papers, which noted that "no one denies that a newspaper can properly be enjoined from publishing the copyrighted works of another." *New York Times Co.,* 403 U.S. at 731 n.1 (White, J. and Stewart, J., concurring). Current treatises reflect this judicial consensus. "[C]ourts have found no constitutional obstacle to enjoining, pursuant to federal legislative mandate, the unlawful use of a registered trademark or copyright." Floyd Abrams & Gail Johnston, *Communications Law in the Digital Age 2010: Prior Restraints,* 1026 PLI/Pat 247, 261 (2010); James L. Oakes, *Copyrights and Copyremedies: Unfair Use and Injunctions,* 38 J. Copyright Soc'y 63, 71 (1990) ("A pirated or copied edition, record, movie, song or other work . . . cries out for an injunction").

The Supreme Court's most detailed treatment of the interrelationship between the First Amendment and copyright, the seminal case of *Harper & Row Publishers, Inc. v. Nation Enterpr,* 471 U.S. 539, 560 (1985), stressed that far from conflicting with the First Amendment, the Copyright Act actually furthers the very interests which the First Amendment protects. "First Amendment protections," the Court noted, are "already embodied in the Copyright Act's distinctions between copyrightable expression and uncopyrightable facts and ideas." The Constitution supports the explicit protection of such expression and creativity, the Court stated, within a framework that defends both the right to speak and the ability to profit from speech. "Mlle Framers intended copyright itself to be the engine of free expression," explained the Court, and "[Il]y establishing a marketable right to the use of one's expression, copyright supplies the economic incentive to create and disseminate ideas." *Id.* at 558. Copyright law thus fortifies protections for speakers and creators, in a First Amendment context, while stimulating future creativity.

The evident constitutionality of injunctive relief for copyright violations does not mean, to be sure, that injunctions must automatically or always be issued in response to a copyright violation. The Supreme Court has recently held to the contrary, warning against the error of a "categorical grant" of injunctive relief for patent infringement in *eBay Inc. v. MercExchange. L*547 U.S. 388, 394 (2006), and the Second Circuit has applied that conclusion in a recent, celebrated copyright case, *Salinger v. Colting,* 607 F.3d 68 (2d Cir. 2010). What *no* court has ever denied is that injunctions are a valuable and constitutional response to copyright violations.

Legislative Summary

I turn to a discussion of the bill itself. COICA is designed to enforce federal copyright and trademark law in the age of the Internet. It aims to combat the "theft of American intellectual property" on a scale that costs "American creators and producers billions of dollars per year," as this Committee's Legislative Report documented, and which results in "hundreds of thousands of lost jobs annually.- S. Rep. No. 111-373, at 2 (2010).

COICA does so by strengthening the measures that the Attorney General may pursue, with court approval, to address infringing content. The bill buttresses injunctive relief to not only order offending websites to cease breaking the law, but also to compel domain names, advertising companies, financial transaction providers and Internet service providers to cease cooperating with websites that are breaking the law.

The bill does not address all types of infringement online. It focuses only on websites that are dedicated to profiting from infringing content or activities. COICA would establish a statutory category of websites that are "dedicated to infringing activities." This term is defined as a web-site that is "marketed" or "primarily designed" for infringement, or has no other "commercially significant purpose or use" besides infringement, as defined under current copyright and trademark law, and which would otherwise be "subject to civil forfeiture." Thus for copyright violations under COICA, a website must be "dedicated to infringing activities" and offering goods or services in violation of title 17 U.S.C, or facilitating such violations by means such as downloading, streaming, transmitting or linking. For trademark violations under COICA, a website must be "dedicated to in-fringing activities" and offering, selling or distributing goods, services or counterfeit materials in violation of section 34(d) of the Lanham Act (15 U.S.C. 1116(d)).

COICA does not alter the available remedies for private parties seeking to redress infringement. Nor does it limit the defenses that may be offered, including but not limited to that of fair use. What the bill does, beyond the current copyright framework, is add to the remedies available to the Attorney General, who would be authorized to commence actions against websites "dedicated to infringing activities." Under CO1CA, a federal district court "may" issue a temporary re straining order, a preliminary injunction or an injunction "in accordance with rule 65 of the Federal Rules of Civil Procedure." By incorporating Rule 65, COICA applies the procedural protections that federal law currently affords all litigants in civil actions in the United States.

Under Rule 65, courts "may issue a preliminary injunction only on notice to the adverse party. For temporary restraining orders to be issued without notice, Rule 65 requires that two conditions must be met. "[S]pecific facts in an affidavit or verified complaint [must] clearly show that immediate and irreparable injury, loss, or damage will result before the adverse party can be heard in opposition." And "the movant's attorney certifies in writing any efforts made to give notice and the reasons why it should not be required." Hearings for orders without notice are to be held "at the earliest possible time, taking precedence over all other matters," under Rule 65, and the adverse party may move to dissolve or modify an order on two days' notice to the moving party. All these protections are incorporated into COICA.

For websites registered in the United States, COICA provides for *in rem* actions to be commenced located in the judicial district where a domestic website's domain name registrar is doing business. Once court orders are issued against domestic domains, a federal law enforcement officer shall serve the registrar, or if the registrar is abroad, then the registry. A registrar or registry receiving such an order is required to suspend or lock the domain name.

For foreign websites, COICA provides for in rem actions in the District of Columbia against the domain names of such websites, provided that the Attorney General simultaneously sends notice to the registrant of the domain name by postal mail and email, (using the addresses that the registrant provided to the domain name registrar), and provided that the Attorney General publishes notice of the action, as a court may direct, after its filing. Once court orders are issued against foreign domains, a federal law enforcement officer may serve such orders on three entities that work with the website in question. First, the order may be served on advertising services companies, which shall take "reasonable measures" to prevent their networks from providing advertisements to the website named in the order. Second, the order may be served on financial transaction providers, which shall stop payment transactions between U.S. customers and the website named in the order. And which shall inform the website that it is not authorized to use the transaction provider's trademark. Third and finally, the order may be served on Internet service providers ISPO, which shall take "technically feasible and reasonable steps" to block the domain name in the United States. COICA enumerates several protections for ISPs in this process, stipulating that they "shall not be required" to modify their network or facilities to comply with such orders; nor to take steps involving "domain name lookups" that are performed by entities other than their "own domain name system server"; nor to continue taking preventive actions under the order once access to the domain name has been "disabled by other means." Under COICA, all three such entities may decide, at their discretion, how to communicate their actions to users or customers. In the event of a willful and knowing failure to comply with such orders, the Attorney General may seek injunctive relief directly against the entity in question. In such actions, COICA provides that the technological inability to comply with the underlying orders shall serve as a defense.

Entities taking actions reasonably designed to comply with court orders issued under COICA are granted immunity from causes of action based on such compliance. They are also exempted from liability for voluntarily taking the actions stipulated against websites dedicated to infringing activity in COICA, provided that such actions are taken based on the reasonable belief that the websites are dedicated to infringing activity.

First Amendment Considerations

Having discussed the broad constitutional and copyright framework for COICA, and described what the bill does in basic terms, I now turn to two potential First Amendment issues in analyzing CO1CA: the breadth of the regulatory framework's impact on speech, and its procedural protections in a First Amendment context.

Potential Overbreadth

It is a fundamental principle of First Amendment jurisprudence that government restrictions on speech should be narrowly tailored to avoid unnecessarily burdening protected speech. Courts apply strict scrutiny to statutes that potentially interfere with protected speech, with special attention for rules that may sweep too broadly. Like any statute impacting speech, Congress must consider the potential overbreadth of COICA's statutory structure and remedies in light of these First Amendment considerations.

COICA is not constitutionally overbroad. First, it sets a rather high bar in defining when a website or domain is eligible for potential actions by the Attorney General. Second, its remedies are focused on preventing infringing content at the distribution point where website operators choose to infringe. Finally, the application of Federal Rule 65 serves as a check on overbreadth.

COICA is not designed to regulate the entire Internet. Nor is it designed to counter the vast array and forms of online infringement, which are subject to various laws already on the books. COICA focuses, instead, on a narrow category of entities which are not simply trafficking in some infringing content, or occasionally breaking federal laws, but which are primarily and continuously devoted to providing and selling infringing content in the United States. Since COICA specifically defines a rigorous standard of websites that are "dedicated to infringing activities," actions under COICA require a showing that a target website is both violating federal law and operating with the main function of continuous infringement. Therefore, any website devoted to legal activities, such as commentary, socializing or commerce, cannot be pursued under COICA if it occasionally or even repeatedly practices infringement.

For websites and domains that meet COICA's definition, injunctive relief would be issued to address infringement at its distribution point. Thus an individual choosing to use a website or domain to practice infringement faces relief at the point of infringement, be that a particular web-site address or a domain name devoted to infringement. This approach constitutes a narrowly tailored means to prevent future infringement, with a court making the final determination as to whether and how to craft injunctive relief "against the domain name used by an Internet site ... to cease and desist from undertaking any further activity in violation" of COICA, S. 3804 (Reported in Senate) at 17. Such relief tracks equitable remedies in traditional copyright law, such as forfeiture or impoundment, 17 U.S.C. § 506(b) (forfeiture); 17 U.S.C. § 503 (impoundment). In the online context, distribution may occur only at a single website address, in which ease injunctive relief may block that address via orders served on the domain name registrar, registry or ISP. Or distribution may occur across a domain, in which case injunctive relief may block the domain via orders served on the domain name registrar, registry or ISP. Some protected and non-infringing content may he implicated in this process, but such content would have to be hosted in conjunction with an entity that is dedicated to infringement. Even without such a high bar, of course, the presence of non-infringing speech generally does not provide a copyright violator with immunity from enforcement actions. The First Amendment allows government regulations to prevent piracy that clearly have an incidental impact on non-infringing speech. *United States v. Elcom Ltd.*. 203 F. Supp. 2d 1111, 1129 (N.D. Cal. 2002) (noting that the First Amendment allows the government to pursue online infringement with an "incidental restriction" on First Amendment freedoms, so long as the traditional test is met that the "means chosen do not burden substantially more speech than is necessary to further the government's legitimate interests.") (internal citations omitted). Furthermore, and independent of a potential statutory framework such as that set forth in COICA, courts already approve, on a case-by-case basis, copyright seizures of domain names that can result in the blockage of some non-infringing content. Indeed, some such seizures apply current forfeiture laws to permanently seize a domain name as property. *United States v. n'Shack.net et al.,* 2010 WL 2666284 (S.D.N.Y. June 29, 2010) (treating domain names hosting infringing videos as forfeitable property under 18 U.S.C. §§ 2323(a) and ordering their seizure).

If an order under COICA does result in blocking some non-infringing content, COICA is sufficiently narrow to accommodate the immediate publication of that content elsewhere and the future publication of the content on the same domain. First, by definition, any non-infringing content is not specifically enjoined by the order, so it may still be legally posted anywhere else online. Second, such content can be unblocked or reposted *on the same* website or domain name in the future, once the infringing content at issue is removed. Indeed, the content can be unblocked or reposted precisely because the domain name itself, as property, is not forfeited by an order pursuant to COICA. Thus after the infringement issue is resolved and the site operator is in compliance with federal law, the domain name can post its archived non-infringing content.

In addition, it is worth noting that a website may meet COICA's "dedicated to infringement" standard based on its links to other websites providing infringing content, apart from whether or not the linking website technically hosts infringing content on its own site or servers. COICA provides that such websites may be dedicated to infringement by providing "aggregated links to other sides or Internet resources for obtaining" infringing content. Just as with posting infringing content. however, such a site must meet the high bar of being "marketed" or "primarily designed" for infringement, or having no other "commercially significant purpose or use" besides infringement. 'This is consistent with case law regarding online copyright infringement, since "Plinking to infringing material" can create liability, 1003 PLI/Pat 35 at 43. When a website links to infringing content, or links to technology to facilitate infringement, courts look to whether the web-site operator knowingly linked to facilitate violations of the law. *Universal City Studios, Inc, v. Reimerdes, 111* F. Supp. 2d 294 (S.D.N.Y. 2000) (holding defendant violated Digital Millennium Copyright Act by linking to program to unlock DVDs for unauthorized copying, and requiring knowing linking for the purpose of disseminating the program); *Bernstein v. JC Penney, Inc.,* 50 U.S.P.Q.2d 1063 (C.D. Cal. 1998) (plaintiff did not have a claim for mere linking to website without knowledge of infringing material on the site). Injunctions issued specifically against linking, in order to thwart copyright infringement, have also been held to be consistent with the First Amendment. *Universal City Studios, Inc. v. Corley,* 273 1[7].3c1429 (2d Cir. 2001). Furthermore, in recent enforcement actions against domain names, the U.S. Department of Homeland Security specifically seized "'linking' websites" that provide "links to files on third party websites that contain illegal copies of copyrighted contact." (Aff.1113) *United States v. The Following Domain Names: HQStreams.com* et al., 2011 WI. 320195 (S.D.N.Y. Jan 31, 2011). Given these precedents, potential actions pursuant to COICA against websites dedicated to infringing content based on extensive and continuous linking to facilitate infringement appear to rest on a solidly constitutional foundation. As for overbreadth in the linking context, it appears clear that neither a few inadvertent links to infringing material on an otherwise lawful website, nor some links to infringing websites for the purposes of public information or education, could be held to meet COICA's threshold.

Procedural Protections

The procedural protections under COICA are so strong, uniform and constitutionally rooted that it is no exaggeration to observe that any complaints in this area are not really with the bill, but with the Federal Rules of Civil Procedure itself, which governs all litigants in U.S. federal courts.

COICA incorporates Rule 65 to provide the process governing how a judge "may" issue a temporary restraining order, preliminary injunction, or permanent injunction. Thus website operators subject to COICA would benefit from the same procedural safeguards afforded litigants in all other U.S. civil actions. For preliminary injunctions, those safeguards require notice in advance. For temporary restraining orders, the safeguards include first, the requirement that temporary restraining orders issued without notice must be based on specific facts showing the prospect of immediate and irreparable damage "*before* the adverse party can be heard in opposition" (emphasis added); and second, a written certification by, in this case, the U.S. government's attorney, explaining efforts made to give notice and the reasons it should not required in this instance. Subsequent hearings for orders without notice are a first priority under Rule 65, which also grants the adverse party the option of moving to dissolve an order with two days' notice.

In addition to those well-established procedures, COICA also explicitly requires the Attorney General to conduct service of process by sending notice of an intent to proceed under COICA to the domain name registrant. Consistent with the objectives of Rule 65, this requirement provides an opportunity to operators of allegedly infringing websites to defend themselves before an order is issued. In the event that operators prefer to respond later, or only learned of injunctive action later because they did not provide accurate contact information to their registry, they also retain their rights to seek later relief from the order by disputing the allegations or appealing to the interests of justice. It is worth noting that federal copyright law disfavors the submission of false contact information to a domain name registrar, treating the knowing provision of "materially false contact information to a domain name registrar" as a rebuttable presumption of willful infringement. 17 U.S.C.A § 504(c); *Chanel, Inc. v. Cui,* 2010 WL 2835749 (S.D.N.Y. July 7, 2010) (entering default judgment for permanent injunction against product trademark infringement and finding willful conduct based, in part, on defendant's repeated submissions of "false information in registering domain names" used for infringement). Indeed, the rules for registration of domain names require the provision of accurate contact information. Registrar Accreditation Agreement, section 3.7.7.1 (May 21, 2009), available at http://www-w.icann.org/en/registrars/ra-agreement-21may09-en.htm#3 (registrants required to provide registrar accurate and reliable contact details). Finally, since COICA states that courts "may" issue preliminary injunctions or injunctions, the range of available remedies includes the prospect of a final- not preliminary-resolution of the dispute.

Once COICA's required procedural protections are satisfied, it is still possible that some operators of allegedly infringing websites will knowingly decline to participate in U.S. court proceedings. Such a choice, after legitimate notice and procedural safeguards are provided, can lead to *ex parte* proceedings and default judgments. Courts routinely enter default judgments in civil lawsuits, including comparable online copyright eases. After initial notice has been served, courts grant permanent injunctive relief for copyright violations in default judgments without additional attempts at notice. *Disney Enterprises, Inc. v. Farmer,* 427 F.Supp. 2d 807 (E.D. Term. 2006) (issuing permanent injunction barring infringement of copyright by website distributing copyrighted movies over peer-to-peer network, with default judgment entitled without additional service of notice on defendant): *Priority Records, LLC v. Bradley,* 2007 WL 465754 (F.D. Mich. Feb. 8, 2007) (issuing permanent injunction in default judgment against defendant using online distribution system to download and distribute copyrighted recordings).

Conclusion

I am aware that COICA has been criticized on First Amendment-related grounds by organizations such as the American Civil Liberties Union and certain human rights groups, organizations for which I have the highest regard. The core of their concern about the bill seems anchored in the view that the United States would be less credible in its criticism of nations that egregiously violate the civil liberties of their citizens if Congress adopts COICA.

I disagree. Copyright violations are not protected by the First Amendment. Entities "dedicated to infringing activities" are not engaging in speech that any civilized, let alone freedom-oriented, nation protects. That these infringing activities occur on the Internet makes them not less, but more harmful. The notion that by combating such acts through legislation, the United States would compromise its role as the world leader in advancing a free and universal Internet seems to me insupportable. As a matter of both constitutional law and public policy, the United States must remain committed to defense both the right to speak and the ability to protect one's intellectual creations. The legislation does not impair or overcome the constitutional right to engage in speech; it protects creators of speech, as Congress has since this Nation was founded by combating its theft.

Respectfully submitted,
Floyd Abrams*

cc: Directors Guild of America
American Federation of television and Radio Artists
Screen Actors Guild
International Alliance of Theatrical and Stage Employees
Motion Picture Association

---

* I thank my associate and colleague, Ari Melber, for his assistance in all aspects of the preparation of this submission.

February 15, 2011

The Honorable Patrick Leahy Chairman
United States Senate Committee on the Judiciary
224 Dirksen Senate Office Building Washington, D.C. 20510-6275

Re: Targeting Websites Dedicated to Stealing American Intellectual Property

Dear Chairman Leahy:

In advance of tomorrow's hearing before the Senate Committee on the Judiciary, we write to support your policy objectives in convening a discussion about the problem of online copyright infringement and counterfeiting. We understand that enforcing our copyright and other intellectual property laws can be a difficult and frustrating challenge, and we look forward to the exchange of views that the hearing will provide.

We also write to highlight some concerns with the Combating Online Infringement and Counterfeits Act (COICA), the bill introduced in the 11th Congress that attempts to address online infringement. While we support the goals of the bill, we worry that the draft passed by the Committee last fall has significant unintended consequences. Because of the breadth of its provisions, it threatens to chill First Amendment freedoms over the 21st century's most important platform for speech and democracy engagement — the Internet.

1. Requiring domain name service (DNS) providers to delist entire domain names based on the criteria outlined in the bill would have the effect of chilling lawful speech.

We are concerned that the bill's approach — blocking top-level domain names when a site "offer[s] goods or services ... that ... enables or facilitates a violation of title 17, United States Code" — will have the unintended consequence of chilling entirely lawful speech.

Consider the following example: David Pogue writes a popular blog, Pogue's Posts, for the New York Times. Pogue often writes reviews of consumer electronics products, including smartphones, laptop computers, and digital cameras. Pogue's blog posts assist consumers in purchasing these devices, and each of these devices can certainly be used to break copyright infringement laws. Does that mean that Pogue's blog, as well as the *entire* nytimes.com domain name, should be subject to *in rem* action? By the same token, should apple.com be subject to *in rem* action because some people buy Apple computers and use them to stream unlawful content? Surely not. And yet subjecting both of these websites to liability is a plausible reading of the bill as proposed last fall.

2. The bill's immunity provisions could enable non-governmental actors to censor content online with impunity.

We are concerned that the bill's immunity provisions, which authorize domain name registries, financial transaction providers, and other service providers to disconnect domain names so long as the service provider "reasonably believes the site is dedicated to infringing activity," have the potential to dramatically chill user-generated content online. In short, the bill allows private entities to substitute their own judgment for that of law-enforcement officials and censor content without consequence. Under the proposed legislation, user generated content the kind of noncommercial content that makes the Internet such a varied forum for discussion may be the most likely to suffer, as ordinary users will be the least likely to have either the resources or the technological know-how to contact DNS providers and contest the decision to take down lawful websites. Two user-generated content sites — both blogs dedicated to hip-hop music that claim they comply with the widely accepted existing legal framework established by the Digital Millennium Copyright Act — have already been seized by the federal government. To authorize network operators to engage in similar disconnections with statutory immunity gravely threatens the value of the open Internet as a media infrastructure enabling and empowering diverse voices.

3. Authorizing United States courts to exercise jurisdiction over foreign domain names threatens to balkanize the Internet and runs counter to this country's global Internet freedom agenda.

Finally, we are concerned that this legislation would allow United States courts to exercise jurisdiction over foreign domain names. Even if disconnecting foreign domain names could have positive policy outcomes, the costs would be far too great, and the practice could lead to regional balkanization of the Internet if other governments adopted similar strategies. Instead of one Internet with the benefits of global interconnection, Americans could face greater difficulty reaching foreign content, and our counterparts abroad could be cut off from the innovations of American companies and the speech of American thinkers. These consequences seem particularly grave when one considers that while COICA may employ DNS interference in pursuit of a legitimate objective — combating online infringement -- other regimes may feel no hesitation in deploying similar techniques to suppress dissenting views or immobilize opposition movements when such actions violate their domestic law. The United States should not adopt a domestic policy that implicitly condones the very kinds of practices we attempt to condemn abroad.

Again, we look forward to the opportunity for dialogue afforded by tomorrow's hearing. We understand that these arc difficult problems to solve. At this point, we ask merely that you consider these unintended potential consequences as you evaluate policy proposals forward. We look forward to further discussions of policy solutions that effectively combat online infringement and preserve the Internet as a vibrant, open medium for speech, culture and democratic engagement. We look forward to working with you and the members of the Committee on this issue.

Very truly yours.
Saseha Moinrath
Open Technology Initiative, New America Foundation
Apama Sridhar, M. Chris Riley: Free Press Action Fund

WRITTEN TESTIMONY SUBMITTED FOR THE RECORD OF DANIEL CASTRO

Senior Analyst
Information Technology and Innovation Foundation (ITIF) on "Targeting Websites Dedicated to Stealing American Intellectual Property" before the Senate Committee on the Judiciary U.S. Senate
February 12, 2011

Legislation introduced in Congress in 2010, such as S. 3804, the "Combating Online Infringement and Counterfeits Act" (COICA), would take an aggressive and needed stand against online piracy and counterfeit goods, a growing problem that hurts American consumers and costs Americans jobs. Critics of the legislation argue that this bill would hurt free speech, encourage censorship in foreign countries, and cripple the technological infrastructure on which the Internet runs. Not only is this criticism untrue, but more robust enforcement of digital copyrights would likely lead to a stronger Internet ecosystem and more innovative content and services for consumers.

The Problem of Digital Piracy

Software, video games, movies, music, books, photos, and other media are increasingly available to users online. Many users go online and pay for digital content or applications through sites like Amazon, 'Tunes or Netflix. And the advent of new services like Google TV suggests that consumers will increasingly use the Internet to enjoy video programming on their PCs, in their living rooms and on their mobile devices. But all too many Internet users are choosing to download pirated digital content from illegal sites or peer-to-peer (P2P) networks. The problem has become some pervasive that at least 1 in 4 bits of traffic on the Internet is related to infringing content.[5] The Information Technology and Innovation Foundation (ITIF) has previously documented how Internet users can easily go online and, with just a few clicks, find pirated copies of full-length Hollywood movies or television programming to watch for free or software programs to use on their computers.[6] Many of these sites earn advertising dollars from major companies. For example, in ITIF's 2009 review of the websites The Pirate Bay and isoHunt, we found brands such as Amazon.com, Blockbuster, British Airways, and Sprint appearing on these sites.[7]

Online piracy has a significant impact on the U.S. economy. While the exact cost of piracy is difficult to measure, the impact is substantial, with one estimate finding that the U.S. motion picture, sound recording, business software, and entertainment software/video game industries lost over $20 billion dollars in 2005 due to piracy, and retailers lost another $2 billion, for a combined loss of over $22 billion.[8] Online piracy harms the artists, both the famous and struggling, who create content, as well as the technicians—sound engineers, editors, set designers, software and game programmers—who produce it. Piracy ultimately also hurts law-abiding consumers who must pay higher prices for content, enjoy less content or relatively lower quality content, or pay higher prices for Internet access to compensate for the costs of piracy

Potential Legislative Responses

In December 2009, ITIF proposed a number of policies to help reduce online copyright infringement, especially in countries that turn a blind eye to copyright enforcement.[9] These recommendations include the following:

---

[5] David Price, "An Estimate of Infringing Use of the Internet," Envisional (2011), http://documents.envisional.com/docs/Envisional-Internet_Usage-Jan2011.pdf.

[6] Daniel Castro, Richard Bennett, and Scott Andes, "Steal These Policies: Strategies for Reducing Digital Piracy," Information Technology and Innovation Foundation (Washington, DC: 2009), http://www.itif.orefiles/2009-digital-piracy.pdf.

[7] Ibid.

[8] Stephen Siwek, "The True Cost of Copyright Industry Piracy to the U.S. Economy," Policy Report 189, The Institute for Policy Innovation, September 2007.

[9] 5Castro, Bennett and Andes, "Steal these Policies."

- Create a process by which the federal government, with the help of third parties, can identify websites around the world that are systemically engaged in piracy
- Enlist ISPs to combat piracy by blocking websites that offer pirated content
- Enlist search engines to combat piracy by removing websites that offer infringing content from their search results
- Require ad networks and financial service providers to stop doing business with websites providing access to pirated content
- Create a process so that the private sector can consult with government regulators on proposed uses of anti-piracy technology
- Fund anti-piracy technology research, such as content identification technology
- Pursue international frameworks to protect intellectual property and impose significant pressure and penalties on countries that flout copyright law

Many of these recommendations have been considered in recent legislation, such as COICA, introduced by Senators Patrick Leahy (D-VT) and Orrin Hatch (R-UT) in 2010. COICA would provide important new tools to crack down on online infringement of intellectual property. The legislation would not target minor violations of copyright, but rather would target "Internet sites dedicated to infringing activities" which it defines as a site that is "primarily designed, has no demonstrable, commercially significant purpose or use other than, or is marketed by its operator...to offer" unauthorized access to copyright-protected content.

Response to Criticism of Legislation

Critics of COICA make three general objections: 1) that the legislation would impair free speech; 2) that the legislation would encourage censorship in foreign countries; and 3) that the legislation would cripple the technological infrastructure on which the Internet runs. All of these objections are unfounded.

Freedom of Speech

First, some critics oppose the legislation on the grounds that it would hurt free speech, a groundless accusation. Not all free speech is protected. As Justice Holmes in *Schenck v. U.S.* famously argued, freedom of speech does not include the freedom to falsely yell "Fire" in a crowded theater (or more recently "Bomb!" on an airplane).[10] Nor does it entail a freedom to establish a website for the sole purpose of enabling online piracy, even if the site posts a few statements expressing the owners' political views.

Neither does the idea of a "free and open" Internet mean that every website has the right to exist. Certainly, most people would agree that some websites should not be permitted to remain online, such as sites devoted to hosting child pornography or illegal scams. The purpose of this legislation is not to shut down a personal website that accidentally links to a copyrighted image or websites that use material protected by fair use, but to shut down websites whose principal purpose is to engage in egregious infringement of intellectual property.

Yet critics of the legislation, such as the Electronic Frontier Foundation (EFF), complain that free speech will be hurt if the government blocks "a whole domain, and not just the infringing part of the site."[11] While certainly most infringing sites will contain at least some non-infringing content, it is not an injustice to block the entire site. As noted, the legislation only applies to sites where the principal purpose of the site is to engage in digital piracy. Such frivolous complaints are equivalent to

---

[10] The man who said 'bomb' on an airplane," San Francisco Chronicle, August 6, 2010, http://www.sfgate.com/cgibin/blogs/crime/detail?entry_id=69558 and "Woman accused of airport bomb threats," United Press International, April 21, 2008, http://www.upi.com/Top_News/2008/04/21/Womansaccused-of-airportibombsthreats/UP1-38521208794796/.

[11] 7Richard Esguerra, "Censorship of the Internet Takes Center Stage in 'Online Infringement' Bill," Electronic Frontier Foundation, September 21, 2010, http://www.eff.oredeeplinks/2010/09/censorship-internet-takes-center-stage-online.

arguing that the justice system would be unfair to shut down a bar found to be repeatedly serving alcohol to minors even if some of its customers were of legal age or a pawn shop that serves as a front for moving stolen goods even if a few of its items were acquired legally.

Others present a similar criticism of the legislation under the guise of protecting free speech when their objection is really to an expansion of government authority. This mentality is exemplified by Bruce Schneier who as a matter of course argues against virtually any action by government to police abuses on the Internet.[12] These kinds of objections come from a purely anti-government ideology that rejects any attempt to give government more power, even if that is appropriate power to enforce laws against criminals.

Foreign Censorship

Critics also claim that COICA would set a negative precedent and harm the United States internationally by giving political cover to the "totalitarian, profoundly anti-democratic regimes that keep their citizens from seeing the whole Internet."[13] Critics, such as the 87 Internet engineers who signed EFF's letter to the Judiciary Committee, argue that the legislation would "seriously harm the credibility of the United States in its role as a steward of key Internet infrastructure." Others, including groups like the American Library Association, Consumer Electronics Association, Net Coalition and Public Knowledge, argue that "COICA's blacklist may be used to justify foreign blacklists of websites that criticize governments or royalty, or that contain other 'unlawful' or 'subversive' speech."[14]

---

[12] 8For example, with regards to the Obama Administration's plans to expand wiretapping online Schneier writes, "it's bad civic hygiene to build technologies that could someday be used to facilitate a police state." Bruce Schneier, "Web snooping is a dangerous move," CNN.com, September 29, 2010, http://www.cnn.com/2010/OPINION/09/29/schneier.web.suryeillance/index.html.

[13] Esguerra, "Censorship of the Internet Takes Center Stage in 'Online Infringement' Bill."

[14] Letter from Public Knowledge et al. on "S. 3804, Combating Online Infringement and Counterfeits Act (COICA), September 27, 2010, http://www.publicknowledge.Orefilesidocs /JointLetterCOICA20100929.pdf.

Again, these criticisms do not stand up to a serious analysis. This is equivalent to arguing that the United States should not put rioters who engage in wholesale property destruction and violence in jail because it simply encourages totalitarian governments to use their police to suppress their citizens.

More narrowly, some critics, such as Wendy Seltzer at Princeton University's Center for Information Technology Policy, argue that other countries would use anti-piracy efforts as a ruse for cracking down on political dissidents.[15] Such activities are not without precedent—Russian police have raided advocacy groups and opposition newspapers that have spoken out against the government in the name of searching for pirated software![16] Yet while certainly some unscrupulous countries might claim their actions are equivalent to that of the United States, it would be demonstrably untrue. There is simply no comparison between a country using clear and transparent legal means to enforce intellectual property rights online and a country censoring political speech online, even under the guise of protecting copyrights. Moreover, to argue that abusive regimes operating without the rule of law would somehow act more abusively because the United States cracks down on cybercrime is a stretch at best. If this were the case, we should have seen a dramatic increase in Internet censorship after nations like France and the U.K recently passed laws to crack down on online copyright theft.

In fact, if this law would have any effect on foreign nations it would be to embolden them to take stronger steps to crack down on digital piracy, a problem that is even worse in many foreign nations and one that contributes to a deteriorating balance of trade for the United States as foreign consumers steal U.S. software, music, video games, movies, books, photos, and other digital content.

---

[15] Wendy Seltzer, "Copyright, Censorship, and Domain Name Blacklists at Home in the U.S.," Freedom to Tinker, September 21, 2010, http://www.freedom-tostinker.com/blog/wseltzer/copyright-censorship-andsdomainsname-blacklists-homesus.

[16] Clifford Levy, "Russia Uses Microsoft to Suppress Dissent," New York Times, September 11, 2010, http://www.nytimes.com/2010/09/12/worldieurope/12raids.html.

Weaken the Internet

Finally, some opponents of stricter online IP enforcement argue that this legislation "will risk fragmenting the Internet's global domain name system (DNS)."[17] To understand the debate, you must understand how DNS works. DNS is like a global phonebook for the Internet providing users a number that corresponds to each name. Before a user can visit a domain name (e.g., www.itif.org), his or her computer must first discover the IP address associated with that web address (e.g., 69.65.119.60). DNS servers provide this service to users by translating domain names into IP addresses through a recursive process. Most users rely on the DNS servers of their local ISP for this service and it is these DNS servers that are the principle target of COICA. If a site appeared on the government blacklist, e.g., www.watchpirated-videos.tv, then the DNS servers would be instructed to no longer resolve an IP address for that domain. And without this IP address, users cannot visit these infringing websites.

Groups like EFF claim this will "undermine basic Internet infrastructure" and lament that it will keep 1SPs from "telling you the truth about a website's location.[18] While such fiction may be useful in generating fear about COICA, the simple fact is that using DNS to block access to websites or servers is not new or particularly challenging—it has been used for blocking Spam and protecting users from malware, for example, for many years. In addition, many DNS resolvers routinely return different answers to users as part of a service, such as to provide parental filters, correct typos in URLs, or to provide search results in lieu of a basic "domain not found" error.[19]

Other critics, such as the Center for Democracy and Technology, argue that COICA will set a precedent where ISPs will be required to block other "illegal or unsavory content" creating "a controlled, ISP policed

---

[17] Peter Eckersley, "An Open Letter from Internet Engineers to the Senate Judiciary Committee," Electronic Frontier Foundation, September 29, 2010, http://www.eff.orgideeplinks/2010/09/opensletter.

[18] Esguerra, "Censorship of the Internet Takes Center Stage in 'Online Infringement' Bill."

[19] For a more detailed rebuttal of some of the technical fears about COICA, see Daniel Castro, "No, COICA Will Not Break the Internet," Innovation Policy Blog (2011), http://www.innovationpolicy.oreno-coica-will-notsbreaksthe-internet.

medium.[20]Such an end result is antithetical to the worldview of CDT (and other opponents of this legislation) that the Internet should be free of private-sector control regardless of the consequences. This "slippery slope" argument is fundamentally illogical. The analogy would be like saying that if we pass laws against a person committing physical assault on another person, then it is only a matter of time before we pass laws against people bumping into each other rudely on the street. Such stubborn and entrenched views do not reflect the kind of flexible policymaking that most people agree is necessary for the fast-paced world of the evolving Internet. Rather than relying on tradition to justify Internet policy, a better approach would be to look at the practical implications of specific policy proposals in the present.

Why the Criticism?

So what's really behind these criticisms? They all reflect these groups' and individuals' overarching view of the Internet as a medium whose chief function is to liberate individuals from control by, or dependence on, big organizations. For these groups, the Internet is first and foremost about individual freedom, not about collective responsibility. They see the Internet as a special place, above and beyond the reach of the kinds of rules that govern the offline world. Yet, for most of the rest of us, the Internet is no different than the rest of society where we have rights and responsibilities and where laws against certain behaviors exist. We play by the rules and we expect others to do the same, and when they do not, we expect society (through the actions of democratically elected governments) to step in and punish those who commit crimes. All of these objections listed here reflect this fundamental Internet exceptionalist ideology, and as such are largely attacks not so much on this particular legislation, but on

---

[20] "The Dangers of S. 3804: Domain Name Seizures and Blocking Pose Threats to free Expression, Global Internet Freedom, and the Internet's Open Architecture," Center for Democracy and Technology, September 28, 2010, http://cdt.orgifiles/pdfs/Leahy_bill_memo.pdf.

any legislation that would put limits on Internet freedom, even if it's the freedom to falsely yell "fire!" in a crowded theatre.

Because of their overriding focus on individual freedom and not on collective benefit, critics of the legislation fail to understand that stronger enforcement of intellectual property would be beneficial to American consumers and businesses. For example, delivering video content to the TV is expected to be the next driver of broadband access and services but for this business model to work, content owners and creators should be able to ensure their rights are protected. Online piracy not only results in the unauthorized distribution of content, it hurts the ability of content producers to create legitimate business models for selling digital content. As the saying goes, "It's hard to compete with free." While many companies have rallied to the challenge and created compelling businesses to sell content legally, on the whole, illegal content still remains widely available and commonplace.

Conclusion

COICA is important because it recognizes that online piracy is no longer about college students trading files in their dorm room, but instead it has grown in to a multi-million dollar international business. Sites hosting pirated content or linking to pirated content can generate a significant amount of revenue from online advertising and sales. COICA would provide a mechanism to not only cut off access to these sites, but also cut off their funding mechanisms to make operating online piracy sites unprofitable.

Should we throw out freedom of speech and long-held legal protections like due process just to protect intellectual property online? Of course not. But neither should we abandon the Constitutional provisions which support protecting intellectual property. As with any law enforcement initiative, efforts at reducing online piracy involve balancing costs and benefits. While street crime could be reduced by doubling the number of police, most communities find an equilibrium where the marginal cost of an additional police officer does not outweigh the corresponding reduction in crime. With regard to Internet piracy, it is hard to argue that this equilibrium has been reached and that society would not be better off with greater efforts to stop digital piracy. While not all anti-piracy efforts should be embraced—for example, policymakers are wise to shy away from expensive digital rights management (DRM) technology mandates—the government should make a serious effort to combat piracy through reasonable approaches like COICA. The extent of piracy is so large, and the costs of enforcement quite reasonable, that it is clearly in the public interest to take more aggressive steps to curb it. Legislation such as COICA provides an opportunity for the U.S. government to get serious about enforcing intellectual property rights online.

STATEMENT OF THE CENTER FOR DEMOCRACY AND TECHNOLOGY

Submitted to the committee on the Judiciary, United States Senate
Patrick Leahy, Chairman
Regarding the Hearing: "Targeting Websites Dedicated to Stealing American Intellectual Property"
February 16, 2011

The Center for Democracy and Technology (CDT) appreciates the opportunity to submit this written statement for the record of the February 16, 2011 hearing on "Targeting Websites Dedicated to Stealing American Intellectual Property." CDT is a nonprofit public policy organization dedicated to keeping the Internet open, innovative, and free.

CDT supports the goal of reducing copyright and trademark infringement. In particular, we agree that there are websites the main purpose and activity of which is to enable and promote infringement. These sites are true "bad actors" and they deserve to be the target of law enforcement.

CDT has significant concerns, however, about some of the *mechanisms* proposed in the legislation developed by this Committee last year, the Combating Online Infringement and Counterfeits Act (COICA). Specifically, we would urge the Committee to take a hard look at the provisions of COICA that focus on the blocking and seizure of Internet domain names. These domain-name provisions would be almost entirely ineffective at achieving their goal of reducing infringement. At the same time, they would threaten unintended collateral damage in a number of areas, including suppressing lawful speech; exacerbating cybersecurity risks; and encouraging a dangerous jurisdictional scrum in which each country tries to use the domain name system to assert domestic jurisdiction over foreign websites. In short, the bill's domain-name provisions would fail any serious cost-benefit test and simply cannot be justified. The Committee should not proceed with COICA or with legislation proposing similar domain-name focused remedies.

This statement discusses why COICA's domain-name provisions would be ineffective. It then reviews the types of collateral damage that those provisions would risk.

1. Ineffectiveness

The domain-name seizure and blocking contemplated in COICA can be easily circumvented, and thus will have little ultimate effect on online infringement. The domain name system (DNS) performs a relatively simple function: translating text URLs (like www.cdt.orq) into machine-readable IP addresses (like 72.32.6.120). Importantly, this function is wholly unrelated to the content available at any given site. Neither seizing nor blocking a website's domain name *removes* the site from the Internet. The servers are still connected and users can still reach the site, including any infringing content.

There are a number of ways a targeted site may still be reached. First, the site's operator could simply register a new domain name for the site. There is ample evidence of just how easy and likely this is in the wake of

Immigration and Customs Enforcement's (ICE) seizure of over 100 domain names between June 2010 and February 2011. For example, all of the sports-streaming sites connected to the ten domains seized earlier this month quickly reappeared and are easily located at new domains.

Second, the site's operators could simply publicize its IP address, which users could then bookmark in lieu of saving or remembering the domain name. This is exactly what happened when Wikileaks's DNS service provider terminated the controversial site's account in December 2010; the IP address was immediately and widely available.[21]

Third, a site's operators could distribute a small browser plug-in or other piece of software to allow users to retrieve the IP addresses of the operators' servers. Such simple tools would make the process of following a site around the web virtually automatic.

Fourth, in the case of blocking by ISPs, users could easily switch DNS-lookup providers to avoid blocking orders. Since most operating systems come with DNS server functionality built in, savvy users could set up local DNS resolvers on their own computers, thus avoiding any DNS servers that have been ordered to block. In addition, third-party public DNS servers are widely available, and more would inevitably spring up outside the United States to avoid being subject to blocking orders. For Internet users, pointing DNS requests to these unfiltered servers would be simply a matter of updating a single parameter in their operating systems' Internet settings. Users who want to engage in infringement will thus easily be able to route their traffic around DNS providers that enforce blocking orders. For users to whom this seems complicated, more sophisticated users may create and distribute software tools to make the process easy.

All of these circumvention techniques are likely to occur as domain-name seizure and blocking become widespread. These sites have a highly motivated and relatively savvy user base, and word will spread quickly as to how best to circumvent any blocking. This means that any impact on

---

[21] Rob Pegararo, "WikiLeaks sinks, resurfaces (repeat as necessary)," Washington Post Faster Forward blog. December 3, 2010, hltp://voices.washinotonoost.comitasterlorward12010/ 12/wikileaks sinks res_urfaces rep,html.

infringement from seizing or blocking domain names is likely to be ephemeral at best.

In short, the main impact of COICA's domain-name provisions would be to drive website operators to domains administered by non-U.S, registrars and registries and website users to alternative (but equally easy) Internet navigation methods. The more common the interference with the domain name system, the more the workarounds would become routine. The workarounds themselves are trivial and would quickly go viral. Thus, seizing and blocking domain names as contemplated in COICA would be almost entirely ineffective at stopping infringement.

2. Collateral Damage

Interfering with the domain name system in an effort to combat infringement websites would threaten unintended collateral damage in a number of areas.

A. Overbreadth: Impact on Lawful Speech

The version of COICA approved by the Committee last year would affect lawful speech, for several reasons.

First, seizing and blocking domain names each target *entire websites,* which may contain a mix of lawful and unlawful content. This stands in sharp contrast to the notice and takedown provisions of the Digital Millennium Copyright Act (DMCA).[22] Under the DMCA process, specific infringing material is identified. That material, and only that material, is then targeted for takedown. Under COICA's domain-name provisions, an enforcement action would affect anything and everything on the website.

The risk of impairing access to lawful content might be mitigated if COICA only targeted pure infringement hubs. In fact, however, the bill has the potential to sweep much more broadly than that. The bill uses the phrase "dedicated to infringing activities," but its definition of that term is

---

[22] 17 U.S.C. § 512 (c)(3).

broad enough to encompass sites that, far from being "dedicated" to infringement, are actually multipurpose sites featuring a wide variety of content. This is because section 2(a)(1) of the bill includes in the definition any site that is subject to civil forfeiture under 18 U.S.C. § 2323 -- which covers any property "used, or intended to be used, in any manner or part to commit or facilitate" criminal copyright infringement. Criminal copyright infringement, defined in 17 U,S.C. § 506, includes any willful infringement committed for financial gain or involving $1,000 worth of goods. So in the end, COICA could be used against any website involved in at least $1,000 worth of infringement, regardless of how much lawful activity also occurs on that site. Measures aimed at such a site's domain name would affect all of that lawful content and speech, not just infringement.

Second, the bill's process for targeting infringing websites does not involve any prior, adversarial hearing. A website can petition to have a court order reversed after-the-fact, but the initial court order to block or seize the domain name occurs without the targeted website having an opportunity to defend itself. Given the one-sided nature of the presentation to the court, with law enforcement making its case unopposed, the risk of mistakes or overaggressive action is high.

This risk is evident from news reports about several of the recent domain-name seizures conducted by ICE pursuant to the civil forfeiture provisions of criminal copyright law. Several of the domain names seized in November were for music blogs that contained links to copyrighted songs. The operators of some of those blogs claim that the songs were supplied by the record labels themselves, for promotional purposes.[23] To be clear, CDT expresses no opinion about whether these blogs were authorized to post links to these songs or whether that activity was infringing. But there are significant questions about whether these blogs

[23] Ben Sisario, "Music Web Sites Dispute Legality of Their Closing," New York Times, December 19, 2010, httzl/www.nvtimes.com/2010/12/20/businessimedia/20music.html; see also Mike Masnick, "It Newly Seized Domains Were Purely Dedicated To infringement. Why Was Kanye West Using One?," Techdirl, November 30, 2010, ht01./Www.tecildint,C9Inladide.00101130/00M1 312049/if-newlyrseized-domains-werely: d d' ate-infringement- why -was-kanie-west-using-one.shtml.

were such "bad actors" that their entire domain names should be seized. Seizing the domain name affected not just the links to potentially infringing songs, but all of the commentary on the blogs.

In another example, earlier this month ICE seized domain names associated with a Spanish site that had been ruled lawful and non-infringing after extensive litigation in Spain.[24] Again, CDT expresses no opinion about whether the site's activity violates U.S. law. But the outcome in Spain suggests that the site operator, rather than being a clear-cut infringer, might at least have some serious legal arguments that it could offer in its defense. Its domain names were seized nonetheless.

Looking ahead, nothing would prevent COICA's domain-name provisions from being used against user-generated content sites — that is, websites that enable *users* to store, post, and share data. Such sites have many lawful uses, but can in practice be widely used for infringement as well. There is substantial ongoing debate and litigation about whether and when such sites should bear some responsibility and/or liability for infringing activities by users. But at a minimum, that is a question that should be decided only upon a full, adversarial judicial proceeding. By short-circuiting that process, COICA could affect lawful platforms for user speech.

A final reason why COICA's domain-name provisions may affect lawful speech relates to the existence of subdomains. Many web hosting services are constructed in a way such that thousands of individual sites, created and maintained by thousands of individuals, share a single domain name. For example, the service might be located at "webhost.com" and the individual sites might be joe.webhost.com and bob.webhost.com. If some infringement sites were hosted on this kind of platform, COICA's domain-name remedies would affect not just the actual offenders, but the *entire platform.* This is because the registrar and registry only have the ability to

---

[24] Nate Anderson, "US Customs begins pre-Super Bowl online mole-whack," Ars Technics, February 2, 2011. httpllarstechnica.com/tech-policvinews12011/02/us-custorm-be_gins-pre-sliper-bowl-mole-whacking.ars; see also Mike Masnick, "Homeland Security Seizes Spanish Domain Name that Had Already Been Declared Legal," Techdirt, February 1, 2011, http:/f.www.techcacomiglicks/20110291/10252412910/homelandsecurit -seizes-s anish-domain-name-that-had-alread -been-declared-legshtml.

seize or block the entire domain; they have no ability to take action at the subdomain level. As a result, a great deal of lawful speech could be affected.

In short, COICA's domain-name provisions would impede access to some material that is not itself infringing, but that simply shares a domain name with infringing material.

This overbreadth, in turn, raises serious constitutional questions. There is a strong argument that COICA targets an instrumentality of speech (domain names) and that it creates a prior restraint, effectively trying to censor the owner of a domain name based on his or her illegal activity in the past. Especially given how ineffective COICA's domain-name provisions would likely be in achieving their stated goal, as discussed above, the bill could be vulnerable to a First Amendment challenge.

B. Technical Impact and Cybersecurity

Seizing and blocking domain names presents a number of technical challenges that could have an impact on the Internet's reliability, security, and performance.

First, for ISPs, compliance with blocking orders may come at the expense of implementing the DNS Security Extensions (DNSSEC). For over 10 years, Internet engineers have been working to develop and implement a set of standards for addressing security flaws in the domain name system. DNSSEC is finally being deployed; the Office of Science and Technology Policy calls it a "major milestone for Internet security."[25] But having DNS lookup providers either pretend a site does not exist or redirect users to a site they have not requested (such as to a site saying "access to the site you were seeking is being blocked due to a court finding of copyright infringement") is flatly inconsistent with DNSSEC. The incompatibility is technical; DNSSEC uses cryptography to prevent DNS responses from being tampered with or falsified. A DNS resolver using DNSSEC simply is not able to give a cryptographically signed response that is false. DNS lookup providers could try to avoid the incompatibility

[25] http://www .whitehouo .gov Iblog12010107 1221a-major-milestone-internal-security.

by declining to respond to certain DNS requests at all, but this carries drawbacks that providers might prefer to avoid. Congress should avoid steps that would prevent or discourage Internet service providers from implementing this important security standard.

Second, blocking at the service provider level carries security risks for Internet users beyond the tension with DNSSEC. Most users today rely on their ISP to perform domain-name lookup functions. But as explained above with regard to ineffectiveness, switching to another lookup provider is trivial. The more ISPs and other major DNS providers are required to block lookup requests for websites that users want to reach, the more users will switch to independent, non-!SP DNS servers, And critically, they will not switch to other trustworthy U.S.-based DNS providers, but to DNS services located outside of the reach of U.S. law.

This would do more than just render service-provider-level domain-name blocking ineffective. 1SPs' DNS servers offer a crucial window into network usage; migration away from these servers would undermine ISPs' ability to observe and track botnet activity and other cybersecurity threats on their networks.[26]

In addition, it would put users at the mercy of potentially unscrupulous foreign DNS servers, which could redirect user traffic for phishing or bolnet purposes. Though they may be unaware of it, users place an enormous amount of trust in their DNS provider to route requests to the proper sites. ISPs have incentive to maintain that trust, but other DNS operators — especially those with an interest in evading the blocking of sites dedicated to commercial infringement — will likely not share that same incentive. By creating strong incentives to rely on potentially untrustworthy DNS providers, COICA as introduced would create a new and very dangerous opportunity for security risks and crime online.

Finally, encouraging many residential customers to rely on out-of-country DNS servers could undermine the efforts of CDNs (content delivery networks, such as Akamai) to improve the overall speed and efficiency of the Internet as a whole. CDNs rely on the approximate

---

[26] See Letter from DNS security researcher Dan Kaminsky regarding COICA, available at httn://www. ipAlicknowledge.orgifilestdocs/COICA Kaminsky lettgr.pdf.

location of users' DNS lookup servers (based on IP address) to choose the best location from which to deliver content. As users change their DNS settings to use foreign name servers, this signal will become a less reliable proxy for a user's location. For example, a CDN might assume a Maryland user using a Russian DNS provider is in Russia, undermining the benefits of CDNs and distributed hosting and increasing Internet congestion.

These security and reliability harms flow directly from the use of domain-name remedies to address infringing content. In light of how ineffective the approach is likely to be, this should raise serious questions as to whether the approach is worth the risk.

C. International Implications

From an international perspective, Congress should think twice before endorsing domain-name blocking and seizure as common tools for enforcing domestic U.S. law against foreign websites. If other countries were to follow this example, the result would be a dangerous jurisdictional scrum. Other countries, citing the U.S. example, could try to seize or block the domain names of U.S. websites that are lawful here but that violate some foreign law. This risk is not limited to repressive regimes. The scope of protection provided by the First Amendment remains the most expansive in the world, and speech protected in the United States remains proscribable in many other democratic countries. Local access to such speech remains a frustration to governments in those countries, and they would welcome a U.S.-based precedent to justify blocking it.

To take a concrete example, in 2000, a French court ruled that a Yahoo auction site violated French law because it contained postings for Nazi memorabilia.[27] U.S. courts refused to enforce that judgment, because the site's activity was lawful in the United States. Taking the approach set out in COICA's domain-name provisions, however, in the future a foreign country with a similar complaint could try to seize or block the site's domain name. If the registrar or registry for the domain name in question

---

[27] UEJF and Licra v. Yahoo! Inc. and Yahoo France, Tribunal de Grand Instance de Pans, May 22, 2000, httb://www.iuriscnanetitxtriurisfricti/yauctions20000522,htm.

has an office in that foreign country, it could be ordered to de-register the name.

COICA's domain-name provisions could also serve as precedent for a variety of actions that the United States would characterize as censorship. Already, some countries erect national Internet "firewalls," in an effort to suppress access to certain speech. Over forty countries (and growing) now filter the Internet to some degree, and even many liberal democracies like Australia and France are considering mandatory regimes in which the government requires ISP5 to block certain websites.[28]

Historically, the U.S. State Department has been the strongest global voice against such balkanization of the Internet. Indeed, Secretary of State Clinton has made the concept of a single, global Internet a cornerstone of U.S. foreign policy on Internet matters, as she reaffirmed just yesterday in a major speech,[29] But if the United States sets the precedent that any country can order the blocking of a domain name if some of the content at that name (wherever its physical location) violates the country's local laws, it is hard to see what credibility the United States would have as it urges other countries not to block access wherever they see fit.

To be clear, CDT does not suggest that the United States should not take action against infringement and encourage other countries to do likewise. The concern is simply that, by trying to use domain names as the means for fighting infringement, COICA would signal U.S. acceptance for the proposition that countries have the right to insist on removal of content from the global Internet as a tactic for enforcing domestic laws - and nothing would limit the application of this approach to copyright infringement and counterfeiting.

---

[28] See Australian Department of Broadband, Communications, and the Digital Economy, "ISP Filtering," http://www.dbcde.uov.auflunding and prograrnsthybersatetv olan/internel service provider isp filtering: see also Projet de lot d'orientation 0 de programmation pour la performance de la securite interieure, passed by the French Senate on February 8, 2011 and available at htlp://www senat.lr/petite-loi-ameli/20102011/262.html (in French; the bill includes a requirement that ISFs block access to Internet sites when ordered by an administrative authority).

[29] Secretary of Stale Hillary Rodham Clinton, "Internet Rights and Wrongs: Choices & Challenges in a Networked World," Speech at George Washington University, February 15, 2011, hltpl/www.state.govisecrelarylrm/2011/02/156619.htm.

In countries where rule of law is weak or entirely absent, that approach would open the door to serious misuse. Once the United States sends the green light, the use of domain-name seizures and blocking to silence other kinds of content considered unlawful in a given country - from criticism of the monarchy in Thailand to any speech that "harms the interests of the nation" in China - would surely spread. In short, the international precedent set by COICA's domain-name provisions would worsen the balkanization of the Internet and undermine the effort to protect the ability of Internet users, human rights defenders, and citizen journalists to speak and access content online.

D. Compliance Costs

Under COICA, law enforcement would issue orders calling on third parties such as registrars, registries, Internet service providers, payment networks, and advertising networks to take action against specific websites. A substantial portion of the costs of the administration of the bill, therefore, would all on such third parties. While the expense to third parties of complying with COICA is not a primary focus for CDT, the Committee should take account of such costs in conducting a cost-benefit analysis of the tactics proposed in the bill. Given the minimal effectiveness of measures targeting domain names, CDT believes there is little justification for asking Internet service providers, registrars, and registered to bear the cost of carrying out such measures on behalf of law enforcement authorities.

CTD does not oppose efforts to fight websites that are truly dedicated to infringing activities. But since domain name remedies would be ineffective at curbing infringement while carrying a variety of risks and costs. CDT believes it would be a serious mistake for Congress to enact COICA or any legislation similarly focused on using domain names to control infringement. In addition, any measures that aim to sidestep regular judicial process would, at a minimum, need to be much more narrowly tailored than COICA and would require carefully crafted procedural safeguards. In particular, CDT's understanding is that COICA was intended to target sites that have no redeeming qualities, whose whole focus is enabling blatant copyright infringement. As discussed above, however, COICA's definition of "dedicated to infringing activities' reaches much farther than this targeted purpose. COICA likewise envisioned taking strong action against selected websites based on *in rem* proceedings with no adversarial hearing and very little in the way of procedural safeguards to ensure that only true "bad actors" would be affected. For all of these reasons, CDT urges the Committee not to move forward with the approach suggested in COICA.

CDT appreciates the opportunity to offer this statement and stands ready to work with the Committee on this and other important issues of internet policy. For more information please contact Daid Sohn, dsohn@cdt.org, or Andrew McDiarmid, andrew@cdt.org.

STATEMENT OF EDWARD J. BLACK

President and CEO Computer & Communications Industry Association
February 16. 2011

On behalf of the Computer & Communications Industry Association, I appreciate the committee's consideration of this testimony on the matter of seizing domain names associated with infringing activities online. This written testimony addresses the general issue of seizing domain names, and then focuses on the last legislative incarnation of that policy, S. 3804. It identifies risks related with domain name seizure and cautions against adopting S. 3804 in any form, as the bill would not only prove ineffective but also endanger cybersecurity. The Computer & Communications Industry Association joins with prominent Internet engineers,[30] human

---

30 See Letter from 89 Internet engineers to the members of the Senate Judiciary Committee, available at <http://www.publicknowledge.org/files/docs/COICA_internet_engineers_letter.pdf>; Dan Kaminsky, DNS Filtering and S.3804, 'Countering Online Infringement and Counterfeiting Act' (Oct. 2010), available at <http://www.publicknowledge.org/files/docs/COICA_Kaminsky_letter.pdf>.

rights advocates,"[31] law professors,[32] educational groups:[33] and other technology organizations[34] in opposing S. 3804.

I. Summary

This written testimony argues that attacking allegedly unlawful content at the architectural layer of the Internet is a dangerous precedent to set, one which will further empower oppressive and authoritarian regimes to the political and economic detriment of the United States. Moreover, such a strategy is likely to prove ineffective and is already yielding false positives. This testimony also argues that much of 5.3804, the Combating Online Infringement and Counterfeiting Act ("COICA"), represents dangerous and unworkable responses to the problem of infringement. Not only is COICA unlikely to remedy the problem of foreign infringement, but it also threatens cybersecurity and is overbroad in its sweeping coverage of domestic sites and lawful products and services. In addition, COICA will

---

[31] *See* Letter from American Civil Liberties Union, Center for Democracy & Technology, Electronic Frontier Foundation, Freedom House, Human Rights First, Human Rights Watch, Rebecca MacKinnon, Reporters Sans Frontières, and World Press Freedom Committee to Chairman Patrick J. Leahy and Ranking Member Jeff Sessions, United States Senate (Oct. 26, 2010), *available at* <http://www.publicknowledge.org/files/docs/COICA_human_rights_letter_0.pdf>.

[32] *See* Letter from 49 law professors to the Senate Judiciary Committee (Nov. 16, 2010), *available at* <http://www.publicknowledge.org/files/docs/LawProfCOICA.pdf>.

[33] *See* Letter from Gregory A. Jackson, Vice President for Policy & Analysis, Educause, to Chairman Patrick J. Leahy and Ranking Member Jeff Sessions, United States Senate (Sep. 27, 2010), *available at* <http://www.publicknowledge.org/files/docs/COICA_EDUCAUSE_letter.pdf>; Letter from Cameron P. Wilson, Director of Public Policy, Association for Computing Machinery, to Chairman Patrick J. Leahy and Ranking Member Jeff Sessions, United States Senate (Sep. 28, 2010), *available at* <http://www.publicknowledge.org/files/docs/COICA_USACM_Letter.pdf>.

[34] *See* Letter from American Association of Law Libraries, American Library Association, Association of College and Research Libraries, Association of Research Libraries, Center for Democracy and Technology, Computer and Communications Industry Association, Consumer Electronics Association, Electronic Frontier Foundation, Home Recording Rights Coalition, NetCoalition, and Public Knowledge to Chairman Patrick J. Leahy and Ranking Member Jeff Sessions, United States Senate (Sep. 27 2010), *available at* <http://www.publicknowledge.org/files/docs/JointLetterCOICA.pdf>; Letter from Markham C. Erickson, Executive Director, NetCoalition, to The Honorable Patrick Leahy, Chairman, Senate Committee on the Judiciary (Nov. 15 2010), *available at* <http://www.publicknowledge.org/files/docs/COICA_NetCoalition_letter.pdf>.

further embolden authoritarian governments abroad, and lacks traditional safeguards to prevent its abuse at home. The solution to addressing infringement abroad is to persuade our trading partners to enforce the intellectual property laws that they have enacted an objective in which we have already invested considerable political capital.

II. Seizing Domain Names

The Internet is an amazing tool for global c-commerce that has opened up many new markets to U.S. firms. It also resembles a giant copying machine which resists control by any one person, company or government. The result is that, in addition to adding S2 trillion to annual U.S. GDP,[35] the Internet upsets old business models — for better or worse — and occasionally complicates the enforcement of intellectual property rights online.

Over the past year, domain name seizures have figured prominently in the online enforcement effort. This conversation has largely ignored the reality that, as Secretary Clinton stated only yesterday, "walls that block the Internet... are far easier to erect than to maintain." The challenges of using Internet architecture to police content has not stopped numerous governments, authoritarian and democratic, from trying to restrict Internet freedom. As a general rule, it is antithetical to the economic interests of the United States to validate the strategy of regulating Internet architecture to police content. As recent events have demonstrated, authoritarian governments cannot stand the openness and democratic nature of the Internet, and seek any excuse to regulate it. Even democratic governments occasionally feel the temptation to control the Internet, and it is of paramount importance that the United States lead by example.

---

[35] According to the National Economic Council this yields over $6,500 per person. Exec. Ofc. of the President, Nat'l Econ. Council/OSTP, *A Strategy for American Innovation: Driving Towards Sustainable Growth and Quality Jobs*, Sept. 2009, at 5, *available at* <http://www.whitehouse.gov/administration/eop/nec/StrategyforAmericanInnovation>.

Nevertheless, under a very narrow set of circumstances, the extreme approach of attacking unlawful activity at the architectural layer of the Internet may be a necessary option of last resort. However, as evidenced by mistakes already made, domain name seizure must be exercised carefully. As a broad enforcement tool, domain name seizure is in many cases unwise and unwieldy.

With respect to infringers located inside the United States or otherwise within the reach of U.S. law enforcement, a domain name seizure may be followed by arrest and prosecution. Domain name seizure thus serves to cease immediate infringing activity, but only as an initial approach to a more traditional law enforcement approach. If a domain name seizure is not followed by an arrest, most infringers easily re-register their domains. Aside from yielding more fees for domain name registrars, this exercise results in little effect.

Because infringers overseas are not being arrested concurrently with the domain name seizure, they generally re-register with immunity. For example, in June 2010 nine domain names were seized by the United States Immigration and Customs Enforcement Agency ("ICE") under the banner of a new initiative called "Operation In Our Sites.[36] Only a few days after the seizure and initiative were announced on a lot at Walt Disney Studios in Burbank, CA, at least two of the seized domains were back online under different domain addresses.[37] After ICE shut down the tvshack.net domain of Swedish company TV Shack, the site's operators relaunched at tvshack.cc, a domain administered by the Australian territory of the Cocos Islands. When the .cc domain was seized, sites appeared at tvshack.bz and tvshack.org.uk. Additionally, the seized Movie-Finks.tv site appeared back online at its new www.watch-tv-movies.info address.

In addition to the case with which infringers re-register, several mistakes have been made. For instance, ICE seized several sports-

---

[36] Michael Cieply, "9 Domain Names Seized in Fight Against Internet Theft," Media Decoder Blog, *N.Y. Times* (June 30, 2010), *available at* <http://mediadecoder.blogs.nytimes.com/2010/06/30/in-anti-theft-effort-officials-seize-9-domain-names>.

[37] Erick Schonfeld, "TV Shack Flouts the Feds by Moving Video Piracy Site to Offshore Domain," *TechCrunch* (Jul. 6, 2010), *available at* <http://techcrunch.com/2010/07/06/tv-shack-piracy>.

streaming sites just before the Super Bowl, including Spanish website Rojadirecta.[38] Rojadirecta is of special note because ICE's seizure comes after, and despite, Spain's determination that the site is legal.[39] Thus, ICE's actions as to Rojadirecta are particularly troubling in their complete disregard of another country's sovereign determination of legality. Even assuming that Rojadirecta were a clearly illegal site, the efficacy of seizing rojadirecta.com is dubious at best. After the seizure of the .com domain, users began using rojadirecta.cs, as the U.S. Government has no control over .is, the Spanish ecTLD. Internet traffic statistics from Alexa Internet, Inc. suggest that rojadirecta.es is now receiving *more* daily traffic than rojadirecta.com was receiving prior to seizure. This is hardly cause for declaring victory.

For another troubling example, one need look no further than the November 2010 seizure of hip hop blogs OnSmash and RapGodFathers.[40] The seizure of these blogs illustrate the tensions between a common marketing technique in the music industry called "leaking", where labels, agents, or artists themselves send popular websites new songs and videos to post in order to garner attention, and the immediate sanctions implemented through ICE's "Operation In Our Sites" initiative.[41] Similarly, in his recent letter to ICE Director John Morton, Senator Ron Wyden (D-OR) called into question the November seizure of dajazl.com based on an ICE special agent's ability to download four songs that were legally provided to dajazl.com's operator for purposes of distribution.[42]

Domain name seizure therefore seems unwise in many circumstances. It has the unfortunate result of implying that international IP norms are

---

[38] Bianca Bosker, "Rojadirecta.org One of Several Sites SEIZED by U.S. Authorities," *The Huffington Post* (Feb. 2, 2011), *available at* <http://www.huffingtonpost.com/2011/02/02/rojadirecta-org-seized_n_817458.html>.

[39] Id. See also Letter from Senator Ron Wyden to The Honorable John Morton, Director, U.S. Immigration and Customs Enforcement 2 (Feb. 2, 2011), available at <http://www.scribd.com/doc/48143849/Wyden-Ice-Letter-to-Holder-and-Morton>.

[40] *See* Ben Sisario, "Piracy Fight Shuts Down Music Blogs," *N.Y. Times* (Dec. 13, 2010), *available at* <http://www.nytimes.com/2010/12/14/business/media/14music.html?_r=1&ref=todayspaper>.

[41] Ben Sisario, "Piracy Fight Shuts Down Music Blogs," *supra* n. 11.

[42] Letter from Senator Ron Wyden to The Honorable John Morton, Director, U.S. Immigration and Customs Enforcement 2, *supra* n. 10.

impotent, as well as highlighting the apparent control of the U.S. Government over Internet architecture. This is occurring at a time when various governments are proposing to transfer Internet governance functions to a United Nations entity, in the hopes of exerting more control over Internet governance. Furnishing more arguments for that troublesome campaign, particularly when the law enforcement gains are dubious, is imprudent.

Finally, domain name seizure is a blunt instrument. While in some cases, all of the content of a site will be infringing, in many cases this will not be the case. As mentioned in the cases of OnSmash and RapGodFathers above, songs and videos will often be given to the website by the artist herself, her agent, or even the label. Such "leaking" of new and upcoming material is a common marketing technique within the music industry. ICE's current seize-now-and-worry-about-it-later approach opts to hit operators with the excessively harsh sanction of not only seizing the domain, but also stigmatizing the operator with 10E's placeholder screen notifying visitors of the seizure, all without confirming whether or not the content has been posted with consent. COICA's approval of such a procedure will only serve to chill speech and completely shut clown an innovative and useful marketing tool, as operators will likely cease posting material, even if they have been given permission to do so, for fear of the potential ICE repercussions.

Ill. Domain Name Seizure as Proposed by 5.3804 (COICA) Will Be Ineffective and Risky

CO1CA aims to address foreign websites that are otherwise beyond the reach of the U.S. legal process and are exclusively dedicated to making infringing content available to users in the U.S. and elsewhere. Unfortunately, COICA's scope goes far beyond its stated intent, and its remedies are not even likely to be effective.

A. COICA's Domain Name Blocking Will Be Ineffective

Like the current domain name seizure exercises, COICA will have little practical impact on reducing infringement. COICA's primary strategy is to require that certain Internet intermediaries "de-list" sites from the Domain Name Server ("DNS") system — the virtual Internet "White Pages" that connect web servers' easy-to-remember domain names (like enn.com) to their unique IP address number (157.166.226.25). Yet users can simply point their browsers to IP addresses instead of domain names, or easily configure their computers to use one of millions of offshore 'phone books' (DNS servers), thereby circumventing the restriction. Moreover, COICA's domain name provisions will have limited effect on non-U.S. Internet users, since their DNS servers cannot be compelled to purge domain name entries by U.S. authorities.

A COICA-based seizure of 'enn.com' means that "ennsecim' will no longer direct to the IP address 157.166.255.19. The website will not disappear. Instead of typing `enn.com' into their browser bar, users will simply enter the II-digit string that is the IP address, and access CNN. A domain name seizure or a domain name block is like tearing a page out of a phonebook to prevent people from dialing the "bad" number. The relevant page may be missing from the phonebook — the DNS server but the "bad" phone line — the IP address — hasn't been disconnected. Everyone who knows the number may still dial it. Moreover, users can circumvent the blocking by employing another phonebook (DNS server) through a simple change of their browser settings. Even *supporters* of COICA have conceded that changing DNS servers is "incredibly easy.[43]

When Wikileaks' DNS server was under cyberattack in late 2010, the site's IP address was a top search result on all major search engines, and could also be easily discovered on numerous online forums or in news articles discussing the dispute. Users simply copied *"213.251.145.96¨* into the address bar of their browser and easily accessed Wikileaks. Ultimately,

[43] Daniel Castro, "No, COICA Will Not Break the Internet," Innovation Policy Blog, The Information Technology and Information Foundation (Jan. 18, 2011), *available at* <http://www.innovationpolicy.org/no-coica-will-not-break-the-internet>.

the cyberattack on Wikileaks' server that caused the site's domain name to fail had little effect on the site's availability.

B. COICA Will Have Troublesome Collateral Consequences

The scope and application of COICA (i) is significantly broader than its stated intent; (ii) is inconsistent with existing law; (iii) deputizes the private sector into law enforcement without compensation; and (iv) sets bad precedents. COICA unnecessarily applies to domestic sites, and the breadth of its definitions improperly sweeps in online retailers, web platforms and cloud storage services, as well as entirely legal products and services sold on lawful websites. Moreover, it endangers cybersecurity and sets had precedents for broader blocking by foreign governments.

COICA Inappropriately Extends- to Domestic Sites. Although it purports to address the "worst of the worst" foreign pirates, COICA in fact applies to U.S. domestic websites, permitting U.S. law enforcement to forego standard due process procedures that should be afforded to Americans. This is unnecessary, given the current strong 1P enforcement in the United States.

As the committee is aware, it remains unclear how COICA would interact with the Digital Millennium Copyright Act (DMCA).[44] Insofar as COICA is an extraordinary remedy, to be used only in cases where a foreign website cannot be reached through regular U.S. legal channels, COICA currently does not address its potential to supersede the DMCA's provisions that allow website operators the opportunity to appear in court and defend themselves against allegations of hosting infringing content.[45] COICA thus appears to be both duplicative and inconsistent with existing protections.

COICA Overbroad Definition Sweeps in Legitimate Online Sites and Legal Products and Services. COICA defines as infringing all websites that offer goods or services that enable a violation of copyright law. As years of litigation have shown, iPods, VCRs, personal computers,

---

[44] *See* Letter from Markham C. Erickson, Executive Director, NetCoalition, to The Honorable Patrick Leahy, Chairman, Senate Committee on the Judiciary, *supra* n. 5.

[45] *Id.* at 1-2 (discussing 17 U.S.C. § 512(g)(3)).

photocopiers, and countless consumer electronics all *enable* violations of copyright law. Yet under COICA's definitions, legitimate sites selling these electronic products are "dedicated to infringing activities."

Due to the many uses of "or" in COICA's definition of what sites are "dedicated to infringing activities", COICA sweeps in many legitimate domains. Any domain name may be seized so long as the site "is marketed by... a person acting in concert with the operator... to offer goods or services... that enable... a violation of title 17... when... such activities are the central activities of the Internet site." COICA § 2(a)(I)(B)(i)(1-11). Under COICA's definition, Best Buy's website may be "dedicated to infringing activities." If Best Buy advertises that one may buy iPods and PCs on bestbuy.com, the domain could be subject to a COICA seizure, since iPods and PCs "enable" "violation[s" of title 17 and selling iPods and PCs is central to bestbuy.com's activities. Unless COICA aims to punish all consumer electronics vendors, this provision in particular demands revision.

In addition, because COICA lacks any willfulness requirement, any service used in infringement totaling more than $1,000 may be targeted. This affects numerous legitimate online services, and appears even to include the U.S. Postal Service, given the recent indictment of a Baltimore man who received over $265,000 for infringing software he distributed online and via U.S. Mail.[46] Neither the online services nor the Post Office are guilty parties in this offense.

COICA endangers cybersecurity. Dan Kaminsky, the famous security researcher credited with "saving the Internet" has said COICA is dangerous.[47] Kaminsky, who discovered a critical security bug in the architecture of the domain name system (which now bears his name), has noted that one of CO1CA's risks arises from the fact that patching the "Kaminsky bug" requires users to trust DNS servers. COICA undermines

---

[46] *See* "Maryland Man Indicted for Infringement of Commercial Software Programs," ICE News Release (Jan. 14, 2011), *available at* < http://www.ice.gov/news/releases/1101/110114baltimore2.htm>.

[47] Jack Schofield, "How Dan Kaminsky Saved the Internet", The Guardian (Dec. 2, 2008) *available at* <http://www.guardian.co.uk/technology/blog/2008/dec/02/dns-kaminsky>; *see also* Dan Kaminsky, *DNS Filtering and S.3804, 'Countering Online Infringement and Counterfeiting Act'*, *supra* n.1.

that trust by demanding that DNS servers occasionally deny users' requests — effectively lying about where sites are. COICA could thus impede efforts to patch this security flaw by driving users to unsecure, offshore servers.[48] First, COICA's requirement to block certain domain names will encourage users to switch from the name servers provided by their ISPs over to offshore servers, thus hindering the U.S. government's ability to respond to cyber attacks. Such a shift could also hinder network managers' ability to monitor activity over their networks and the ability to get any necessary software patches out to users. The ease with which users can adopt offshore name servers which will not be bound by COICA's requirements would therefore undermine COICA's impact while increasing the exposure of the U.S. infrastructure to cyberattack.[49]

By requiring ad *hoc,* manual editing of DNS databases, COICA may also impede the implementation of DNS Security Extensions (DNSSEC), a ten-year project to increase Internet DNS security.[50] DNSSEC figures prominently in the White House's strategy for increasing security on the .gov, .edu, and .us top level domains (TLDs).[51]

Moreover, the Pirate Bay has recently announced that it will start providing its own uncensored DNS server. Users will he told that if they use Pirate Bay's `phonebook,' they will have a censorship-free experience. Such a DNS server may become an attractive nuisance target for cyberattacks designed at exploiting its control over traffic, and it is uncertain whether Pirate Bay or any other ideologically motivated provider of a DNS server will have the requisite security. The operator of an unofficial, unsecure DNS server might decide to redirect Internet traffic for a political purpose. The result is that its DNS server might one day direct users of `bankofamerica.com' or 'whitehouse.gov' to a malicious site, rather than their intended destination.

---

[48] *See* Letter from Markham C. Erickson, Executive Director, NetCoalition, to The Honorable Patrick Leahy, Chairman, Senate Committee on the Judiciary 3, *supra* n.5.

[49] *Id*

[50] *See* Kaminsky, *supra.*

[51] White House Strategy for American Innovation: Securing Our Economic Growth and Prosperity (Feb. 2011) Appx. A *available at* <http://www.whitehouse.gov/innovation/strategy/appendix-a>.

COICA sets bad precedents that will be used to justify ·Preign blocking of U.S. services. COICA's expansive interpretation of the jurisdiction of the Federal Government, and its effectively extraterritorial application of U.S. law, all come at a time when authoritarian governments are seeking greater control over Internet architecture, and foreign officials are demanding that the ITU, a UN agency, take control of Internet governance functions from the U.S.-based independent non-profit ICANN.[52] Furthermore, the precedent of COICA may invite retaliation against U.S. businesses and will disadvantage U.S. efforts to maintain a free and open Internet. Similar concerns have motivated human rights advocates who fear that the U.S. is setting a precedent of filtering and blocking websites based on content that will abandon the moral high ground in the Administration's efforts to secure the ability for Internet users across the globe to access the legal content of their choice[53] - efforts which were reaffirmed just yesterday by Secretary Clinton in her speech on Internet Freedom at George Washington University. Human rights advocates also argue that COICA could lead to other countries using similar policies to prohibit access to legal U.S. content or, even worse, be used for political repression.[54]

C. COICA Lacks Proper Safeguards

Traditionally, law enforcement assistance bills contain proper safeguards to guard against abuse. COICA lacks such safeguards, including compensation to intermediaries when they are forced to provide services to the Federal Government, and restrictions on misuse.

CO/CA's Mandate for the Private Sector is a Government Taking. Unlike most other law enforcement assistance measures, COICA forces

---

[52] Omar El Akkad, "The Internet Needs Peacekeepers. Is Canada Ready?" *The Globe and Mail* (Nov. 12, 2010), *available at* <http://www.theglobeandmail.com/news/national/time-to-lead/internet/the-internet-needs-peacekeepers-is-canada-ready/article1795954/>.

[53] *See* Letter from American Civil Liberties Union, Center for Democracy & Technology, Electronic Frontier Foundation, Freedom House, Human Rights First, Human Rights Watch, Rebecca MacKinnon, Reporters Sans Frontières, and World Press Freedom Committee to Chairman Patrick J. Leahy and Ranking Member Jeff Sessions 1, *supra* n.2.

[54] *Id.* at 1-2.

communications intermediaries to provide law enforcement assistance to the government free of charge. Whereas CALEA, ECPA, and the USAPATRIOT Act amendments all reimburse intermediaries when they are compelled to provide government services, COICA requires private entities to provide free, expeditious service to the Federal Government without any reimbursement or compensation.

COICA includes a "vigilante- provision that immunizes registrars and registries, financial transaction providers, and advertising services who voluntarily take Internet restricting actions against an Internet site if they "reasonably believes the Internet site is dedicated to infringing activities." Sites erroneously targeted are entitled to no protection and, if a site is intentionally targeted by a competitor, the vigilante provision appears to immunize that competitor from any penalty, so long as this blocking is justified with the fig leaf that the site was believed to be "dedicated to infringing activities."

IV. Alternatives to COICA

Fruitless tinkering with Internet architecture will not substitute for demands upon nations in the international trade community that they uphold the existing international IP laws they have committed to as a condition of participating in the global marketplace via the World Trade Organization. The U.S. can address true pirate sites operating abroad by insisting that foreign countries uphold their international commitments and enforce copyright law against the offenders. The U.S. has signed numerous Free Trade Agreements, and is one of over 150 nations that have joined the TRIPS Agreement, both of which require signatories to adhere to 'gold-standard' international IP norms. The USTR can bring countries who refuse to enforce their IP law before the WTO and demand that they be punished, as it has successfully done with China.[55] If the U.S. is unwilling

[55] Panel Report, *China – Measures Affecting the Protection and Enforcement of Intellectual Property Rights*, WT/DS362/R (Jan 26, 2009), *available at* <http://www.wto.org/english/tratop_e/dispu_e/cases_e/ds362_e.htm>

to enforce trading partners' commitments to protect IP, then it will have squandered precious political capital in securing these agreements in the first place. The benefits of an international approach — in addition to avoiding the Internet-crippling security risks posed by COICA — are that when sites are taken down, they disappear worldwide. COICA, on the other hand, would merely inconvenience U.S. Internet users, imposing minor, transitory hurdles that COICA supporters concede are easily defeated.

Conclusion

In conclusion, I urge the committee to avoid putting an American seal of approval upon a strategy most frequently employed by strongmen and despots. The threat to Internet freedom posed by government control over the private sector-maintained Internet architecture is immense. Perhaps even more importantly, as we have already seen, it would not address the stated problem. The approach to insufficient law enforcement must be more law enforcement, not government authority over Internet domains.

STATEMENT OF THE CONSUMER ELECTRONICS ASSOCIATION

February 16, 2011

On behalf of the Consumer Electronics Association (CEA), I would like to express our concerns with certain provisions of the 5.3804, the "Combating Online Infringement and Counterfeits Act" ("COICA") as introduced at the end of the last session. It is our sincere hope that the concerns outlined below are addressed and reflected in the reintroduction of this legislation in the 112th Congress.

CEA is the preeminent trade association promoting growth in the consumer electronics industry. CEA members include product and component manufacturers, Internet providers and both small and large retailers. Our industry accounts for more than SI65 billion in annual sales in the United States, and directly employs approximately 1.9 million United States workers. We support strong intellectual property enforcement. In fact, our members' businesses rely on robust and balanced intellectual property law that protects the rights of authors and inventors while preserving and encouraging innovation, free expression, and competition.

Our primary concern is that the scope of S.3804 (111th) was significantly broader than its intended purpose of shutting down "rogue" or foreign websites solely engaging in the exchange of pirated content or goods. Instead, it could have inadvertently subjected domestic lawful retailers and consumer electronics manufacturers, as well as legitimate communications storage and data-sharing companies, to unwarranted burdens, expense, litigation, and loss of property.

As written, S.3804 (111th) inappropriately borrowed broad definitions, relating to civil causes of action, and injected them into a one-sided, harsh, punitive, and inappropriate context. These definitions put at risk any site that could be characterized as "enabling and facilitating" a violation of Section 17 of the Copyright Act (COICA § 2(a)(1)(B)(i)(1-11). It sweeps up good faith conduct that occupies gray areas under the Copyright Act and the Digital Millennium Copyright Act, as to which our highest courts have differed over outcomes. By establishing this threat without customary civil process, it would erode the Supreme Court's landmark Betamax decision that protects technology products with substantial non-infringing uses. The 1984 Betamax holding, which reversed a holding of the U.S. Court of Appeals for the Ninth Circuit, is commonly referred to as the "Magna Carta of the Innovation Industry", and is crucial to our ability to build and sell new innovative products without fear of crippling lawsuits.

If the Internet had existed when suit was filed against the Betamax VCR in 1976, and adjudicated in 1979 (lawful), 1981 (unlawful), and 1984 (lawful), the websites of retailers selling VCRs on-line could have been subject to seizure from 1976 through 1979, and again from October, 1981 until January, 1984, when the Supreme Court finally ruled that offering a VCR for sale was not copyright infringement. Today, under the same definitions, a consumer electronics retailer's web site could be subject to seizure by the Department of Justice since printers and computers for sale on it (and central to the site's activities) could be used to "enable" "violation[s]" of title 17. While the targeting of legitimate commerce was undoubtedly not intended by the bill's drafters, the text as written does in fact authorize such overreaching and harmful actions.

Our concern is further heightened by the inclusion of a so-called "vigilante" provision that provides complete immunity for registrars and registries, financial transaction providers, and advertising services, allowing them to take voluntary action against an Internet site if the entity "reasonably believes the Internet site is dedicated to infringing activities." As written, under this "vigilante provision" there is no Department of Justice discretion involved in determining which sites meet the standard of infringement. Due process will be denied for those websites targeted, and to add insult to injury, no remedy in terms of replacement of lost revenue was proscribed for a site that was targeted, mistakenly or purposely for competitive reasons.

The "vigilante" provision provides registrars with incentives to be hyper-inclined to take action against any site alleged even without proof—to be engaged in infringing activities. For example, a U.S. District Court awarded Summary Judgment to YouTube in a lawsuit brought by Viacom in which damages of $1 billion were claimed. As introduced, S.3804 arguably empowered Viacom to approach a registrar with evidence that YouTube was "dedicated to infringing activities" and the registrar could have removed YouTube.com. Given this provision, the registrar would have full immunity and YouTube would have no legal recourse.

Finally, the definitions use of "enable or facilitate," invites a claim that the law establishes a new secondary liability concept, making U.S. Internet companies liable for inadvertently "enabling" or "facilitating" the conduct of third parties. This runs contrary to 13 years of well-settled federal policy under the Digital Millennium Copyright Act. Such claims could ensnare legitimate U.S. social media platforms, video sharing sites, auction sites, third-party retail sites, grey-market sales sites, and countless sites that are overwhelmingly lawful and integral to the U.S. economy.

As an industry that relies on intellectual property protection, we suffer the damaging effects of counterfeit products in international trade. We are committed to working closely with copyright owners to shut down web sites that are truly dedicated to piracy. However, we urge this committee to proceed deliberately with this legislation and make the necessary revisions to ensure that COICA does not inadvertently criminalize legitimate U.S. retailers, internet companies, and manufacturers.

Respectfully submitted,
Michael Petricone
Senior Vice President, Government Affairs

THOMAS M. DAILEY: TESTIMONY BEFORE THE SENATE COMMITTEE ON THE JUDICIARY

Vice President and Deputy General Counsel Verizon Communications Inc.
February 16, 2011

Chairman Patrick Leahy (D-VT)

I. Introduction

Chairman Leahy, Ranking Member Grassley, members of the Senate Judiciary Committee, thank you for the opportunity to testify today and to present Verizon's perspectives on the Combating Online Infringement and Counterfeits Act ("COICA"). Verizon supports the efforts of Congress, the Department of Justice ("DoJ") and rights-holders to combat the theft of intellectual property carried out through the unlawful sale of goods and copyrighted works on websites. We believe that responsible members of the Internet ecosystem should work with Congress, law enforcement and the courts to take efficient, effective and judicially-sanctioned steps to address this important problem. However, we also note that one of the greatest strengths of the Internet is its ability to promote the open and free-flow of information, ideas and commerce. While Verizon supports the use of strong actions against online actors who egregiously flaunt U.S. law from abroad, we also have always stood solidly on the side of the free flow of information on the Internet — domestically and internationally.

As a major provider of the global internet, we respect and protect the rights of users to pursue their individual and collective desire to connect, create and collaborate. That is why the use of new approaches like those in COICA requires careful consideration in the broader context of our nation's larger global interests in the growth and health of the Internet, including the promotion of U.S. commercial interests. Verizon believes that the further changes described below are necessary and will help to address these important interests and ensure that the mechanisms described in the bill remain efficiently and effectively focused, but we also urge the Committee to consult further with a broader base of stakeholders about its policy impacts before Congress acts.

II. Discussion

A. The Legislation Should Minimize the Impact on Service Providers

Because COICA shifts the burden of protecting the property interests of others to network operators, these newly imposed obligations should be limited in nature and scope. Accordingly, Verizon appreciates the fact that the Committee has included in the legislation a number of provisions designed to minimize the bill's impact on Internet service providers ("ISPs). For example, the limitation that ISPs will be required to take action only pursuant to a judicial order in a lawsuit filed by the Department of Justice will help ensure that ISP resources are not drained by myriad private investigative efforts and that COICA is properly and narrowly invoked.

Similarly, the legislation properly limits the steps a service provider is required to take to prevent a domain name from resolving to that domain name's Internet protocol ("IP") address. For instance, a service provider is not required to modify its networks or take any steps with respect to domain name lookups not performed by its own domain name servers. Finally, because an ISP is acting pursuant to court order, the legislation takes appropriate steps to protect the service provider from liability. The legislation clarifies that nothing under COICA affects a service provider's limitations on liability under Section 512 of the DMCA, and includes appropriate immunities for taking action in compliance with the legislation or arising from a judicial order issued under it, and protections against liability based on actions taken by subscribers to circumvent DNS restrictions or a service provider's good faith inability to restrict access to a domain name subject to judicial order.

B. Portions of the Legislation Which Verizon Believes Require Amendment or Clarification

The overbroad or inappropriate exercise of the powerful tools that would be created by COICA would not only place undue burdens on service providers, but would also run counter to U.S. interests in other areas of national import, including promotion of a "global" Internet — an Internet that is not split up by specific national interests or regimes. To limit these dangers while facilitating action against egregious online actors, Verizon believes a limited number of further changes are required to ensure that COICA becomes and remains a narrowly tailored tool that is able to be used, as this Committee's December 17, 2010 report (the "Senate Report") envisions, to help prevent inadvertent access to the "worst of the worst" Internet sites.

First, the bill must be clarified to ensure that service providers are required to take action only with respect to their U.S.-based DNS servers. *Second,* the legislation should expressly forbid private rights of action and require that DNS restrictions are imposed only where they are the least burdensome form of remedy. *Third,* from an operational perspective,

COICA should be modified to ensure that i) actions against nondomestic domain names are properly and narrowly tailored; ii) the list of restricted domain names is properly administered and service providers receive timely notification from the DoJ of domain names that no longer require restriction, and appropriate limits are placed on the number of domain names that can be subject to restriction and that cost recovery be made available to service providers which request it. We address each of these issues in turn, below.

I. Judicial Orders to Restrict Access to Domain Names Should be Limited to U.S.-Based DNS Servers

The bill should clarify that judicial orders issued pursuant to it apply only to service providers' DNS servers located in the United States. While Verizon believes that the scope of the bill's domain name restrictions is intended to apply only to a service provider's U.S. customers and operations, some service providers — including Verizon -- maintain DNS servers that are located in countries outside our borders that serve customers outside the U.S. For example, Verizon's overseas affiliates maintain DNS servers abroad that are available to Verizon's non-U.S. based enterprise customers. A judicial order directing a service provider to restrict access to domain names on its international servers -- and therefore to international Internet users — not only increases the burden on and cost for service providers, it may create an extra-territorial impact that could open the legislation to legal challenge in foreign courts against which the bill does not and cannot provide immunity.

Clarifying the legislation in this way would not materially undermine the bill's goals. For technical and other reasons, we believe most U.S. broadband customers utilize DNS servers designated by their service provider, and we further believe that most U.S. service providers utilize U.S.-based DNS servers for their U.S. customers. Thus, a judicial order restricting access to domain names through U.S.-based DNS servers only would still carry out the bill's sole objective of limiting inadvertent access to illegal websites by consumers in the United States.

Accordingly, to accomplish the clarification that a judicial order shall only apply to a service provider's U.S.-sited DNS servers, we urge the Committee to make the following highlighted change to §2(e)(2)(B)(i)(1)(bb):

> "(1) such entity shall not be required - .(bb) to take any steps with respect to domain name lookups not performed by its own domain name system server or domain name .system servers located outside the United States."
>
> The Bill Should Expressly Prohibit Private Rights of Action and Ensure that Domain Name Restrictions are Imposed Only Where they are the Least Burdensome Form of Remedy.

Verizon strongly believes that only the DoJ should be authorized to bring an action under the bill and that the law should expressly state that no private right of action is available. The legislation represents a new approach to dealing with the harmful effects of online infringement. Legally mandated restrictions on access to information available through particular domain names, and the resulting creation of a unique, U.S.-specific DNS capability, is something that should be approached with caution and control, with the added protection that only DoJ review brings.

The DoJ is in the best position to offer an unbiased and disciplined review of requests for enforcement under this bill, requests that are intended to restrict access to information on the Internet and which will inevitably create divergence between U.S. distributed and globally-available DNS information. Having the DoJ serve this important oversight role will help insure that cases brought arc properly and narrowly tailored to effectuate the expressed purpose of the legislation of targeting, as the Senate Report notes, the "worst of the worst" Internet sites. Conversely, private plaintiffs, unlike the DoJ, are acting in their own interests and are far less likely to weigh the costs that their enforcement requests impose on third parties and, more broadly, U.S. national interests in promoting a global Internet. Allowing private litigants to seek judicial orders restricting access to publicly-available websites elevates the risk of over-broad implementation of domain name restrictions.

This concern is not hypothetical. Private parties seeking the identity of Internet subscribers have, at times, swamped the capability of certain ISPs to respond to lawful requests. Recently, for example, plaintiffs in a somewhat different but related context subpoenaed the identities of nearly *ten thousand* Internet subscribers from multiple ISPs, seeking to identify the names of alleged peer-to-peer infringers of certain movie titles. This mass copyright suit swamped the capacity of certain third party ISPs who were subpoenaed to respond, and required those ISPs in some cases to seek protective orders to deal with the extraordinary numbers of IP lookups they were asked to perform.

We also urge the Committee to include a proviso that no relief may be ordered against a service provider unless the relief is the least burdensome among comparably effective forms of relief for that purpose. For example, if content available through a foreign-registered domain name is actually hosted on servers located in the U.S., DoJ should be required to pursue shutdown of that U.S.-based website before seeking a domain name block under COICA against the foreign-registered domain name associated with it. Such language can help ensure that the relief is carefully tailored to achieve the intended purpose.

Accordingly, we propose the following amendment to Section 2(i) to address private right of action point (new language is in *bold italics):*

> (i) NO PRIVATE RIGHT OF ACTION; SAVINGS CLAUSE
>
> (1) IN GENERAL—Nothing in this section shall be construed *to create any private right of action, nor* to limit or expand *any* civil or criminal remedies available to any person (including the United States) for infringing activities on the Internet pursuant to any other Federal or State law."

In addition, we propose that the following subsection be added to Section 2(e)(2)(B)(i) to address the "least burdensome" approach point:

> "(III) no relief may be ordered against a service provider unless it is the least burdensome among comparably effective forms of relief for that purpose;"

3. Proper Implementation of the List of Nondomestic Domain Names and Proper Notification to Service Providers of Domain Names No Longer Subject to Restriction are Critically Important.

Implementing a workable mechanism to enable DNS server restrictions on a dynamic list of domain names across potentially dozens or hundreds of U.S. service providers will require considerable coordination and collaboration, and clearly documented processes. Accordingly, Verizon urges the Committee to amend the legislation to instruct the Attorney General to work with service providers to develop administrative procedures and controls in several areas.

First: procedures need to be developed that will insure actions taken against nondomestic domain names are limited to just the domain names that are currently the subject of a judicial order. Such procedures are necessary to reduce the risk of over-blocking and to minimize the administrative burdens associated with ongoing implementation of a dynamic list of domain names.

Second: procedures need to be developed that will insure all U.S. service providers are given prompt notice of a court order to restrict access to a domain name(s). Such procedures are necessary to ensure that domain name restrictions arc implemented consistently across all service providers in the U.S. The compliance burden should not fall on just a few service providers, nor should U.S. customers of one service provider have their DNS queries returned unresolved while U.S. customers of another service provider do not. A significant amount of logistical effort will he required to ensure uniformity and transparency in the implementation of this program across all U.S. service providers.

Third: the legislation should instruct the Attorney General to work with service providers to implement efficient mechanisms by which the DoJ will post, maintain and update the list of domain names where access needs to be restricted, and notify service providers promptly when a domain name needs to be removed from the list. Service providers should not be left to try to assemble, track and maintain lists of domains to be restricted over time. Ideally, there will be a single point of reference, maintained by DoJ, that will contain a list of domain names that are subject to judicial orders, and this single point of reference would be affirmatively updated by DoJ, with notice to service providers when domain names have been added to or removed from the list of restricted domains.

These administrative procedures and safeguards are important for several reasons. First, clear rules of the road make sense as a matter of administrative efficiency for DoJ and the service providers affected. Second, network performance issues can potentially result from restricting large numbers of domain names in service provider DNS servers, so the domain names subjected to a judicial order need to be properly and narrowly tailored and the list of restricted domain names needs to be properly maintained. Third, if a domain name no longer needs to be restricted, it should properly and expeditiously be removed from the list to avoid imposing the restriction longer than legally necessary.

The current version of the bill is silent on these important administrative controls and procedures, but it does provide a vehicle in Section 3 to clarify that Dot should be tasked with implementing them. Verizon strongly recommends that the legislation be amended to address these administrative concerns by adding the following subsection to Section 3 of the bill:

> "The Attorney General shall —
>
> (7) develop, in consultation with service providers, procedures by which the Attorney General will — identify the specific nondomestic domain names to be the subject of a judicial order under this section; notify all service providers of the domain names which will be subject to such judicial order; maintain and timely update the list of such domain names; and promptly notify service providers when a domain name needs to be removed from such list."

4. The Bill Should Limit the Number of Domain Names to which Access can be Restricted and Provide for Cost Recovery.

The legislation should limit the volume of requests service providers are required to implement and instruct the Attorney General to provide a mechanism for cost recovery. As currently envisioned, this bill is just one tool, intended to be used to address only inadvertent access to the "worst of the worst" Internet web sites. As a practical matter, however, given the tens of millions of domain names in existence, and the virtually limitless number of possible domain names across the .com, .net, and hundreds of country-specific and new top-level domain names, it is reasonable to assume that the volume of domain names to be blocked under COICA will quickly increase. As the restricted domain names list lengthens, depending on a service provider's infrastructure, one might expect to see performance degradation and delay in the process of DNS queries not just for the restricted domain names, but for all queries to such servers. This type of impact might hit disproportionately on small and rural broadband providers who may not have the means to invest in the latest and best server technology.

Therefore, in order to ensure that the list of domains be restricted under COICA remains a list of the then-current, worst examples of websites engaged in illegal activities, there needs to be a hard limit set on the number of domain names that service providers are required to administer. Such a limit will serve as a natural check on an overly-expansive use of COICA.

In addition, Verizon believes some form of cost recovery is required for the time taken to implement changes in service provider DNS systems. Service providers may need to hire new personnel and make equipment upgrades in order to respond expeditiously to the volume of orders, and will need to take time to re-configure their DNS servers every time they receive a blocking order. Requiring compensation to service providers for the time required to comply with COICA -- like hard caps on the numbers of domains to be blocked — will help serve as a natural cheek on the expansion of the use of COICA.

Such cost recovery mechanisms are not new and have been built into other laws where network providers are required by law to comply with law enforcement requests for assistance. For example, the Electronic Communications Privacy Act ("ECPA") contains provisions for the reimbursement of costs to communications providers for assistance in accomplishing an interception or in providing certain information that is subject to a lawful request. We believe, simial cost reimbursement – tied to the volume of domain names for which access is restricted – is appropriate to offset service provider costs of complying with judicial orders under COICA.

Accordingly, Verizon proposes addition of the following subsection to Section 2(e)(2)(B)(i) to address the domain name cap and cost recovery issues:

> "(IV) no service provider may be required to prevent access under this section to more than 100 domain names at one time, unless the Attorney General arranges for a mechanism through which rights owners who submit information to initiate an investigation under this section furnish the government with funds sufficient to reimburse the service provider for its actual, non de minimis costs associated with blocking more than 100 domain names at one time; provided that, for sei-vicc providers with fewer than 100.000 users the foregoing thresholds shall be set at 50 domain names;

Thank you for this opportunity to present Verizon's perspectives regarding this legislation.

STATEMENT OF U.S. SENATOR AL FRANKEN

February 16, 2011

Mr. Chairman, thank you, and Ranking Member Grassley, for holding this important hearing. As you likely know, I am a copyright holder, and like Mr. Turow, I am well aware of how important it is that we protect the intellectual property rights of today's writers, artists, and innovators. When I first started writing for television in the seventies and eighties, the Internet didn't exist, and we didn't need to worry about foreign websites illegally distributing the latest TV shows and blockbuster movies online.

Every year, American industry loses tens of billions of dollars as a result. Confine sales of copyrighted content and counterfeit goods. That's not just profit in the pocket of a movie producer or music mogul. It comes out of the pockets of the hundreds of crew and craft services staff who work on these movies and television shows. It is also money in the hands of American factory workers who produce legitimate, branded goods. It's money in the hands of engineers who develop the technology behind those goods, and its money in the hands of store owners who sell those goods, whether they're Red Wing boots or Prince CDs.

We need to stop online piracy, and we need to give law enforcement the tools it needs to do it. That's why I supported the Combating Online Infringement and Counterfeits Act last year when it came up here in the Judiciary Committee.

But I have also been a strong advocate of preserving the unique nature of today's free and open Internet, and I want to thank the Chairman for adopting changes that I suggested last year to make sure that the bill did not inadvertently hurt free speech. I am pleased that his staff has committed to continuing to work with myself and other members of the Committee on this issue. We need to work together to make sure that any legislation that is introduced this Congress is narrowly tailored and will not unwittingly lead to the blocking of legitimate speech that is protected by the First Amendment. We also need to make sure that we are giving legitimate U.S. businesses and domestic blogs sufficient due process protections before their sites are suddenly shut down.

I also think it is essential that we move cautiously before we create a structure that will direct Internet service providers to block content at the domain name level. Senator Feinstein raised this issue at last year's mark-up, and she reminded us of a letter we received from 90 engineers and architects of the Internet who were particularly concerned about the domain name remedy that was created under your bill. I agree with her concern about maintaining the integrity of the Internet, and I hope we can examine this issue further at today's hearing to make sure this is the best approach.

I'm very pleased that we have this opportunity to talk more about ways our Committee can help protect intellectual property rights. I'm confident that we can address these issues that I have raised because our goals are not incompatible with the underlying purpose of protecting musicians, writers, and innovators in America. I look forward to working with the Chairman to help produce an even stronger hill this year.

STATEMENT OF THE HONORABLE CHUCK GRASSLEY UNITED STATES SENATOR, IOWA

Prepared Statement of Senator Chuck Grassley
Senate Committee on the Judiciary
"Targeting Websites Dedicated to Stealing American Intellectual Property"
Wednesday, February 16, 2011

Mr. Chairman, I appreciate your holding this hearing on this very important subject. I agree that increased online theft of intellectual property has really become a rampant problem. There's a lot of interest in going after criminals who engage in pervasive piracy and counterfeiting online. That's because the impact of copyright piracy and sale of counterfeit goods imposes a huge cost on the American economy — lost jobs, lost sales, and lost income. In fact, these detrimental impacts go far beyond the American economy. One recent report estimated that counterfeiting and piracy have resulted in 2.5 million jobs lost in G20 economies, and that the global value of counterfeited and pirated goods exceeds 5650 billion dollars. Those are staggering numbers.

Piracy and counterfeiting also can present serious health and safety problems. Counterfeit products such as ineffective pharmaceuticals, defective electrical products, tainted toothpaste, malfunctioning equipment, and sub-par materials, all pose a danger to the American public. Addressing this problem would help protect consumers against harmful counterfeit and pirated products.

A large chunk of this piracy and counterfeiting is done online. That's because the internet reaches across the globe and is mostly anonymous. Moreover, part of the problem is that many internet websites that engage in offering infringing content and counterfeit goods are actually foreign owned and operated. These websites appeal to American consumers because they reside at familiar top level domains, such as .com or .net. These websites also appear to be legitimate because they have corporate advertising and credit card acceptance.

Today we'll hear testimony on the scope of intellectual property theft over the internet and what efforts have been undertaken to combat this scourge. I'm interested in hearing whether the witnesses support or have concerns with the legislation that the Senate has proposed to address the problem. I'm certain that everyone supports the underlying goals of S. 3804, the Combating Online Infringement and Counterfeiting Act, a bill that was introduced in the last Congress.

That said, a number of concerns have been raised about that bill, and it is appropriate for the Committee to look into those concerns to determine whether they are legitimate and should be addressed. Certainly, we should act responsibly so that we do not harm consumers, innovation, or economic growth.

GO DADDY :BEFORE THE UNITED STATES SENATE COMMITTEE ON THE JUDICIARY HEARING ON "TARGETING WEBSITES DEDICATED TO STEALING AMERICAN INTELLECTUAL PROPERTY"

Statement of Christine N. Jones, Executive Vice-President, General Counsel, & Corporate Secretary
The Go Daddy Group, Inc.
February 16, 2011

Introduction

Thank you, Chairman Leahy, and members of the Committee, for the privilege of speaking before you today. We at The Go Daddy Group appreciate the efforts of the Committee and of our federal government to stop the use of the Internet for nefarious purposes such as online infringement and counterfeiting. We are honored by the opportunity to share with you our opinions and recommendations regarding the best methods for combating online infringements and counterfeits.

As the world's largest domain name registrar and website hosting provider, with millions of customers all over the globe, we are very familiar with the ease with which trademarked and copyrighted material may be improperly acquired and utilized through the Internet. Selling counterfeit materials or engaging in trademark infringement is now as easy as copying and pasting an image or downloading files in a peer to peer network. Based on our leading position in the industry, we feel that we are uniquely situated to provide insight on legislative and private industry efforts to curtail the proliferation of online intellectual property infringement.

Go Daddy's Commitment to Intellectual Property Rights

Go Daddy currently has more than 46 million domain names under management, and provides web hosting services for more than 5 million websites. In addition, our company offers over 50 products and services, including SSL certificates, website builders, and online business tools, which help our customers establish a trusted presence on the Internet.

On behalf of our customers and our own business, we understand and are strong supporters of the rights of intellectual property holders to protect their trademarks and copyrights. A vast number of our customers earn their livelihood from the successful businesses they have been able to establish online through the use of our products and services. It is critical to their businesses that they have the ability to protect their online brands, and that the intellectual property they have spent time and money to develop is not stolen by competitors who would unfairly copy their work.

Go Daddy itself holds a vast amount of intellectual property that we vigorously police and protect. We have more than 330 trademarks and copyrights that are registered all over the world. We currently hold 37 issued patents, with more than 197 patent applications pending. Given the importance of intellectual property to our business, and our own challenges in monitoring and defending our trademarks and copyrights, we strongly believe that intellectual property owners need the ability to protect their works. We also support the enactment of federal legislation that will assist intellectual property owners in these efforts.

Current Efforts to Combat Online Infringements and Counterfeits through Domain Name Redirection and Website Takedowns

A. Go Daddy Routinely Works with Courts and Law Enforcement to Disable Access to Domain Names and Websites Connected to Infringing Content

As a private domain name registrar and hosting provider, Go Daddy should not and does not make legal determinations as to whether particular domain names or websites are being utilized for intellectual property infringement or counterfeiting purposes. In our view, seizures and takedowns of domain names and websites should occur only in the context of a law enforcement investigation or court order. Moreover, our government and courts must always be vigilant to ensure that the vigorous pursuit of online infringers and counterfeiters does not result in the censorship of lawful speech or activity on the Internet. That being said, there is no doubt that Go Daddy and our fellow registrars and hosting providers can and should play a significant role in assisting courts and law enforcement to disable access to domain names and websites that are used for criminal activity, including infringement or counterfeiting.

Our company has led the industry in working with law enforcement to ensure that the Internet is not used for criminal activities involving infringement and counterfeiting. Unlike many other Internet companies of our size, Go Daddy staffs large, 24/7 abuse and trademark infringements departments, whose sole mission it is to identify and help stop unlawful conduct online. Our staff routinely works with courts and law enforcement.

From the local to international level to shut down domain names and websites through which infringers and counterfeiters operate. Any time we are notified by a court or a federal or state prosecutor that there is criminally infringing material on our systems, we work rapidly to disable access to that material.

There are numerous cases in which the seizure or disabling of access to domain names or websites has been instrumental in stopping online infringements and counterfeits. Late last year, for example, the U.S. Immigration and Customs Enforcement agency ("ICE") was able to execute seizure orders against 84 domain names of commercial websites engaged in the illegal sale and distribution of counterfeit goods and copyrighted works. The coordinated federal law enforcement operation targeted online retailers of an array of counterfeit goods including sports equipment, shoes, handbags, athletic apparel, and sunglasses, as well as illegal copies of copyrighted DVD boxed sets, movies and software. Once the goods were confirmed as counterfeit or otherwise illegal, [CE obtained seizure orders for the domain names of the websites that sold the goods. The domain names were redirected pursuant to the court orders, and individuals attempting to access any of the related sites found banners advising them that the site's domain name had been seized by federal authorities. The same federal initiative has successfully obtained and executed seizure warrants against nine domain names of websites that offer pirated copies of first-run movies.

Go Daddy has been involved in many other government initiatives directed towards taking counterfeit merchandise offline. In March of 2010, we worked with the United Kingdom's Metropolitan Police Service to shut down or redirect nearly 200 domain names and websites used to sell counterfeit merchandise including clothing, shoes and jewelry. We recently worked with the Federal Bureau of Investigation to disable the domain names of more than two dozen overseas websites that were selling counterfeit Tiffany & Co. jewelry. We are currently involved in an investigation by the Computer Crime Division of Scotland Yard to shut down websites that sell counterfeit tickets to sporting events. To date, we have successfully disabled access to approximately 60 such websites by redirecting their domain names.

Finally, we continue to lead the charge to stop the proliferation of rogue online pharmacies and websites selling counterfeit medications. In 2010 alone we worked with the Federal Drug Administration and the U.S. Drug Enforcement Agency to investigate and take down over 36,000 such websites.

B. Go Daddy Works Directly with Intellectual Property Owners to Help Them Protect Their Rights

In addition to our ongoing work with law enforcement, Go Daddy also works directly with intellectual property owners to protect their creative work. We strongly encourage all businesses, authors and artists to be vigilant in policing their creative efforts, and we have instituted numerous, extremely effective, policies and procedures to help intellectual property holders protect their rights online. This includes a wealth of resources that educate our customers and other interested parties about the best practices for monitoring and protecting their intellectual property.

For example, we have developed and publish thorough trademark and copyright infringement policies, which include information about how IP owners may gain rights to domain names they believe infringe on their trademarks, or effect the removal of websites that contain infringing content. The policies are prominently displayed on our website, and describe the method through which intellectual property owners may submit complaints to us regarding infringing content. Our abuse and infringements teams continuously monitor and respond to complaints submitted through these procedures. Last year, we processed over 13,000 such complaints.

Our copyright infringement policy is compliant with the standards set forth in the Digital Millennium Copyright Act (DMCA). We follow a set of voluntary standards we established in 2002 in the trademark context, as well, based on the DMCA's successful approach. In the case of trademarks, the information we require to open an investigation includes a copy of the trademark or trade name that is claimed to be infringed, the jurisdiction or geographical area to which the mark applies, the goods or services covered by the mark, the date of first use of the mark, and evidence relating to the content that the complaining party believes to be infringing on the mark. Similarly, with respect to copyright complaints, we ask complaining parties to submit documentation that demonstrates their right to the infringing content. This includes identification of the copyrighted work claimed to have been infringed, identification of the material that is claimed to be infringing, and the complaining party's contact information.

We initiate investigations into intellectual property complaints almost immediately after receiving the background information requested in our infringements policy. In the event that the disputed content appears on one of our corporate websites, for example, our social networking site, Go Daddy Community, or our video sharing site, www.Video.me, we often temporarily remove the challenged material from the site. We may also suspend the posting party's Go Daddy account, or, if the material is solely stored on a Go Daddy server, we may deny the posting party the ability to access the challenged material.

We also notify the poster of the allegedly infringing material of the complaint against his or her content, and provide that party with information regarding how to respond to the complaint. A response from the posting party must include an affidavit that the party has a good faith belief in his or her right to use the material. The response must also include a consent to the jurisdiction of the Federal District Court, and confirm that the poster will accept service of process of a complaint relating to the alleged infringement. In this way, we ensure that the intellectual property owner is able to effectively locate and bring a legal action against the posting party.

Where an intellectual property owner has a complaint not about content on a website, but about infringement contained in a domain name itself, for example, if an individual has infringed on the Verizon trademark by registering vvvw.verizoon.com and causing that domain name to resolve to content that would otherwise violate Verizon's registered trademarks, Go Daddy and other ICANN-accredited registrars are bound by the Uniform Domain Name Dispute Resolution Policy ("UDRP"). The UDRP provides the terms and conditions through which private disputes concerning the registration and use of Internet domain names, including trademark-related disputes, may be resolved, Go Daddy follows the UDRP when we receive a trademark concern or dispute specifically focused on a domain name.

Under the UDRP, private trademark-based domain name disputes must be resolved by agreement, court action or arbitration before a registrar such as Go Daddy can cancel, suspend or transfer a domain name. However, once Go Daddy receives notice of a filed UDRP dispute, we immediately "lock" the disputed name. Our locking of the domain name offers several protections to the intellectual property holder. Once locked, the registrant cannot transfer the domain name to another registrar, change contact or other details about the domain name in the Whois database, or update the DNS information regarding the name. In this way, the IP owner can be assured that it won't lose the ability to obtain the domain name through, for example, the registrant's obfuscation of his or her true identity, or transfer of the name to an overseas registrar. The lock we institute remains in place until we get a final decision from the UDRP arbitration panel making a determination as to which party has rights to the domain name, or the dispute is otherwise resolved through a signed legal agreement or court order.

Finally, it should be noted that our Terms of Service and other legal agreements are carefully crafted to require our customers to confirm that neither their domain name nor their website content infringes upon or otherwise violates the rights of any third party, including intellectual property rights. Our customers must agree that they are not registering a domain name or operating a website for any unlawful purpose, and that they will not knowingly use their domain name or website in violation of any applicable laws or regulation, including the laws that exist to protect the rights of intellectual property owners. Whenever we are notified of a violation of our agreements in this area, we take swift action to either ensure the removal of infringing material, or to disable or redirect the offending website.

Comments Regarding Senate Bill 3804: The "Combating Online Infringements and Counterfeits Act"

Go Daddy is a strong supporter of legislative proposals designed to curtail the proliferation of online infringement and counterfeiting. We applaud the efforts of this Committee in supporting initiatives that will assist the government and private industry to combat illegal activity on the Internet. We have reviewed the most recent draft of Senate Bill 3804, the proposed "Combating Online Infringements and Counterfeits Act, " and are pleased at its focus on clarifying the process through which the government can target and disable domain names that are used for criminal purposes. We also appreciate the Bill's inclusion of an immunity provision for organizations that act in accordance with its provisions — we are confident that Go Daddy's ongoing efforts would afford us with statutory immunity under the Bill. However, we do feel that some modifications to the Bill could make it even more effective for its intended purpose.

For instance, the Bill in its previously submitted form focuses primarily on domain names, rather than on websites that display infringing content or merchandise. We would suggest that the Bill's focus be expanded to address the role of website hosting providers in combating online infringements and counterfeits. The inclusion of hosting providers in the Bill would clarify the role of web hosts in disabling access to criminal websites with domain names over which the U.S. government cannot obtain jurisdiction.

Domain name registries, domain name registrars, and website hosting providers are, for all intents and purposes, three different entities when it comes to legal and administrative issues. In our experience, it is not uncommon for domain name registrants who engage in infringing and counterfeiting activities to register multiple domain names, often under numerous identities. These registrants also regularly engage in the continuous transfer of their domain names and websites between different registrars and hosting providers. Thus, for any particular website that displays infringing or counterfeit content, the registry, the registrar, and the hosting provider may be three different, unaffiliated entities, and may be located in three different jurisdictions domestically or overseas.

This is particularly true of criminal websites that utilize country code top level domain names, or ccTLDs, which are issued by numerous countries around the world. Go Daddy, like many other registrars, offers a wide variety of ccTLDs through various registries, many of which are based overseas. Many of the registries that offer ccTLDs do not provide registrars with the ability to suspend or redirect these domain names. In these instances, to institute a proceeding against the domain name, the government would need to direct its action to the ccTLD registry. These are often located overseas and not subject to jurisdiction by the U.S. government. Based on the difficulty of reaching overseas registries, and the inability of the registrar to take action in these cases, it would be helpful if the Bill provided the government with the ability to direct the (hopefully domestic) hosting provider to shut down the site.

The Bill also potentially affects the doctrine of secondary liability for web hosts. Once a domain name is identified on the list proposed to be maintained by the Justice Department as "dedicated to infringing activities," it is unclear what obligations the hosting provider has with respect to other sites owned by the same individual. We would like future versions of the Bill to clarify that hosting providers will not be expected to affirmatively monitor their customers' hosted websites in order to avoid the risk of secondary liability for trademark or copyright infringement.

We would also ask that the final version of the Bill include a notice provision for websites that display user-generated content, such as Go Daddy's social networking or video sharing websites. Current law specifically recognizes that website operators are not obligated to affirmatively monitor and police the user-generated content displayed on their sites. However, site operators *are* required by the DMCA to promptly respond and take action when notified of infringing content on their sites. The Bill in its current form theoretically raises some conflicts with the DMCA's notice provision, in that the Attorney General could cause a domain name affiliated with a website containing user-generated content to be disabled, even where the site operator is unaware of the infringing content and would be happy to remove the material if it were notified of the same.

From a procedural standpoint, when an Attorney General action or court order is issued to disable a domain name, we would respectfully request that the order or action be initially directed to the domain name registrar, rather than to the registry. Because it is the registrar that typically has the most contact with the registrant of a domain name, we are very often involved in criminal investigations that are outside the scope of the Bill (for example, child pornography investigations involving registrants). The registry in many instances has no knowledge of these highly confidential and sensitive matters, and we have experienced several occasions in which the sudden disabling of a domain name by a registry disrupted weeks or months of work by law enforcement agencies who were investigating serious criminal activity by the registrant. We would like to see the registrar named as the primary contact for courts and law enforcement regarding all criminal and civil matters relating to domain names. Registrars could then facilitate and coordinate concurrent actions by international, federal and local governments with respect to particular names.

Finally, we would ask the Committee to consider revisiting and clarifying the concept of when and how a website will be determined to be "dedicated" to infringing activities. The definition in the current version of the Bill refers to sites that are "primarily designed" to do one or more of certain activities, and then refers to those activities as "the central activities of the Internet site or sites accessed through a specific domain name," We question how the determination will be made as to when a site is "primarily designed" to conduct a certain activity and how the " central activities" of a website will be identified. We are concerned that without clear and precise definitions regarding the types of activities that are considered unlawful, the Bill could be attacked as a potential means of suppressing free and open expression and thought online.

Conclusion

Go Daddy is proud of our long history of working to preserve the integrity of the Internet, including our efforts to combat intellectual property infringement and counterfeiting. We have documented proof that our efforts in this area work. In 2010 alone, Go Daddy suspended almost 7,000 websites which were determined to contain content that infringed the rights of a trademark or copyright owners. We locked over 5,500 domain names that were the subject of trademark disputes or UDRP proceedings, and ultimately transferred more than 3,200 of those names to the rightful registrants. Based on these successes, there is no doubt that domain name registrars and hosting providers, working closely with the courts and law enforcement, have a significant role to play in taking down online bad actors.

Go Daddy will be pleased to support thoughtful federal legislation that streamlines and clarifies the methods through which we and our fellow members of private industry can work with the government to take criminals offline. However, effectively combating online infringements and counterfeits will require all of our online counterparts to join the tight. Each of what we call "The Big Five" major players online -- domain name registrars, hosting service providers, payment card processors, Internet service providers, and online advertising providers — must institute efforts similar to those used by Go Daddy, and work hand-in-hand with courts and law enforcement to keep infringers and counterfeiters off the Internet. In the absence of such concerted efforts, the criminals that Go Daddy works so hard to take offline will soon reappear, almost certainly as customers of one of our more lax competitors.

Thank you.

Blue Sky

BRIAN A. KEANE

The Honorable Richard Blumenthal
United States Senate
Washington, DC 20510

February 15, 2011

Dear Senator Blumenthal:

Last year, Senator Leahy and Senator Hatch along with 18 cosponsors introduced bipartisan legislation that would combat online copyright infringement and the sale of counterfeit goods, S.3804, the "Combating Online Infringement and Counterfeits Act." Knowing that you have been a leader on protecting consumers from online harms, I hope that you will be an original co-sponsor of Senator Leahy's legislation when it is reintroduced this year.

Blue Sky Studios is located in Greenwich, CT and currently employs 400, mostly high skilled animators and engineers. The financial success of our movies like Ice Age, Horton Hears a Who, and our soon to be released movie Rio, is threatened when Rogue sites – many of which are hosted outside the U.S. and not reachable by current U.S. law – entice people to illegally download or stream our movies. These Rogue sites have become increasingly sophisticated in both design and operation, and often deceive consumers into believing they are legitimate. In addition to undermining the growth and stability of companies like Blue Sky and threatening American jobs, many of these sites represent a severe safety risk to consumers who unwittingly purchase dangerous and illegal products. We believe that the legal tools the Rogue site legislation would provide to the Department of Justice are essential to helping address these illegal websites and ensuring that the Internet is a safe and vibrant marketplace.

Senator Leahy's bill was carefully crafted to adhere to constitutional requirements that protect free speech and provide appropriate due process for all affected parties. We therefore urge you to become an original co-sponsor of this legislation when it is introduced and we look forward to working with you in support of its enactment.

Sincerely,

Brian A Keane

Brian Keane
Blue Sky Studios

Statement of Senator Patrick Leahy (D-Vt.)

Chairman, Senate Judiciary Committee, Hearing on "Targeting Websites Dedicated to Stealing American Intellectual Property"
February 16, 2011

I thank the witnesses who are here today to testify about how we can make some progress in the fight against online copyright infringement and the sale of counterfeit goods. Last Congress, I introduced legislation, cosponsored by 12 other Senators on this Committee, to combat "rogue websites" which do nothing but traffic in infringing material. I thank those Senators, including Senator Hatch who was the lead cosponsor and a longtime leader on intellectual property issues, and our new Ranking Member, Senator Grassley.

That legislation was approved unanimously by the Senate Judiciary Committee, 19-0. Understand, however, that there are still some concerns on both sides of this issue. Some intellectual property owners argue that the legislation did not go far enough; others are concerned it may go too far. I expect that is why Senator Coburn requested we hold this hearing — to give all sides an opportunity to address the issue.

While we work to address concerns, let us also be Blear that the problem of online infringement is real; it is substantial; and it is a drain on our economy, which costs American jobs. Copyright piracy and the sale of counterfeit goods are reported to cost the American economy billions of dollars annually and hundreds of thousands of lost jobs. A January study found that nearly 24 percent of all Internet traffic worldwide is infringing. That is a staggering number, and the problem is growing. That is why inaction is not an option, and we must pass online infringement legislation in this Congress before rogue websites harm more businesses, and result in more lost jobs.

What these rogue websites do is theft, pure and simple. They are no more than digital stores selling stolen, and in the case of counterfeits, often dangerous products. If they existed in the physical world, everyone would agree that they should be shuttered and their proprietors arrested. We cannot excuse the behavior because it happens on the Internet and the owners operate overseas. The Internet needs to be free and open — not lawless.

Every one of the witnesses here today has an interest in an Internet marketplace that remains vibrant and continues to expand. I suspect no one here condones rogue websites. After all, we all have an interest in keeping Internet activity lawful. If we lose confidence that the products we are purchasing online are the real thing, rather than counterfeit, it hurts the entire Internet ecosystem.

I know some market participants have become more aggressive on their own initiative since we began consideration of a legislative approach to this problem last June. I want to commend them; after all, legislative action alone cannot possibly achieve the effects of self-policing in the private sector. MasterCard, for instance, has been working closely and productively with the intellectual property (IP) community to make sure they are not processing payments from sites that are trafficking in illegal goods. I know Visa has begun discussions with the IP community as well, and I appreciate that.

In some cases, voluntary conduct is not enough, and court orders are necessary to ensure appropriate action, AT&T first suggested in written comments an approach that allows law enforcement to seek a court order that could be used by AT&T and other Internet service providers (ISPs) to prevent rogue websites based overseas from reaching the U.S. market with stolen goods. I applaud their leadership. That model not only became the basis of our legislation last year, but is also consistent with the work law enforcement has done recently in seizing domain names from rogue websites pursuant to court orders. The seizure approach has its limits, which is why legislation is needed.

I am confident that we will pass legislation to target rogue websites this year. I want to hear from all sides as we move forward, but I refuse to accept that addressing the problem is too difficult because people who want to steal will always find a way. That is like saying that we should not prosecute drug crimes or child pornography because bad people will find a way to do bad things anyway, I am a former prosecutor, and that line of argument is unacceptable.

I look forward to working closely with Chairman Smith and other Members of the House who have been leaders on this issue and share a concern about the magnitude of the problem and its effect on our economy and job creation. And I look forward to continuing to work with Senator Grassley and the members of this Committee. This is one of those issues - like patent reform - in which we can work on a truly bipartisan and bicameral basis. After all, if the Chamber of Commerce and organized labor can come together in support of legislation to address this problem, then so can Democrats and Republicans in both the House and Senate.

Statement of Motion Picture Association of America, Inc. Before the Senate Judiciary Committee

Dirksen Senate Office Building, Room 226 Washington, D.C.
February 16, 2011, 10 A.M.

A. Background and Introduction

We want to thank the Committee for this opportunity to submit this Statement regarding rogue Internet sites on behalf of the MPAA and its member companies. The MPAA is the primary voice and advocate for the American motion picture, home video and television industries in the U.S. and around the world. MPAA's members are the leading producers and distributors of filmed entertainment: Walt Disney Studios Motion Pictures, Paramount Pictures Corporation, Sony Pictures Entertainment Inc.; Twentieth Century Fox Film Corporation; Universal City Studios LLP; and Warner Bros. Entertainment Inc.

Motion picture and television production is a major private sector industry in all 50 states, directly employing over 296,000 people across the

United States. These are high quality jobs—both in front of the camera and behind the scenes—with an average salary of nearly $76,000, 72 percent higher than the average salary nationwide. Our on-location production activity also supports more than 115,000 small businesses across the country—over 90% of which employ fewer than 10 people—with film productions infusing on average 5225,000 per day into a local economy. Nationwide, the motion picture industry generates in excess of $15 billion in public revenues, and we consistently boast a positive balance of trade in every country in which we do business.

B. Rogue Websites Create Consumer Confusion and Damage the Motion Picture and Television Industry

While high-speed broadband networks bring immense opportunities for the exchange of information and ideas, the inappropriate use of the networks can facilitate the anonymous theft and rapid, ubiquitous illegal distribution of copyrighted works. It is not an overstatement to say that, the rampant theft of if' strikes at the heart our nation's economy, our core values of reward for innovation and hard work, and our ability to compete globally. In short, Internet theft puts at risk one of America's great export industries.

The most pernicious forms of digital theft occur through the use of websites. The sites, whose content is hosted and whose operators are located throughout the world take many forms, but have in common the simple fact that all materially contribute to, facilitate and/or induce the distribution of copyrighted works, such as movies and television programming.

"Rogue" websites, as they are frequently called, typically engage in one or more of the following forms of online theft of copyrighted content:

- Streaming an unauthorized copy of a copyrighted video;
- Downloading an unauthorized copy of a copyrighted video;

- Streaming or downloading of an unauthorized copy of a copyrighted video by linking to a torrent or other metadata file that initiates piracy;
- Linking to a specific offer to sell an unauthorized copy of a copyrighted video;
- Hosting an unauthorized copy of a copyrighted video.

These rogue websites are increasingly sophisticated and take on many attributes of legitimate content delivery sites, creating additional enforcement challenges and feeding consumer confusion. Among the steps taken by rogue websites to deceive consumers into believing they are legitimate are:

- The use of credit card companies, such as Visa and MasterCard, to facilitate payments to rogue websites.
- The use of "e-wallet" or alternative payment methods such as PayPal, Moneybrokers, AlertPay and Gate2Shop to allow for the receipt of payment from the public for subscriptions, donations, purchases and memberships.
- The use of advertising, often for mainstream, Blue Chip companies, on the websites.
- Reward programs for frequent purchasers.

All of these elements combine to create a feeling of legitimacy that results in unknowing consumers purchasing illegal content and enriching the criminals profiting from these rogue sites.

The impact of this activity is documented in a recently published report by Envisional, an independent Internet consulting company. Envisional's "Technical Report: An Estimate of Infringing Use of the Internet" estimates that almost a quarter of global Internet traffic and over 17 percent of U.S. Internet traffic is copyright infringing. This is a staggering level of theft that cannot be sustained without significant damage to the motion picture industry and the workforce it supports.

C. Action by the Congress and the Administration Will Curtail the Negative Economic Impact of Online Theft

We have enjoyed a long history of working with the Committee and have been encouraged by the emphasis that the Administration has placed on intellectual property rights and enforcement. Since Victoria Espinel was confirmed by the Senate over 13 months ago we have seen increasing cooperation from our partners in the private sector intermediaries—whether pay processors, ad brokers, or ISPs. The combined efforts of the Department of Justice, ICE and the IPR Center have not only put rogue sites out of business but have raised awareness with the public, deterred had actors, and resulted in many websites voluntarily ceasing criminal activity or going legal.

In fact, an MPAA evaluation of ICE's "Operation In Our Sites, v.1.0" demonstrated the positive effects of the Administration's involvement. Of the top 304 infringing websites that were monitored during the 2010 calendar year, including both sites that compile links to stolen content and sites that allow unauthorized streaming, nine were seized during both phases of "Operation in Our Sites". An additional 81 websites, over one quarter of the landscape (26%) voluntarily stopped offering illegal content or completely shut down, and of the 81 sites, 12 transitioned to legal movies or TV, or became promotional websites that do not offer illegal content. This is a significant development.

Last week the IPEC released its first annual report to Congress pursuant to the PRO-IP Act and the report reiterated not only the detrimental impact of copyright infringement on the economy but also the need to work with the Congress to update intellectual property law to improve law enforcement effectiveness. To quote:

> "The digital environment is at its core an economy of intellectual property. Digitalization of goods, services, data, ideas and conversations creates intrinsically new assets, often built on or derived from assets for which there are existing protections. The application of intellectual property rules to the digital environment are therefore essential to

enabling creators to be rewarded for their work. Lack of intellectual property enforcement in the digital environment, by contrast, threatens to destabilize rule-of-law norms, with severe effects on jobs and economic growth. Undermining respect for rule-of-law values impacts a range of other policy goals affected by the Internet (e.g., privacy),In short, criminal laws and intellectual property laws that apply in the physical world are based on a tradition of rules, checks and balances that must be applied to and tailored to the digital world."

We believe that rogue sites legislation, combined with the Administration's work with intermediaries and enforcement by the IPR Center, will go a long way towards shutting down the unauthorized distribution of copyrighted works and close a gap in the intellectual property law.

Again, we thank Chairman Leahy on behalf of our member companies for the opportunity to provide this Statement. We look forward to working with you, Ranking Member Grassley, Senator Hatch and other members of the Committee on crafting legislation to deal with this criminal activity.

TESTIMONY OF NETCOALITION BEFORE THE UNITED STATES SENATE COMMITTEE

226 Dirksen Senate Office Building, Washington, DC 20510
February 16, 2011

The members of NetCoalition[56] share Chairman Leahy's concern over websites that are dedicated to stealing American intellectual property. We support the objective of combating offshore counterfeiting and online infringement, and we understand the frustration over the challenges of targeting websites that reside beyond the borders of the United States. We pledge to work with Chairman Leahy and other members of the Committee

[56] NetCoalition serves as a public policy voice to leading Internet and technology companies, including Amazon.com, Bloomberg LP, eBay, Google, IAC, Yahoo!, and Wikipedia.

on the Judiciary to address these concerns. However, combating foreign sites that are engaging in activity that is unlawful in the United States is complicated and challenging. Such an effort raises legal, political, and technological concerns.

During the last Congress, on November 18, 2010, the Committee on the Judiciary approved S. 3804, the Combating Online Infringement and Counterfeits Act ("COICA"). The legislation had 19 cosponsors and was approved by the Committee 19-0. The Committee had not conducted a legislative hearing on It R. 3804, and there was a considerable amount of concern with the legislation, including concerns that were raised by NetCoalition. At the time, Chairman Leahy pledged to work with concerned parties to address these concerns, even as the bill was being approved by the Committee.

Senator Feinstein noted that the Committee needed "to be careful to try to avoid unintended consequences on legitimate businesses." She further noted that 90 engineers and others involved in developing the architecture and standards for the operation of the Internet were opposed to the bill and particularly concerned about the domain name remedy. She also noted that the Committee ought to explore whether the model adopted in the Unlawful Internet Gambling Enforcement Act, which imposes obligations on payment systems, would be a preferable model to use in combating offshore websites.

Senator Coburn indicated that certain Internet service providers, search engines, Federal agencies in charge of intellectual property, and other interested parties had outstanding concerns over some provisions in the legislation. He noted the need for further discussion of those issues.

Given the concerns raised with S. 3804, we appreciate that Chairman Leahy is holding a hearing to address some of the issues that were raised with S. 3804. We also appreciate the pledge by Committee counsel to work with NetCoalition and other stakeholders to address our concerns before a new version of legislation is introduced.

In anticipation of a productive conversation about how to craft legislation in this area, we believe it would be helpful for the Committee to understand the concerns that were raised with S. 3804 in the 111th Congress. The following summarizes those concerns.

Concerns with S. 3804, the "Combating Online Infringement and Counterfeits Act."

The sponsors of COICA intend to address the problem of foreign websites that arc otherwise beyond the reach of the U.S. legal process and are dedicated to nothing but making infringing content available to U.S. users, essentially "the worst of the worst foreign-based sites with no legitimate content whatsoever.

Unfortunately, the scope of the proposed bill goes far beyond the stated intent of the sponsors and it continues to raise significant legal, political, and technological concerns.

Technological Concerns

The bill's primary, technical means of enforcement---requiring ISPs to manually interfere with the Domain Name Service ("DNS") that connects a website name to the actual website--will not effectively prevent users from accessing the website in question and do nothing to remove the underlying infringing content.[57]

A DNS provider, which today is normally the user's Internet access provider (e.g., Verizon, Comcast, AT&T, corporate enterprise server) serves as a "phone book" that connects the commercial domain name of a website (e.g., *'NAkw .site* in_question.com) to the Internet Protocol number of the actual site (e.g., 123.456.789.123). The site's Internet Protocol number may have an almost unlimited number of names that correspond to the site. The bill would require the DNS provider to "de-list" the domain name with the corresponding number for the site through a manual intervention into the directory. (This is similar to crossing out an entry in the virtual Internet phone book. The IP address is not disconnected, it

---

[57] See Exhibit 3 (Dan Kaminsky, "DNS Filtering and S. 3804, 'Countering Online Infringement and Counterfeiting Act."

merely becomes "unlisted.") This DNS "spoiling" procedure required by the bill is not effective for the following reasons.

1. The user can simply type the numeric IP address into the browser.
2. Operators of the websites in question can easily offer alternative, offshore DNS servers that will allow users to end-run the DNS spoiling and thwart the effectiveness of the bill.
3. Individual users seeking to access a website in question can easily change a single setting on their computers to avoid their 1SP's DNS servers and instead connect to an offshore or little-known DNS provider. There are over one million DNS providers that make their servers available to Internet users.
4. Operators of websites in question can easily provide its users with a browser plug-in that ensures the user can reach the site no matter what the user's 1SP is doing to block access to the site.

The DNS blocking requirement and these easy "work-arounds" have the potential to create a tremendous amount of collateral harm to the Internet ecosystem. The following are some of the harms.

1. Increased risk of identity theft, spyware, malware, and other malicious activities. If a user accesses a non-U.S. DNS provider (especially one run by the website in question), this user is at increased risk for spyware and malware. Once the user's computer is infected, the user likely will infect other computers. Moreover, the user will likely rely on that rogue DNS service for all other Internet activity, thereby affecting e-commerce more broadly. There would be no guarantee, for example, that the DNS provider would direct the user to the real online shopping or other desired site.
2. A shift way from U.S. DNS providers diminishes the ability of network managers and cyber-security experts to monitor the overall activity of the network and protect U.S. Internet users from cyber-attacks.

3. If the offshore DNS provider so desires, it can orchestrate a denial of service attack on U.S. Internet sites, using the computers of its increased U.S. audience.
4. With the strong support of the US government, major U.S. DNS providers have spent a decade working to implement "DNS Security Extensions" ("DNSSEC"), which ensure that responses to DNS lookups are cryptographically signed by the authoritative name server. This, in turns, ensures that the DNS lookup cannot be manipulated to direct a user to a site that will expose the user to identity theft and malware. In other words, these new security extensions will make sure that the "www.cnn.com¯ site that is displayed on a user's computer is truly CNN. COICA upends this decade's worth of work to secure the Internet. In fact, for major U.S. DNS providers that have implemented DNS-SEC, it is not clear that they can even technically comply with the requirements of the bill.
5. Manipulation of the DNS lookups is a technique used by certain governments around the world to deny users access to content deemed lawful in the United States (e.g., political speech). Legislating the same technical solution in the U.S. (arguably for content that is lawful in the foreign jurisdiction) will invite retaliation against U.S. Internet companies and lead to geographical balkanization of the Internet.
6. DNS blocking will result in over-blocking of lawful content and other communications such as e-mail. A DNS provider has the ability to control only the second-level domain (i.e., the name immediately to left of the dot in .com). A DNS provider cannot block subdomains, which are widely used today by most corporations, universities and popular websites. A site that qualifies as infringing under the bill may be part of a larger, lawful domain— but the order will require blocking of the entire domain, including traffic associated with that domain such as email. For example, an order to block access to www.site-in-

question.com would result in blocking access to www.blo2.site-in-question.com or www.cmail.site-in-question.com.

7. The Internet was developed to operate efficiently and with multiple redundancies in order to withstand a nuclear attack. This architecture not only makes DNS spoiling technically questionable, but such blocking also interjects an incredible amount of inefficiency into the infrastructure, slowing down the Internet experience for all users.

Legal Concerns

The scope and application of the legislation is significantly broader than its intended purpose and includes new and confusing definitions that are inconsistent with existing copyright law.

1. Contrary to the stated intent of the sponsors, the bill unnecessarily applies to U.S. domestic websites. Under the bill, law enforcement can serve a court order on the registrar or registry for a domestic site. The registrar or registry shall "suspend operation of, and may lock, the domain name."
   a. U.S. law enforcement already has jurisdiction over domestic sites that infringe copyright law. This bill creates an overlapping and inconsistent remedy to law enforcement's existing powers. Indeed, U.S. law enforcement has recently seized a significant number of ".com" and other sites hosted by U.S. registrars or registries, calling into question the need for further legislative authority.
   b. Because of the overbroad definitions in the bill, law enforcement (or a registrar or registry utilizing the bill's "vigilante" provision) could take down a major Internet company's domain for unlawful content on a subdomain. For example, infringing material on a subdomain, e.g., illegalmaterial.usergroup.malprinternetcompany.com, could

result in the entire domain of www.maajorinternetcompany.com being blocked.

2. The bill would create a new cause of action against a site "dedicated to infringing activities." The definition of "dedicated to infringing activities" arguably would implicate major U.S. social media platforms, video sharing sites, e-commerce sites, third-party retail sites, grey-market sales sites, and countless sites that are overwhelmingly lawful and integral to the U.S. economy. There are two ways a site can be "dedicated to infringing activities."
   a. A site is "dedicated to infringing activities" if it is "subject to civil forfeiture" under 18 U.S.C. § 2323. A website is subject to civil forfeiture if it used to sell infringing products with a total retail value of $1,000. This definition sweeps in most open online retailers and open web platforms.
   b. A site also would be "dedicated to infringing activities" if—the site is primarily designed, or has no demonstrable commercially significant purpose or use other than, or is marketed by its operator (1) to offer goods or services in violation of title 17, United States Code, or that enable or facilitate a violation of title 17, United States Code, including but not limited to offering or providing access in a manner not authorized by the copyright owner or otherwise by operation of law, copies or phono records of, or public performances or displays of works protected by Title 17, in complete or substantially complete form, by any means, including by means of download, streaming, or other transmission, provision of a link or aggregated links to other sites or Internet resources for obtaining access to such copies, phono records, performances, displays, goods or services; or (11) to sell or offer to sell or distribute or otherwise promote goods, services, or materials bearing a counterfeit mark, as that term is defined in section 34(d) of the Lanham Act (15 U.S.C. 1116(d); and... when taken together, such activities are the central activities of the Internet site or sites accessed through a specific domain name.

I This definition invents a new secondary liability concept, *i.e.*, "enable or facilitate," and for the first time codifies secondary liability. Today, copyright secondary liability is a judge-made, common law concept. Making U.S. Internet companies liable for "enabling" or "facilitating" third parties that engage in illegal activity runs contrary to 13 years' of well-settled federal policy under the Digital Millennium Copyright Act. This legislation should not be used to re-write the DMCA.

II The definition applies even if the Internet company has no knowledge of the illegal activity or no intent to foster illegal activity: The site is "primarily designed...to offer goods and services... that enable or facilitate a violation of title 17...." A wide range of legitimate products such as personal computers and mobile smartphones "enable or facilitate" a violation of title 17. Accordingly, a site that is designed to sell personal computers or smartphones would fall within this definition. This concept is contrary to well-settled law under the Copyright Act.

III Through its focus on commercial purposes, the definition injects considerable confusion by discounting the well-established *Sony Betarnax* standard that enabled the sale of equipment capable of substantial non-infringing uses -whether commercial or not -- and thereby ushered in a home video market that revitalized the entertainment industry,

IV The definition creates a new trademark liability arguably inconsistent with existing law.

V The phrase "sites accessed through a specific domain name" is unclear.

3. The bill's requirement that a financial transaction provider take "reasonable measures, as expeditiously as reasonable, to prevent or prohibit its service from completing payment transactions between its U.S. customers and the site, and to prevent the use of its trademarks" does not include a technical feasibility qualification,

which is included in the DNS obligations, and needs to be tightened in other ways.

4. The bill would require a service that provides advertisements to Internet sites "take reasonable measures, as expeditiously as reasonable, to prevent its network from providing advertisements to an Internet site associated with such domain name." Some concerns with this provision include:
   a. The online advertising ecosystem is broad and includes many different intermediaries and business models. It is unclear to what parts of the advertising ecosystem this applies and whether exchanges that aggregate advertising space could even comply.
   b. It is unclear what "associated with such domain name" means or to what it is meant to apply. Arguably, an advertiser could be required to cease providing ads to a major ISP's site because the ISP provides access to the unlawful website.
   c. The provision does not include a technical feasibility qualification, winch is included in the DNS obligations.
5. The bill includes a "vigilante" provision that provides complete immunity for registrars and registries, financial transaction providers, and advertising services to take voluntary action against an Internet site if the entity "reasonably believes the Internet site is dedicated to infringing activities."
   a. Under this vigilante provision, there is no government involvement in determining which sites meet the standard. Nor is there any due process or remedy for a site that is mistakenly targeted or purposely targeted for competitive reasons. For example, Viacom recently lost its SI billion lawsuit against YouTube. Under this provision, however, Viacom could approach Verisign with evidence that YouTube is "dedicated to infringing activities" and Verisign's lawyers could remove YouTube.com without any legal recourse for YouTube.
6. Under the bill, the IP Enforcement Coordinator must post a list of domain names affected by court orders on a publicly-available

Internet site. The mere publication of the list may result in constructive knowledge for other Internet intermediaries for purposes of secondary liability, or "red flag" knowledge that disqualifies a service provider from safe harbors under the DMCA. So the list may be used as evidence in copyright lawsuits against any online intermediary, whether or not that entity received a court order under the bill. The bill should he clarified to provide that neither the IPEC list nor any other action could be admitted as evidence establishing knowledge or intent in copyright infringement actions against service providers.

Policy Concerns

1. Jurisdiction. The bill would authorize a U.S. court to exercise jurisdiction over a foreign-registered domain name by virtue of the fact that U.S. citizens can access the site. It is far from clear that the due process clause of the Constitution allows a U.S. court to exercise jurisdiction in this manner. Moreover, this approach would set a dangerous precedent for foreign countries to attempt to control content on U.S. websites. Several years ago, a French court found Yahoo! liable for hosting auctions of Nazi-era materials that were viewable in France. Similarly, an Australian court exercised jurisdiction over Barron's for alleged defamation in an article posted on a U.S. website. And, a French court held eBay liable for the sale of legitimate luxury goods that were being sold lawfully in the United States but violated France's authorized distributor laws. The issue of jurisdiction for Internet-based activities is extraordinarily complex. Until now, Congress has let the courts take the lead on how to apply traditional principles of jurisdiction to the Internet environment. Congress should carefully consider the implications of this aggressive assertion of jurisdiction on U.S. websites that are viewable overseas.

2. Extraterritoriality. In addition to authorizing U.S. courts to exercise jurisdiction over foreign activity, the bill would create extraterritorial remedies. A financial transaction provider would be required to notify foreign website operators that they may not use the financial transaction provider's trademarks. Similarly, an advertising service would be required to stop placing ads on foreign websites. This would be the case even if a U.S. user no longer can access the site or purchase infringing material from it. Again, this could be a troubling precedent that could he exploited by other countries against U.S. businesses.
3. Due Process. Under CO1CA, once a court issues an injunction against the domain name of a website dedicated to infringing activity, the Department of Justice can serve the order on the operators of domain name services, financial transaction providers, and advertising networks. COICA, therefore, allows the Department of Justice to impose obligations on these entities without first giving them an opportunity to be heard in court. In other words, the operators of websites dedicated to infringing activity receive more procedural protections than these innocent service providers.
4. Uncompensated Government Takings of Service. Unlike most other law enforcement tools that mandate that communications intermediaries provide services to the Federal Government, COICA contains no reimbursement for costs. The Communications Assistance to Law Enforcement Act, the Electronic Communications Privacy Act (1 8 U.S.C. § 2706), and the FiSA Amendments of 2008 all provide for reimbursement, generally at the prevailing rate for the service provided. COICA requires intermediaries to provided services for free to the government, however, without any compensation or cost reimbursement.
5. Endorsing the Tools of Government Censorship. Undoubtedly, this legislation's endorsement of the very tools of censorship that have been used by regimes around the globe to disrupt political speech

will be highlighted as justification for those regimes' continued efforts to censor speech. In addition, the U.S. government's disruption of global Internet governance issues will result in increased public pressure for an international governance body such as the United Nations to assume control over Internet governance.

Conclusion

For the foregoing reasons, we hope that the Committee will proceed thoughtfully and carefully as it crafts legislation to address offshore, illegal Websites, We look forward to working with each member of the Committee as it considers this issue.

We appreciate the opportunity to provide testimony on this matter. Please do not hesitate to contact us if you or your staff have any questions or concerns.

September 7, 2010.

Chairman Patrick J. Leahy
United States Senate 433 Russell
Senate Office Building
Washington, DC 20510

Ranking Member Jeff Sessions
United States Senate 335 Russell
Senate Office Building
Washington, DC 20510

Re: S. 3804, Combating Online Infringement and Counterfeits Act (COICA)

Dear Chairman Leahy and Ranking Member Sessions:

Although the undersigned entities support the objectives of S. 3804, the "Combating Online Infringement and Counterfeits Act" (COICA), the bill raises numerous legal, political, and technical issues. If left unresolved, these issues could harm consumers, educational institutions, innovative technologies, economic growth and global Internet freedom. These complicated issues require careful deliberation that we fear cannot he accomplished in the waning days of this session.

The bill enables the Justice Department to bring in rem actions against domestic and foreign domain names of websites dedicated to infringing activities, and, with respect to foreign sites, to obtain judicial orders mandating that Internet services, operators of domain name servers, financial transaction providers, and ad networks discontinue service to the designated sites. In addition, subsection (j) authorizes the Justice Department to maintain a public blacklist of websites that the Department determines "upon information and reasonable belief" to be dedicated to infringing activities. Internet-related services will be encouraged to discontinue service to these websites.

Given the fundamental due process values of our nation and the potential for other countries to enact similar mechanisms to retaliate against U.S. companies abroad, Congress must carefully consider whether it wishes to authorize Justice Department officials to blacklist websites in a manner subject to little process and limited judicial review. Without judicial oversight, these blacklists could reach the websites of political candidates and advocacy groups. Numerous political campaigns have received copyright cease-and-desist letters or infringement notices, including candidates very recently in this cycle from both parties.[58]

The potential for blacklisting for "facilitating" infringement, as so broadly defined in this bill, can undermine U.S. secondary liability law as established in Sorry v. Universal, and ignores the culpable intent

---

[58] Nevada GOP Candidate Faces Copyright Lawsuit, Wash. Post, Sept. 4, 2010; Mu. Democratic nominee for US Senate keeps TV ad despite copyright lawsuit hr For News Network, Wash. Examiner, Sept. 16, 2010.

requirement of MGM v. Grokster. For example, would the listing of a website on the blacklist constitute constructive knowledge for contributory infringement purposes, if a service provider did not discontinue providing service to a website after it was listed? More generally, the new definitions and requirements also raise serious questions about the effect of this bill on existing copyright exceptions, limitations and defenses upon which a significant sector of the U.S. economy relics.

The proposed *in rem* proceeding also raises a host of issues that necessitate thorough review. It is unclear whom may be compelled by such orders, and what obligations can be imposed. The definition regarding which services must comply with *in rem* orders is both broad and vague. Will COICA apply to (a) all ISPs? (b) The root zone server operated by the Internet Corporation for Assigned Names and Numbers (ICANN)? (c) The "authoritative" root zone server operated by Verisign under contract with NTIA? Would a webhost or search engine have to remove all links to designated sites? Such mandates may be unmanageable, and could have a deleterious effect upon the fight to keep Internet governance out of the bureaucracy of international organizations.

It is further unclear what consequences will result from the functionally extraterritorial application of U.S. intellectual property laws. Congress must consider the precedent this bill would set for countries less protective of citizens' rights of free expression. COICA's blacklist may be used to justify foreign blacklists of websites that criticize governments or royalty, or that contain other "unlawful" or "subversive" speech. Just this year, the Secretary of State declared that Internet freedom is nothing less than freedom of assembly online[59] At this time in our campaign to ensure Internet freedom abroad, it is imprudent to endow U.S. law enforcement officials with an unsupervised right to determine who may assemble and who may not.

In sum, COICA - which was introduced only last week - raises a host of global entanglements and serious questions that need to he evaluated thoroughly and carefully. To do so, we believe a hearing on S. 3804, with

---

[59] Hillary Clinton, Remarks on Internet Freedom, Newseum, Jan. 21, 2010, available at h tip ://w ww.state . go v/see re ta ry/rm12 0 1 0/01/135519. Htm.

testimony from impacted industries and user constituencies, should he held before any major legislative action is taken. We look forward to working with you to address these questions, and to ensure that intellectual property laws can be enforced while preserving free speech, due process, and the stability, freedom, and economic potential of the Internet.

Respectfully submitted,

American Association of Law Libraries (AALL)
American Library Association (ALA)
Association of College and Research Libraries (ACRL)
Association of Research Libraries (An)
Center for Democracy and Technology (CDT)
Computer and Communications Industry Association (CCIA)
Consumer Electronics Association (CEA)
Electronic Frontier Foundation (EFT)
Home Recording Rights Coalition (EIRRC)
NetCoalition
Public Knowledge

Cc: Senate Judiciary Committee
Chairman and Ranking Member, House Judiciary Committee

NetCoalition.com

November 15, 2010

The Honorable Patrick Leahy Chairman
Senate Committee on the Judiciary
224 Dirksen Senate Office Building
Washington, DC 20510-6275

Re: S. 3804, The Combating Online Infringement and Counterfeits Act (COICA).

Dear Chairman Leahy:

NetCoalition[60] has serious concerns with S. 3804, the Combating Online Infringement and Counterfeits Act (COICA), which is on the agenda for the Committee's November 18 executive business meeting COICA is intended to address the problem of foreign websites that are otherwise beyond the reach of U.S. legal process that make infringing content available to U.S. users. We understand your frustration that the many actions taken by the Committee to address online infringement, including the PRO-IP Act adopted in the 110th Congress, appear not to have caused a meaningful reduction in the level of infringement. We support your objective of combating counterfeiting and online infringement. Nonetheless, the bill raises significant legal, political, and technical issues that need to be considered and resolved before it progresses. Accordingly, the legislation should not be retorted out in the lame-duck session. Instead, it should proceed by regular order in the 112th Congress.

COICA authorizes the Justice Department to bring *in rem* actions against domain names of websites dedicated to infringing activities. If the domain name has a foreign registry, the Justice Department can serve the order issued against the domain name on the operators of domain name system servers, financial transaction providers, and advertising networks, which would then be required to discontinue providing services to these websites. This new *in rem* proceeding raises a host of questions that necessitate thorough review.

1. Interaction with U.S. Legal Process. It is our understanding that COICA is intended as an extraordinary remedy where a foreign, rogue website is otherwise not reachable by U.S. legal process. Where a website (whether foreign or domestic) is willing to

---

[60] NetCoalition serves as a public policy voice to leading Internet and technology companies, including Amazon.com, Bloomberg LP, eBay, Google, IAC, Yahoo!, and Wikipedia.

400 North Capitol Street, N.W. Suite 585
Washington, D.C. 20001
+1 202-624-1460

appear and defend in U.S. courts, existing legal rules should be applied and COICA should not supplant or supersede those proceedings. This is the approach, for example, that Section 512(g)(3) of the Digital Millennium Copyright Act (DMCA) employs with respect to allegedly infringing content hosted on behalf of foreign users. The current draft does not ensure that COICA will not be used as a weapon against the domain names of sites that are not "rogues," but are instead willing to defend their actions in U.S. courts.

2. Jurisdiction. COICA would authorize a U.S. court to exercise jurisdiction over a foreign-registered domain name by virtue of the impact the foreign website associated with that name may have on U.S. rights holders. It is far from clear that the due process clause of the U.S. Constitution allows a U.S. court to exercise jurisdiction in this manner.

   Moreover, this approach could set a dangerous precedent for foreign countries to attempt to control content on U.S websites. As you may recall, a French court found Yahoo liable for hosting auctions of Nazi paraphernalia that were viewable in France. Similarly, an Australian court exercised jurisdiction over Barron's for alleged defamation in an article posted on a U.S. website. The issue of jurisdiction for Internet-based activity is extraordinarily complex. Until now, Congress has let the courts take the lead on how to apply traditional principles of jurisdiction to the Internet environment. The Committee must carefully consider the implications of this aggressive assertion of jurisdiction on U.S. websites that are viewable overseas.

3. Extraterritoriality. In addition to authorizing U.S. courts to exercise jurisdiction over foreign activity, COICA creates extraterritorial remedies. A financial transaction provider would be required to prevent the use of its trademarks on foreign websites. Similarly, an advertising network would be required to stop placing contextual or display ads on foreign websites. This would be the case even if a U.S. user no longer can access the site or

purchase infringing material from it. Once again, this could be a dangerous precedent that could be exploited by other countries against U.S. businesses.

4. Due Process. Under COICA, once a court issues an injunction against the domain name of a website dedicated to infringing activity, the Justice Department can serve the order on the operators of domain name system servers, financial transaction providers, and advertising networks. These entities would then be required to discontinue providing services to these websites. COICA, therefore, allows the Justice Department to impose obligations on these entities without first giving them an opportunity to be heard in court. In other words, the operators of websites dedicated to infringing activity receive more procedural protections than these innocent service providers.
5. Secondary Liability. The new *in rem* proceeding could also have an unintended impact on copyright and trademark secondary liability. Since secondary liability in these areas is entirely judge-made, it is constantly evolving, and the language of COICA could easily shift the careful balance struck by existing law. For example, the standards in the definition of sites that are "dedicated to infringing activities" differ from those in recent judicial decisions relating to secondary copyright and trademark infringement. The new *in rem* proceeding could affect this precedent. Similarly, as noted above, COICA requires the operators of DNS servers, financial transaction providers, and advertising networks to take certain actions when served with orders issued under this statute. Courts could infer from this provision a Congressional intent that secondary liability be extended to such entities. Although COICA contains a savings clause, it may not be strong enough to prevent these effects on secondary liability.

Furthermore, potential interaction between COICA, secondary liability, and the DMCA safe harbors could unintentionally expand the scope of the legislation, reaching a much broader array of intermediaries than those identified in the bill. For example, once a site is identified as "dedicated to infringing activity," would that constitute "red flag knowledge" sufficient to strip online service providers who provide hosting or search engines of their DMCA safe harbor protections? If so, what would their legal obligations be with respect to such sites? Moreover, because the DMCA safe harbors are limitations on liability, rather than affirmative defenses, under the existing language of COICA sites that fully qualify for the DMCA safe harbors could nevertheless find themselves declared to be "dedicated to infringing activity" because they technically "violate" Title 17 despite enjoying a limitation on resulting liability. These subtle interactions are not fully addressed by the proposed savings clause.

6. Internet Stability. COICA could also undermine the stability of the Internet. By requiring DNS server operators to block domain names, COICA encourages users to take the easy step of switching from their ISP's name servers to offshore name servers. This, in turn, diminishes the ability of the U.S. government and ISPs to respond to cyberattacks. According to computer security expert Dan Kaminsky, "the best place to deploy DNS filters is at the users' ISP name server. But these filters will become useless once users abandon their ISP name servers."[61] The shift away from ISP name servers also diminishes the ability of network managers to monitor the overall activity of the network. ISP name servers "provide and extraordinarily valuable, even predictive, data stream regarding malicious behavior. Losing this stream would materially degrade our ability to secure cyber space." Additionally, a migration away from ISP name servers will make it more difficult to distribute software patches to users. "Now, with DNS [Security Extensions] finally offering the real fix for cache poisoning, we see a proposal that will cause users to avoid the very servers we've spent a decade trying to secure and to get people to use."

---

[61] Dan Kaminsky, DNS Filtering and S. 3804, "Countering Online Infringement and Counterfeiting Act," Oct. 2010.

Significantly, because of the ease of selecting an offshore name server not bound by COICA, COICA will deter few users' intent on accessing infringing content. Thus, COICA would render the Internet more vulnerable to cyber-attacks, but have little impact on infringement.

7. Voluntary Actions. The draft manager's amendment provides a safe harbor from liability for a domain name registrar that voluntarily blocks domain names of websites it "reasonably believes" are dedicated to infringing activity. This provision can be abused for anticompetitive purposes. Many domain name registrars provide other services, and they may take advantage of the safe harbor to block access to a competitor's website. Given the breadth of the definition of a website "dedicated to infringing activity" (see below), it would be easy for the domain name registrar to have a reasonable belief that a competitor's website that allows users to upload content is dedicated to infringing activity.

Furthermore, this provision may have implications for secondary liability. A domain name registrar, financial transaction provider, or advertising network could be sued by a rights holder under a secondary liability theory for failing to take actions that would have been protected by the safe harbor.

8. Definitions. COICA contains undefined or broadly defined terms. Of gravest concern is the sweeping definition of a website "dedicated to infringing activity." A parsing of the definition reveals that any website used for the distribution of copies with a retail value of $1,000 could be considered a website dedicated to infringing activity. Thus, any popular website that allows users to upload content would be subject to COICA's remedies.

Because of the complex and controversial issues COICA raises, it should not be considered during the lame-duck session. Instead, in the 112[61] Congress the Committee should hold a series of stakeholder discussions on the nature of the problem the bill seeks to address, the constitutionality of the *in rem* procedure, the foreign policy implications of this approach, the impact of DNS blocking on Internet stability, and means of mitigating unintended consequences on innocent service providers. After the stakeholder discussions, the legislation should proceed in regular order.

We look forward to working with you and your staff on this issue in the 112th Congress.

Sincerely,
Markham C. Erickson
Partner, Holch & Erickson LLP
and Executive Director, NetCoalition
Cc: Senate Judiciary Committee

DNS Filtering and 5.3804, "Countering Online Infringement and Counterfeiting Act"
Dan Kaminsky, Computer Security Researcher[62] Finder and Fixer of the Kaminsky Bugg[63]

My core concern is one of unintended consequences.

Put simply, if running antivirus software prevented users from listening to pirated copies of the latest Lady Gaga album, users would not run antivirus software. There has long been a bright line in computer security technology -- do not subvert the will of the user, for the user is in the position to opt out of all protections.

By sanctioning the use of DNS filtering to combat copyright and trademark infringement, this bill will directly cause users to opt out of

[62] http://en.wikipeclia.org/wiki/Dan_Kaminsky.
[63] 2M1T Technology Review, "The Flaw at the Heart of the Internet,' November/December 2008, by Erica Naone, available at littp://wwvv.tereviewcorn/weh/21537/. See also, http://www.wired.com/techbiz/people/rnagazine/16-12/ff_karninsky.

using their ISP's name servers.[64] This will lead to more hacks against American assets, for a number of reasons.

First, as the Center for Democracy and Technology correctly notes, changing name servers is a trivial task, taking less than one minute. Which server a user chooses for DNS resolution, however, has consequences. One could easily imagine users being told that to access "The Pirate Bay", they should change their name server to one outside their ISP, and outside the United States. These foreign servers would then not only be used for locating pirated resources, but legitimate ones as well-bank sites, e-commerce sites, even search engines.

Alternatively, users might abandon shared name servers entirely, opting to running their own locally (think of this as a "Pirate Bay Helper" application, itself which might be infected). The DNS depends on shared servers to manage load. Incentivizing large numbers of users to abandon the shared arrangement could have major implications for network stability.

Two years ago, I was part of a major effort to ensure people could trust their own name servers when looking up their banks, their e-commerce sites, or their search engines.[65] This bill would completely undermine that effort and instead create greater security and stability risks for Internet users and the DNS.

Note that it is extraordinarily easy for users to avoid DNS filters. In countries outside the United States where large-scale filtering regimes are in place, we see tremendous awareness and adoption of proxying and VPN technologies, even among the nontechnical. The proposed filter will have no impact on the piracy rate - and it still wouldn't, even if it were ten times more aggressive. Even users that have no interest in infringing content but object to DNS filtering by their local 1SP would gravitate toward alternative DNS servers.

---

64 Section (e)(2)(b)(i) of the bill would impose DNS filtering obligations. That provision authorizes the issuance of a court order requiring service providers and DNS server operators to "take technically feasible and reasonable steps designed to prevent a domain name from resolving to that domain name's Internet Protocol address".

65 Id.

DNS filtering is used now in very limited circumstances. It is one of the few tools that defenders possess to manage hotnets and other very large-scale cyberattacks against the Internet population. The best place to deploy DNS filters is at the users' ISP name server. But these filters will become useless once users abandon their ISP name servers.

We will also lose a significant amount of our "eyes and ears" with respect to attacks. DNS servers are tremendously useful vantage points from which to monitor the overall activity of the network. They provide an extraordinarily valuable, even predictive, data stream regarding malicious behavior. Losing this stream would materially degrade our ability to secure cyber space.

Had this law been in place when we worked to patch major ISP name servers several years ago, it would have severely hampered our success in actually getting safe code to users, since they would have been using other servers, with unknown configurations. Now, with DNSSEC finally offering the real fix for cache poisoning, we see a proposal that will cause users to avoid the very servers we've spent a decade trying to secure and to get people to use.

There is a final concern -- and it's not the constitutional worry. DNS is a global namespace, managed globally, and operated globally. Unilateral action by the United States threatens similar action by other state actors, in forms that are difficult to predict but very clearly not of the form that can be managed through the present global forums run by ICANN.

Ultimately, there are many layers at which piracy can be attacked. Operating at this layer has harmful unintended consequences that will make Americans less safe. DNS filtering is a blunt instrument, a hammer in place of a scalpel.

The DNS works remarkably well right now. It is a core element of how commerce functions. We should not be interfering with this working system, especially not without deliberation and research into unintended consequences.

The New York Times

February 14, 2011

Would the Bard Have Survived the Web?

By Scott Turow, Paul Aiken and James Shapiro

ARCHAEOLOGISTS finished a remarkable dig last summer in East London. Among their finds were seven earthenware knobs, physical evidence of a near perfect 16th-century experiment into the link between commerce and culture.

When William Shakespeare was growing up in rural Stratford-upon-Avon, carpenters at that East London site were erecting the walls of what some consider the first theater built in Europe since antiquity. Other playhouses soon rose around the city. Those who paid could enter and see the play; those who didn't, couldn't.

By the time Shakespeare turned to writing, these "cultural paywalls" were abundant in London: workers holding moneyboxes (bearing the distinctive knobs found by the archaeologists) stood at the entrances of a growing number of outdoor playhouses, collecting a penny for admission.

At day's end, actors and theater owners smashed open the earthenware moneyboxes and divided the daily take. From those proceeds dramatists were paid to write new plays. For the first time ever, it was possible to earn a living writing for the public.

Money changed everything. Almost overnight, a wave of brilliant dramatists emerged, including Christopher Marlowe, Thomas Kyd, Ben Jonson and Shakespeare. These talents and many comparable and lesser lights had found the opportunity, the conditions and the money to pursue their craft.

The stark findings of this experiment? As with much else, literary talent often remains undeveloped unless markets reward it.

At the height of the Enlightenment, the cultural paywall went virtual, when British authors gained the right to create legally protected markets for their works. In 1709, expressly to combat book piracy and "for the encouragement of learned men to compose and write useful books," Britain enacted the world's first copyright law. Eighty years later, America's founders expanded on this, giving Congress the authority to enact copyright laws "to promote the progress of science and useful arts."

Copyright, now powerfully linking authors, the printing press (and later technologies) and the market, would prove to be one of history's great public policy successes. Books would attract investment of authors' labor and publishers' capital on a colossal scale, and our libraries and bookstores would fill with works that educated and entertained a thriving nation. Our poets, playwrights, novelists, historians, biographers and musicians were all underwritten by copyright's markets.

Yet today, these markets are unraveling. Piracy is a lucrative, innovative, global enterprise. Clusters of overseas servers can undermine much of the commercial basis for creative work around the world, offering users the speedy, secret transmission of stolen goods.

The Senate Judiciary Committee is holding a hearing on Wednesday on "targeting Web sites dedicated to stealing American intellectual property," and the White House has pledged to propose a new law to address rampant piracy within the year. But writers and other creative workers should still be worried.

The rise of the Internet has led to a view among many users and Web companies that copyright is a relic, suited only to the needs of out-of-step corporate behemoths. Just consider the dedicated "file-sharers" — actually, traffickers in stolen music movies and, increasingly, books — who transmit and receive copyrighted material without the slightest guilt.

They are abetted by a handful of law professors and other experts who have made careers of fashioning counterintuitive arguments holding that copyright impedes creativity and progress. Their theory is that if we severely weaken copyright protections, innovation will truly flourish. It's a seductive thought, but it ignores centuries of scientific and technological progress based on the principle that a creative person should have some assurance of being rewarded for his innovative work.

Certainly there's a place for free creative work online, but that cannot be the end of it. A rich culture demands contributions from authors and artists who devote thousands of hours to a work and a lifetime to their craft. Since the Enlightenment, Western societies have been lulled into a belief that progress is inevitable. It never has been. It's the result of ahiding by rules that were carefully constructed and practices that were begun by people living in the long shadow of the Dark Ages. We tamper with those rides at our peril.

Last July, a small audience gathered at that London archaeological dig to hear two actors read from "A Midsummer Night's Dream" at the place of its debut, where theater's most valuable walls once stood. While the foundations of the Theater (as it was known) remained, the walls themselves did not. When Shakespeare's company lost its lease, the members dismantled the Theater's timber frame and moved the walls to a new site across the Thames, naming their new playhouse the Globe. Shakespeare's paywall traveled with him.

The Globe would later burn down (a cannon fired during a performance of "Henry VIH" touched off the blaze) and was quickly rebuilt. Its final end came in the mid-17th century, at the outset of a bloody civil war, when authorities ordered the walls pulled down. The regime wasn't motivated by ideals of open access or illusions of speeding progress.

They simply wanted to silence the dramatists, who expressed a wide range of unsettling thoughts to paying audiences within.

The experiment was over. Dramatists' ties to commerce were severed, and the greatest explosion of playwriting talent the modern world has ever seen ended. Just like that.

Scott Turow, a novelist, is the president of the Authors Guild. Paul Aiken is its executive director. James Shapiro, a member of the guild's board, teaches Shakespeare at Columbia.

Public Knowledge

STATEMENT OF SHERWIN SIY

Deputy Legal Director, Public Knowledge
Before the United States Senate Committee on the Judiciary
Hearing on: Targeting Websites Dedicated to Stealing American Intellectual Property
February 16, 2011

Chairman Leahy, Ranking Member Grassley, and members of the Committee:

Thank you for the opportunity to have our testimony included in the record. Public Knowledge has been closely involved in many of the legal and policy debates surrounding online access and digital copyrights, and we are particularly concerned with ensuring that copyright enforcement mechanisms work with, and not against, free speech and the technical requirements of the Internet.

Introduction

In regulating copyright, the law is regulating a form of speech. Addressing these issues in the context of the Internet—a potent outlet for free speech of all sorts—adds additional delicacy to these undertakings. Any technical mechanism that can be used to remove infringing content can be abused to remove disfavored, but constitutionally protected, speech. Any legal remedy that can enjoin the distribution of content can be misapplied or misused in the restraint of speech. This means that both technical and legal measures must be narrowly tailored both in their defined targets for action, and in the scope of the effects of their remedies.

Proposed remedies against online infringers must also take into account the evolving nature of the Internet and the businesses that rely upon it. Overbroad mechanisms can chill not only speech, but also investment in new distributed technologies.

Remedies also must take into account the technical structure of the Internet and its in-built dependencies and limitations. Certain technical objectives can only be achieved at a cost to innocent users' use of the Internet, while others can open up cybersecurity vulnerabilities.

Tailoring Solutions Accurately

The perfect solution to online infringement would act instantaneously, be 100% effective, and would never adversely affect any lawful use or user. The perfect solution would prevent infringement that originated beyond U.S. borders, without acting extraterritorially, affecting cybersecurity, or inviting international controversy. Such a perfect solution, however, does not now exist, and seems unlikely to arise in the future. However, we cannot, in seeking faster and more effective methods, shirk the constitutional obligations to narrowly tailor remedies and provide adequate due process before restraining speech.

Targeting Bad-Faith Actors

This focus on speech is not tangential to copyright enforcement. While there are obvious and notorious infringers whose electronic communications are composed entirely of infringing works, there are also countless other online presences whose infringement status is being hotly debated. YouTube, an established website used by several members of this Committee, is still engaged in litigation over the basic legality underpinning its operations. Less-established sites also face potential liability, whether they provide forums for individuals to share news, ideas, and other content, or seek to improve our ability to store and access our own data. In the end, some of these sites may fall afoul of copyright law despite good intentions. Others are eventually vindicated in court, with their legal status being found to match their good faith actions.

If the Committee is seeking a more immediate remedy to online infringement than what can be provided by civil litigation or criminal prosecution, then a narrower subset of alleged infringers should he targeted than all those who meet the definition of criminal infringement. Currently, many good faith actors can easily find themselves within this definition, especially given the replicable nature of Internet communication. A video-sharing site like YouTube or an online music locker could be distributing or making thousands of copies of works in a single day. If those copies are found to be infringing, the site would then be meeting the section 506(a)(1)(B) prong for criminal infringement. Rather than have its assets seized and its business choked off immediately, such a company should have the ability to defend itself in court.

Limiting Collateral Damage in Enforcement

The remedies included in any proposed solution to online infringement should also be narrowly tailored so as not to affect non-infringing subdomains, users, or uses of targeted sites or domains.

For example, imagine an infringing site located on a subdomain, piratesite.blogplace.com. This infringing site is hosted unknowingly by a larger, general-purpose blog host, Blogplace.com. A remedy requiring the registrar that sold Blogplace its domain name to shut down the domain would affect not only the infringing site, but also all of the other users who hosted sites on Blogplace. The same overbreadth problem would occur should the remedy target the operator of the .com registry.

As an additional problem, websites are not the only aspects of Internet communication that would be derailed by a domain seizure. Any email addresses housed on a domain would be unusable and unreachable. This would deprive the user of an important means of communication, necessary whether or not his email account was relevant to the infringing activities present on the same domain's website.

Ensuring Due Process

The legal structure of the remedies is as important as the scope of their application. As noted above, alleged infringers should have the ability to avail themselves of defense in a court of law. Should there be a need to stop the operations of the allegedly infringing site, an injunction or restraining order could be issued through standard procedures, with parties given the opportunity to make the case to a judge regarding the balance of harms, the public interest, and the likelihood of their success on the merits of an infringement action. By issuing an order directly to the accused party, clearly legitimate activities could continue while the activities at issue are suspended during litigation.

This stands in contrast with methods both proposed and currently being used. Recent actions by law enforcement against accused infringing sites have seized domain names under civil forfeiture statutes that were intended to apply broadly to physical goods—cash currency, contraband, stolen goods, or machinery used in the commission of a crime. Domain names differ from physical goods in several important ways. For one, the seizure of a domain name prevents its use as a communications medium, unlike most physical goods. A domain is used as a contact point for speech (including email addresses as well as websites) in ways that most physical property is not. Secondly, unlike physical property, there is no chance that a domain name can be hidden or disposed of before a trial. The domain will be exactly where it was throughout the entire procedure, viewable by the authorities so long as it is active. Any usage of it can be monitored or enjoined until a resolution of the case on the merits.

International Implications

In seeking solutions to online infringement, particular note has been made of the fact that many online infringers locate their operations overseas. The global nature of the Internet has made it easy for information to flow through national borders. In most cases, this is to everyone's benefit—news from independent sources can reach populations, citizens can exchange political ideas, and creativity and innovation can spread and grow rapidly. A downside of this ease of exchange, however, is that it can be difficult to enforce national laws in a medium designed for international information exchange.

However, recognizing the limits of direct legal jurisdiction does not mean that solutions must be based in alterations of Internet architecture. Attempts to make a global network align neatly with jurisdictional boundaries can be limited in effectiveness, stability, or both. Furthermore, unique sensitivities of foreign policy are bound up in any approach Congress may take in manipulating communications with foreign-based entities.

International Sensitivities and Risks of Technical Retaliation

For example, the United States' historic leadership in information technology has resulted in large parts of basic web and Internet operational infrastructure being housed within the United States and subject to U.S. jurisdiction. Many other countries, friends and foes alike, remain leery of this special relationship between the U.S. government and Internet governance. Attempts to enforce U.S. jurisdiction upon foreign businesses—for whatever good cause—through this situation may exacerbate tensions in the Internet governance space, renewing calls for some other body to manage these tasks. Whether any successor body would have the same commitment to free speech is an open question.

Actions against websites based jurisdictionally upon their use of a U.S.-based registry or registrar could likewise invite territorial escalation. Many U.S.-based sites and businesses use foreign-housed registries, such as .ly, the country code domain for Libya, or use registries that have foreign offices and points of contact. Using registries as a point of attachment for local law invites other countries to do the same, seizing domains that violate local ideas of public order or morality, defamation, or political correctness.

Maintaining a Consistent Message on Internet Freedom

Solutions based on directing U.S.-based Domain Name System (DNS) providers to route traffic away from particular domains raise further problems. The globally-coordinated routing systems of the DNS have been long used because of their consistency and reliability. While it is possible to direct the largest in-country DNS providers to fail to resolve certain domain names, doing so effectively creates a national blacklist for a domain. Doing so sets a country's users apart from the rest of the world, balkanizing the DNS. Other countries that have done the same, for various reasons of censorship or nationalistic impulses, are criticized for this behavior. There is no fundamental reason that each country could not simply designate its own DNS providers to resolve domain names differently, so that a user who types "senate.gov" in Manila might reach the Philippine Senate, rather than the U.S. Senate. Citizens in countries that limit access to the press might direct browsers to washingtonpost.com, wsj.com, or bbc.co.uk to find not independent news sources, but state-controlled propaganda arms instead.

As many other countries develop their information infrastructure, we can see them facing the choice between an American and a Chinese approach to Internet traffic. Increasing the mechanisms by which our government directs the flow of that traffic blurs the distinctions between that stark choices.

Cybersecurity Considerations

Country-specific limitations on DNS providers will create cybersecurity risks as well. Users unable to reach a growing list of sites with their current DNS providers can easily use another one. If domestic DNS providers are made unreliable, users will seek out foreign providers, many of which may not meet the same standards of security as major domestic providers. Actively unscrupulous providers can also redirect users' traffic at will, leaving computers vulnerable to phishing, viruses, and other forms of fraud and computer intrusion. Subverted systems can further be "recruited" by botnets to attack other, unrelated systems. Currently, such security threats are reduced due to a lack of incentives for users to switch DNS providers. Forcing a fragmentation of DNS resolution creates new reasons for users to seek out new services, many of them posing grave cybersecurity risks.

Conclusion

None of this is to suggest that the protection of copyrights is unimportant. However, this Committee must recognize that the same technical and legal tools that can be used to protect copyrights can, if applied over broadly or poorly, can stifle legitimate speech and information. Nor are problems of legal jurisdiction and speedy prosecution usually best remedied by altering the nature of various technical systems. Much more rides upon the technical and organizational realities of the Internet than streaming videos—the same network operations that make infringing streaming easy also underpin the security of e-commerce, the exchange of global free speech and conversation, and the reliability of daily communication. Any attempt by Congress to affect the technological workings of the Internet must take into account the way those vital interests rely upon its structure, and ensure that those values are not harmed.

February 13, 2011

Dear Chairman Leahy and Members of the Senate Judiciary Committee, I strongly support Bill 3804.

Piracy eats away not only at the income of writers, but at the fabric of intellectual property. This blatant disregard for copyright not only devalues us, the creators, but the work we labor to create.

In discussions with people who feel piracy is simply the cost of doing business, or worse, that it's their right as a consumer, I've been told I should be flattered so many people want to read my work--for free--that they probably wouldn't have bought the book anyway, so it's not really a lost sale, that there's nothing I can do about it, so why fight ft. They tell me they can't afford to actually buy the book, but they want to read it. When I suggest the library as an alternative, I'm told the library's too far away or the wait for the book from a library too long.

I'm told not to call it stealing or those who engage in the practice thieves because it annoys them.

It annoys them.

I say respectfully it annoys me when what we, as writers, have created out of our individual minds, hearts, and guts is taken without compensation. When it's taken without our consent. We do not consent to piracy. We do not consent to being devalued out of existence.

The internet is an extraordinary tool, and with it, we can access information with a few keystrokes. But there is a difference, wide and deep, between information and creative property. We use words to express our imaginations, to tell stories that entertain, that bring comfort, offer amusement or solace. Melding that imagination with words to create a book takes work, time, effort, and talent. The storyteller and the book that comes from her through that work, that talent, must be valued and respected. If piracy continues to devastate a writer's income, to erode the ability of the publishers to make the profit necessary to bring those books to the public, where will the next generation of storytellers come from? How can they live if their individual creativity has no value?

The novelist, the novel, the publisher as the gate-keeper can't stand against the growing assault of piracy.

Freedom is essential to us, as people, as Americans. But freedom must co-exist with the rule of law. And the law must address progress along with the benefits and complications it brings with it.

We look to you to make the laws that protect us, that protect our work, that protect and respect creative property. We look to you to stand up for us and against piracy and its growing sense of entitlement.

Without writers there will be no stories. Without stories, the world will be a smaller and much less vibrant place. Please don't let that happen.

Nora Roberts

My name is Scott Turow. I'm the president of the Authors Guild, the largest society of published authors in the U.S., representing more than 8,500 book authors and freelance writers. Our members represent the broad sweep of American authorship, including literary and genre fiction, nonfiction, trade, academic, and children's book authors, textbook authors, freelance journalists and poets.[66] Guild members have won countless honors and all major literary awards, including the Nobel Prize for Literature.[67]

The Authors Guild promotes the professional interests of authors: we're advocates for effective copyright protection, fair contracts, and free expression.

It's a pleasure and an honor to be here this morning. I'd like especially to thank this committee for recognizing the severity of the problem we all face and getting the ball rolling with COICA in the fall, which recognized this central and unavoidable truth: any serious attempt to address online piracy must address the third-party enablers of infringement. Anything that doesn't address those enablers is, frankly, a pretend solution to a real problem.

Our Copyright Policy Inadvertently Encourages Investments in Technologies and Services That Promote Trafficking in Stolen Books, Music, and Movies

After 300 years as one of history's greatest public policy successes, copyright is coming undone. As we meet here this morning, our well-intended policy toward copyright online is undermining our virtual and physical markets for creative works. That policy is in desperate need of

---

[66] The Guild had its beginnings as the Authors League of America, which was founded in 1912 by a group of hook authors (including Theodore Roosevelt, who served as the League's founding vice president), short story writers, freelance journalists and a smattering of dramatists. In the 1920s, the Authors League broke into two groups: the Authors Guild and the Dramatists Guild of America.

[67] Pearl S. Buck (1938) (who served as Authors Guild president), William Faulkner (1949), John Steinbeck (1962), and Isaac Bashevis Singer (1978). One Guild member, Elie Wiese! (1986), has won the Nobel Peace Prize.

update. The Digital Millennium Copyright Act's "safe harbor" for online service providers has turned out to be an exploitable gold mine for unscrupulous online enterprises. That safe harbor allows these rogue enterprises to profit from services that encourage and conceal the trafficking in stolen books, music, and movies, while disclaiming responsibility for that illegal traffic. The DMCA safe harbor has turned copyright's incentives inside out, encouraging massive, global investment in piracy technologies and services.

Our nation's founders gave Congress the authority to enact copyright laws "to promote the progress of science and the useful arts." Copyright laws do this by establishing legally protected markets for creative work. Those laws, and those markets, have worked beyond any reasonable expectation our founders could have had. Copyright's markets have for hundreds of years encouraged authors here and abroad to spend countless hours writing books that they hope readers will value and the marketplace will reward. Nonfiction authors spend thousands of hours immersing themselves in their chosen subjects -- poring over documents, interviewing experts, examining and interpreting facts, theories and events — with the hope that they will be able to contribute something new to public discourse on their subjects and that they will express it in a way that will resonate with readers. Novelists strive to entertain readers and perhaps shed some light on our world and our place in it. Children's book authors devote themselves to reaching our nation's youngest minds, using literature to entertain and enlighten them in ways that no other medium can.

Copyright's markets have also drawn massive, irreplaceable investments from publishers and others in our intellectual and cultural life. Those investments have paid off. Our great research libraries, holding the carefully crafted thoughts, composed over billions of hours by many of our nation's finest minds, are ample proof that copyright has succeeded brilliantly. So is our nation's economic success, nurtured by the hooks that have educated and informed our citizens throughout its history.

We have, inadvertently and with the best of intentions, instituted a policy that not only tolerates, but encourages investments in technologies and services that undermine our markets for creative work. We have, oddly but unmistakably, created the ideal environment for nurturing an innovative, global, networked industry that directly profits from trafficking in stolen books, music, and movies. In a digital age, where tipping points arc always close at hand, the pirate economy can subvert an industry in a heartbeat.

One is tempted to call it a vast underground economy, but there's nothing underground about it: it operates in plain sight, as I will describe. Money clearly suffuses the system, paying for countless servers, vast amounts of online bandwidth, and specialized services that speed and cloak the transmission of stolen creative work. Excluded from this flow of cash are the authors, musicians, songwriters and the publishers who invest in them. The only benefit to the individual author is a parody of a benefit: that the work of the author will be better known. Authors and artists have always been free to give away their work to build an audience, but there had always been the prospect of making a bit of money in the end, that there would be a functioning market to take advantage of that prospect is disappearing before our eyes.

Piracy has all but dismantled our recorded music industry. Any business plan in the music industry must now take into account that piracy is the rule, not the exception. In this environment, about the only value a legitimate provider can add is convenience and safety -- the comfort of knowing that the downloaded music is genuine and contains no malicious code. Finding comparisons for the state of the recorded music. Industry is a near impossibility, because the situation has no precedent. It's as if shopkeepers in some strange land were compelled to operate with a wide-open side doors that would-be customers can sneak out of with impunity, arms laden with goods. In that bizarre place, an ever-growing array of businesses that profit only if the side exit is used eagerly assist the would-be customers, leaving the shopkeeper with only one thing to offer paying customers: the dignity of exiting through the front door.

To get a sense of the scope of the problem we face, I'll describe a couple of businesses operating in the pirate economy.

Case Study #1: BIGuard.com

BitTorrent, a landmark technological development for trading stolen digital works online, is wildly popular. It's estimated to account for 18% of global Internet traffic. According to its website:

> BitTorrent is the global standard for delivering high-quality files over the Internet. With an installed base of over 160 million clients worldwide, BitTorrent technology has turned conventional distribution economics on its head. The more popular a large video, audio or software file, the faster and cheaper it can he transferred with BitTorrent. The result is a better digital entertainment experience for everyone.
> (http://www.bittorrent.cornibtusers/what-is-bittorrent.)

Though its defenders and promoters proudly point to a handful of legitimate uses for BitTorrent technology, everyone knows the real, primary use of the technology: BitTorrent is to stealing movies, TV shows, music, videogames, and now books what bolt-cutters arc to stealing bicycles. A recent study of BitTorrent traffic showed that of the 10,000 most popular files torrented, 63.7% were "non-pornographic content that was copyrighted and shared illegitimately." ("Technical report: An Estimate of Infringing Use of the Internet" by Envisional Ltd. January 2011.) 35.8% of the content was pornographic (the authors of the study did not try to determine how much of the pornographic material was pirated). Of the remaining 0.50% of the 10,000 frequently torrented files, 0.48% could not be identified. That leaves, according to our math, 0.02% -- precisely 2 files out of the 10,000 studied -- that were known to be neither pornographic nor infringing.

Demand is booming for torrented content, so service providers have stepped forward to assist those eager to use BitTorrent technology. Visit the wcbsite BTGuard.com (tagline: "Anonymous BitTorrent Services"), for example, and you'll find an operation that cloaks torrents. There's an animation on BTGuard's home page that illustrates the benefits of its service, using the example of a BitTorrent transfer between two computers in New York. The animation begins with the words "Without BTGuard" (in caps) and "You downloading with BitTorrent." In the animation, the recipient's IP number, which uniquely identifies a recipient's online location is plainly visible, so is the recipient's location: New York. The IP number and New York location of the sender arc also displayed. The animation briefly shows a dashed line representing the BitTorrent transfer proceeding between the two New York computers. Then, in red letters, the animation warns, "BEWARE: EVERYONE KNOWS WHO YOU ARE AND WHAT YOUR DOWNLOADING!"

The animation then restarts, and once again it displays, "You downloading with BitTorrent" but this time it's "With BTGuard. Now the animation shows the torrent's dashed line going from the New York sender to an IP number in Toronto associated with BTGuard's red-and-black logo, before proceeding to the recipient at the other New York location. The animation then reads: "BTGuard gives you a anonymous IP address and encrypts your downloads." It continues: "Not even your ISP will know what you're doing. BTGuard is very easy to use: just install our secure client!" It ends with a red-button call to action "JOIN NOW."

It seems BitTorrent is terrific for sharing stolen works, but the downside is that you might get caught: if IP numbers can be discovered, the traffickers in stolen creative works arc at clear risk. BTGuard and other companies have stepped into the breach.

BTGuard is doing its best to make the benefits of its services clear to the public. On August 14th and 15th of last year, BTGuard (or at least a YouTube user named "BTGuardcom") posted YouTube videos that show how users can "BitTorrent anonymously with BTGuard." These videos, which YouTube reports to have been watched more than 18,000 times in fewer than six months, are also viewable at the BTGuard website. BTGuard.com opened a YouTube channel at apparently the same time. At least one of the commenters at the YouTube channel saw the potential value of the product, but wasn't yet sold: "in the video you never show how it's making you anonymous. Show me that then I'll buy your product."

BTGuard goes to great lengths to reassure users that their systems will protect anonymity, that users won't get caught. At the bottom of its home page, along with "unlimited download speeds" BTGuard promises "no records of usage stored." At the bottom of every page at BTGuard's website is a link for it's "privacy policy: "Neterawled LLC [the apparent owner of BTGuard] is committed to protecting your privacy. Netcrawled LLC does not sell, trade or rent your personal information to other companies. Netcrawled LLC will not collect any personal information about you except when you specifically and knowingly provide such information." Then, in hold letters, the operators promise that no traceable information is gathered: "Netcrawled LLC DOES NOT collect your Internet Protocol (IP) addresses or customer usage."

BTGuard wants its customers to know that not only is its service private, it's also first rate. It boasts that its servers are hosted "at Canada's premiere carrier hotel in Toronto & at the world's largest Internet exchange in Frankfurt, Germany. We have multi-horned bandwidth to multiple tier one networks to provide you with optimum reroute speeds." It lists its "backbone providers" as including such industry leaders as "Leve13, Teleglobe, Deutsch Telekom, Global Crossings, Tiscali, and Cogent Communications."

So here, in a nutshell, is BTGuard's service offering: it will arrange virtual, clandestine "meetings" in Canada for the exchange of large computer files via BitTorrent, and it will do so using state-of-that art facilities. It charges $6.95 per month for this service and accepts payment through PayPal, so subscribers may use their MasterCard, Visa, American Express, or Discover cards. Those in need of cloaking their other online activities can step up to an enhanced service: for $9.95 per month, BTGuard will secure a subscriber's "entire Internet connection: BitTorrent, E-mail, Web Browsing & all other net services become anonymous!"

As with many online enterprises (and nearly all service providers that help customers trade stolen creative work), BTGuard has an affiliate program. BTGuard's program pays a generous $10 per referral and shares 5% of the earnings of webmasters whom affiliates refer to the service. BTGuard compensates affiliates via PayPal, wire, or check. Appearances matter, it seems, BTGuard's affiliate agreement warns that sites that "promote illegal activities" or "violate or infringe upon intellectual property rights" are unsuitable for their affiliate program. BTGuard is forgiving, however, rejected affiliate applicants "are welcome to reapply to the Program at any time."

As with much of the support system for trafficking in stolen creative work, BTGuard is hiding in plain sight. The contact information at the site is Netcrawled LLC, 151 Front Street West, Toronto, M5J 2N1 Canada. Es phone number is 415-762-3688.

Case Study #2: ifile.it

Next, I'd like to discuss to discuss ifile.it, an online file-sharing service that seems to be a one-person operation. Although the proprietor —assume he's male and call him Mr. I for convenience -- appears to work alone, he has know-how and moxie. In a few years Mr. I's been able to bootstrap his little start-up to an operation using two datacenters in North America and at least one in Europe, with year-over-year growth that would make Facebook swoon.

Here's the most useful thing about Mr. I, for our purposes: he's done us the favor of blogging about his efforts. He's not a bad blogger, though his posts are a bit infrequent: he's got some personality, and he's brash. Mr. I gleefully takes shots at one of the file-sharing industry leaders, Rapidshare. Mr. I celebrates his operation's successes as it hits milestones, he posts YouTube videos to show people how a new download feature works, and jumps on the Twitter bandwagon. Mr. I even opens up a Google Project page, an online collaboration tool, with the apparent hope of getting others to develop applications that use his service. In the process of blogging, he gives us an insider's view into the business of facilitating online piracy.

Chronology of a File-Sharing Startup, from Launch to One Million Users

Mr. I launches his blog on January 2, 2008, before his new tile-sharing website, ifile.it, is in beta. Lie's still running his prior website, mihd.net, which apparently was also dedicated to online file sharing. On February 21 he decides to speed up the process of transferring content to sonic of his new servers and moves "a dozen thousand files" onto one of them. On February 29, he apologizes that one of his servers is down for the day, because of some network problems that were "causing me hell for 2 days." Nevertheless, he's live by 10 a.m., which seems to mean that he's no longer in beta with ifile.it.

A series of March 2, 2008, entries in the blog describe many of the details of the file-sharing service. The site's available in about a dozen languages, and it automatically detects a browser's language settings. The site uses "a new distributed filesystem ... sort of similar to Amazon's S3 service but specifically aimed at large file hosting." Mr. I describes ifile.it's support for two types of URLs for download links on March 6: a short one and a descriptive one. "You can share either types of URL's with your friends :)"

On April 1, Mr. 1 thanks his users for helping add languages supported by ifile.it to the list. He reports, "Looking thru' the logs there are some languages such as Japanese, Dutch and Russian which are not *on* the list but are a sizable percentage of our users." He asks for help in adding additional languages to the list. On April 7, Mr. I reports that users will now have usage statistics available to them in their accounts. He gives as an example a user with 65 GB of storage at ifile.it in nearly 3300 files. The user in the example had downloaded 7.41 MB of files in the last five days.

On May 13, 2008, ifile.it hits a milestone, with more than 100,000 members "who registered and activated and use their accounts regularly!" Mr. I provides a graph showing the healthy growth in ifile.it in its first five months. On June 10, Mr. I reports major upgrades: all of ifile.it servers are getting replaced "new Intel quadcore beasts :) also a new internal network will be added to make it easy to balance high loads and bandwidth usage (we use a lot of bandwidth), hopefully this will lead to a marked improvement of the services." On July I, however, 10 servers on ifile.it's new cluster "arc down." On the bright side "The network at the Chicago datacenter is being updated with several Comcast 10gbit connections being added." Mr. I apologizes for the inconvenience.

On July 18, 2008, ifile.it hits a new milestone, 250,000 users.

On August 8, ifile.it increases its upload limit to 250 MB, but then finds that bandwidth is inadequate during peak hours. On August 13 ifile.it doubles its bandwidth at its Chicago network center.

On October 24, Mr. I welcomes "rapidshare refugees". His post describes Rapidshare's business model and is worth quoting at some length:

> I get asked a lot, "how do you plan to compete with the 300lb gorilla in the room called rapidshare?"
>
> Well firstly I would like to think (hope?) that ifile.it doesn't end up like rapidshare, judging by entails received from users this sentiment is shared.
>
> Secondly we don't have to compete, they seems to shoot themselves in the foot every few months, it's sort of amusing as ifile.it doesn't have premium system (not for the foreseeable future anyways) and yet we let people download humongous amounts, in hope that they might become customers one day, I figure the carrot approach is better than the stick and a bit of respect for users is not optional but a requirement.

So welcome aboard and enjoy the ride.

On February 8, 2009, Mr. I asks users to limit heavy downloading to off-peak hours if possible. "[ifile.it] does not block users from downloading at any time but you might find the downloads being slow during peak hours, this is a result of hundreds of thousands of users a day who are not being blocked (unlike other file hosting sites)"

On July 23, Mr. I announces a large number of upgrades to the site and a redesign. He's also posted a YouTube video to describe ifile.it's new upload system. On August 24, he reports that a major site overhaul is complete. His file sharing service can now upload 50 files at a time "(that's quite a crazy amount)" and he's providing an API upload so that developers can more easily "script uploads." He also opens a Google Project so ifile.it users can share their code for the new API. (The Project hub is at http://code.google.com/p/ifile-it/)

Mr. I keeps innovating. On October 19, "thanks to Yahoo Browser+ Plugin" ifile.it offers an advanced uploader "drag and drop" option. Then, on October 30, his site suffers a dedicated denial of service attack. Mr. I promises to "keep an eye on this disturbing development," which caused site usage to drop 20% in an hour."

November 29, 2009, is a red letter day. Mr. I's hard work pays off as he hits a major milestone: "one million registered and verified users." His site is less than two years old.

On February 5, 2010, Mr. I notes that some of his users have built some open source uploaders for his service. They're described at his Google Project Page. He also has posted a new YouTube video.

On March 18, ifile.it gets five new servers (making 45 in all) at a new network operation center in Washington, D.C. The datacenter has multiple 10GB connections through many top level service providers.

On January 31, 2011, a couple weeks ago, Mr. I posts that the maximum file size has been increased yet again, to 1 GB. "Enjoy!"

The Business Model: Ads

Through all of this growth, despite the hardware and bandwidth expenses that Mr. incurs, ifite.it doesn't charge for its services. How does it make money? Through ads at its website. One million users apparently pays for 45 servers and all that bandwidth. Mr. I explains in his blog on July 28, 2008, when some users complained that they have to wait for the downloads of their files to begin. "[B]ut unfortunately the server bills don't pay themselves, *this free service exists thanks to our advertiser (who beside our users they are one of the main stakeholders).* ifile.it doesn't charge users for his file-sharing services." (Emphasis added.)

Mr. I's company, for all of its servers and breathtaking growth, is tiny by piracy industry standards. In a chart prepared by compete.com, we see that the number of unique visitors at ifile.it, measured at 110,184 last month and growing 117% in the last year, barely shows up when compared to the big operators, such as Rapidshare.com and Hotfile, each of which are reported to have had nearly 3 million unique victors in January. We need, urgently, to take the profit out of facilitating piracy.

Recommendations

The Internet presents challenges to our markets for creative works that we have never previously encountered. Infringement that would potentially undermine our domestic markets for creative works has historically taken place within our borders (or could be stopped at our borders), and those who profited from those activities could generally be held personally accountable. That's no longer the ease. Facilitators of piracy now operate in every corner of the globe, and their activities directly undermine our markets for books, music, and movies.

Online trafficking in stolen creative work revolves around one core activity: secret, anonymous online file sharing. Facilitators of online piracy host or provide support for that core activity, and they do it while disclaiming responsibility by taking shelter in the safe harbor protections of our Digital Millennium Copyright Act. A key part of the solution to the piracy problem is to hold those who profit from online file-sharing activities legally responsible for those activities. We therefore urge the committee to consider the following as steps, among others, to address online piracy:

1. Make online file-sharing service providers liable for Facilitating the Trafficking in Stolen Books, Music, and Movies if they

frequently host and distribute stolen creative works or provide services that regularly facilitate the secret or rapid transmission of stolen creative work. Online services that allow anonymous, secret sharing of digital files are clearly subject to enormous abuse. All available evidence suggests that such services will be used as hubs for trading stolen works unless the service provider takes steps to prevent it. Any company proposing to make a business of providing or facilitating file-sharing services should have a clear plan for preventing routine piracy. This should be seen as an essential part of responsibly operating such an enterprise, just as any business has to take care to avoid the public dangers inherent in their operations. Service providers can tackle this issue, just as they've addressed far less destructive menaces such as span, but they need to accept responsibility for the business activities from which they profit.

2. Require online file-sharing service providers to register an agent for service of process for copyright infringement actions with the Copyright Wee as a condition to accepting credit card payments from the U.S. or ad feeds from U.S. online advertising suppliers. Foreign file- sharing service providers can too easily evade our laws while they take money from our residents. Some, such as BTGuard, provide services that encourage the secret transmission of tiles from one U.S. resident to another by cloaking the exchanges through a Foreign Service provider. We wouldn't tolerate this meddling in our domestic market in other areas of commerce, and we shouldn't tolerate it in our markets for books, music, and movies. As a matter of common sense, and as a matter of basic fairness to law-abiding U.S. and foreign file-sharing service providers, all those who directly profit from the U.S. market for file sharing should be subject to U.S. rules.
3. Remove the DMCA safe harbors for online and Internet service providers that provide routine access to online File-sharing service providers that a federal court has found guilty of Facilitating the Trafficking in Stolen Books, Music, and Movies. After a

reasonable notice period, service providers should not be able to disclaim liability for contributory copyright infringement if they provide routine access to a service provider that has been held to be facilitating piracy.

4. Remove the DMCA safe harbors for online and Internet service providers that provide routine access to online file-sharing service providers that have not registered an agent for service of process for copyright infringement actions and for which the Copyright Office has received at least 50 DMCA take-down notices. After a reasonable notice period, allowing adequate time for the online file-sharing service provider to register an agent for service of process for copyright infringement actions, service providers should not be able to disclaim liability for contributory copyright infringement if they provide routine access to an online file-sharing service provider that has been the subject of numerous DMCA take-down notices.
5. Ensure that new legislative action can keep pace with developing technologies. Although online file sharing services are one of today's major piracy threats, illegal streaming is rapidly gaining in popularity and can pull in audio books as easily as it does music, movies, and TV programs. Any congressional solution needs to take the pace of technological change into account, or we'll all be back here in twelve months.

Conclusion

Facilitating online piracy has become far too widespread, because it's far too profitable and easy. To protect and re-establish our markets for creative work, we need bold, immediate reform of our copyright law.

Statement of the U.S. Chamber of Commerce on: "Targeting Websites Dedicated to Stealing American Intellectual Property"

TO: United States Senate Committee on the Judiciary
DATE: Wednesday, February 16, 2011

The U.S. Chamber of Commerce is the world's largest business federation, representing the interests of more than 3 million businesses of all sizes, sectors, and regions, as well as state and local chambers and industry associations.

More than 96 percent of the Chamber's members are small businesses with 100 or fewer employees, 70 percent of which have 10 or fewer employees. Yet, virtually all of the nation's largest companies arc also active members. We are particularly cognizant of the problems of smaller businesses, as well as issues facing the business community at large.

Besides representing a cross-section of the American business community in terms of number of employees, the Chamber represents a wide management spectrum by type of business and location. Each major classification of American business — manufacturing, retailing, services, construction, wholesaling, and finance - is represented. Also, the Chamber has substantial membership in all 50 states.

The Chamber's international reach is substantial as well. It believes that global interdependence provides an opportunity, not a threat. In addition to the U.S. Chamber of Commerce's 1 15 American Chambers of Commerce abroad, an increasing number of members arc engaged in the export and import of both goods and services and have ongoing investment activities. The Chamber favors strengthened international competitiveness and opposes artificial U.S. and foreign barriers to international business.

Positions on national issues are developed by a cross-section of Chamber members serving on committees, subcommittees, and task forces. More than 1,000 business people participate in this process.

TESTIMONY OF STEVEN M. TEPP

Senior Director, Internet Counterfeiting and Piracy Global Intellectual Property Center
U.S. Chamber of Commerce

Chairman Leahy, Ranking Member Grassley, Senator Hatch, and Members of the Judiciary Committee; thank you for your recognition of the problems created by rogue websites and the need for Congressional action in this area. The U.S. Chamber of Commerce appreciates your leadership and the opportunity to submit this testimony.

Recognizing the fundamental importance of intellectual property (IP) protection and enforcement to the future of American business, the Chamber's Global Intellectual Property Center (GIPC) leads a world-wide effort to protect innovation and creativity by promoting strong intellectual property rights and norms around the world. We recognize that these rights are vital to creating jobs, saving lives, advancing global economic growth, and generating breakthrough solutions to global challenges. The G1PC represents a broad spectrum of intellectual property-intensive companies and leads the over 700-member Coalition Against Counterfeiting and Piracy, the largest business coalition dedicated to fighting the growing threat of counterfeiting and piracy to the economy, jobs, and consumer health and safety.

The Harm from Rogue Websites

Rogue websites, those dedicated to counterfeiting and piracy, arc harming our economy, depriving America of jobs and tax revenues, and exposing American consumers to harm and fraud. By perverting the incredible power of the Internet as a tool of legitimate distribution of goods and services, the operators of rogue sites have expanded their criminal enterprises to heretofore unthinkable levels. The existence of online piracy and counterfeiting is well-known, as is its massive scope. But several recent studies lay out the problem in numbers that have stunned even the most jaded.

Last month, the brand protection firm MarkMonitor issued an independent report that identified the traffic to a sample of Internet sites that are notorious for selling counterfeit goods and distributing infringing content. The MarkMonitor report concluded that:

- 26 of the sites selling counterfeit prescription drugs (separate from the counterfeit physical goods analysis) generated 51 million visits per year.
- The combined traffic to 48 of the sites selling counterfeit physical goods is more than 87 million visits per year.
- 43 sites that were classified as sources of 'digital piracy' generated over 146 million visits per day, representing more than 53 billion visits per year -- nearly 9 visits for every human being on earth.

But that was just the beginning. Just a few weeks later, a study released by Envisional found that nearly one fourth of all online traffic worldwide is infringing IP. In the course of this study, Envisional closely examined numerous sites. Among them was a peer-to-peer site that was comprised of 98.8% copyrighted content. And an analysis of the most popular content on the OpenBitTorrent tracker, found that only one file in 10,000 was non-copyrighted.

The harm from this appalling amount of IP infringement was made clear in the stark findings of a report by Frontier Economics just two weeks ago--counterfeiting and piracy have stolen 2.5 MILLION jobs from the G20 economies. The report also found that:

- The global economic value of counterfeiting and piracy is $650 billion a year.
- International trade in counterfeit and pirated products is $360 billion a year.
- Counterfeiting and piracy robbed G20 governments of $125 billion a year in lost tax revenue and other benefits.

At a time when America's need for jobs is so great and our Federal budget deficit is such a major concern, the case for improving IP protection and enforcement has never been clearer: Effectively combatting piracy and counterfeiting saves jobs and promotes legitimate commerce.

Enhanced Legal Tools are Needed to Cut Off Rogue Sites

The enforcement of IP online is complicated by many practical factors, but it is not impossible and it would be a grievous error not to try.

One of the great recent success stories has been the actions of U.S. Immigration and Customs Enforcement (ICE) under Director John Morton. Over the past ten months, and most recently on Monday, ICE, in cooperation with the Justice Department and the IPR Center, has seized the domain names of more than a hundred websites involved in counterfeiting and piracy. While some of these sites have resurfaced with different domain names, many of them have not. This represents a clear win for American consumers, job-seekers, innovators, and creators. The Chamber congratulates the Administration on these past and ongoing efforts and offers its sincere thanks to Director Morton and all the others who have contributed to Operation in Our Sites.

As we know, the Internet knows no national boundaries, but the jurisdictional limits of Federal enforcement agencies do. Thus, the effectiveness of seizing rogue site domain names is limited for addressing counterfeiting and piracy on wholly foreign websites. And many rogue sites are based outside the United States.

Ideally, all countries would improve their IP protection and enforcement systems with the result that the number and reach of rogue sites globally would diminish substantially. Until such time, the United States has a duty to protect its market and consumers from these sites.

Mr. Chairman, your introduction of S. 3804 and its unanimous approval by this Committee was a critical step forward. As we all know, that legislation would have authorized the Justice Department to bring suits in Federal court. Those courts could, upon sufficient proof that a site met the definition of "dedicated to infringement," issue orders to the strategic partners in the tight against online theft - Internet service providers, payment processors, and advertisers – to stop linking and/or doing business with the site. The fundamental premise of that bill, cutting rogue sites off from the American market to protect consumers against fraud and harm and to stem the flow of American dollars to counterfeiters and pirates, is a creative approach to the foreign rogue site problem. As you know, the Chamber enthusiastically supported S. 3804.

Yesterday, we delivered to all Members of Congress a letter on behalf of over 80 businesses and professional and labor organizations, representing over 1.5 million jobs and workers, and over 50 trade associations representing thousands of companies. The signatories to this letter represent a uniquely broad and deep coalition, featuring companies of all sizes and across many sectors of our economy, the entirety of which recognizes the threat and harm of rogue sites and the need for Congressional action. The letter is appended to this testimony.

Mr. Chairman, the Chamber looks forward to working with you, Senator Hatch, Chairman Smith and Ranking Member Conyers on the House Judiciary Committee to help craft the best possible legislation and to enact that legislation this year.

Thank you.

Rogue Sites are Stealing American Jobs and Hurting Consumers!

February 15, 2011

To the Members of the United States Congress:

The more than 80 undersigned businesses and professional and labor organizations, representing over 1.5 million jobs and workers, and more than 50 trade associations representing thousands of companies, urge you to make it a priority to enact legislation that will provide the government with enhanced tools to disrupt the efforts of those who use websites to make illegal profits by stealing the intellectual property (IP) of America's innovative and creative industries. These rogue websites are part of a network of counterfeiting and piracy that a recent study found cost 2.5 million jobs in the G20 economies.

Many of these sites pose as legitimate businesses, luring consumers with sophisticated and well-designed websites. But, in reality, the counterfeit and pirated products these sites distribute are often of poor quality, harmful, and promote fraud. Further, consumers put themselves at risk of identity theft and malicious computer viruses by visiting these sites. Legislation to disrupt these efforts is a major step to make the Internet safer and protect consumers from the dangers of buying in the online marketplace.

IP-intensive industries are a cornerstone of the U.S. economy, employing more than 19 million people and accounting for 60 percent of our exports. Rampant online counterfeiting and piracy presents a clear and present threat that we must do more to address. A recent study examined about 100 rogue websites and found that these sites attracted more than 53 billion visits per year. That averages about 9 visits for every man, woman, and child on Earth. It is not surprising that global sales of counterfeit goods via the Internet from illegitimate retailers reached $135 billion in 2010. What's more, as a consequence of global and U.S.-based piracy of copyright products, the U.S. economy lost $58.0 billion in total output in 2007.

The United States cannot and should not tolerate this criminal activity. As the studies show, the theft of American IP is the theft of American jobs. And rogue sites negatively impact the health and safety of American citizens. Last year, Senator Patrick Leahy and Senator Orrin Latch introduced S. 3804 to combat rogue sites and were joined by an impressively bipartisan group of 18 additional Senators. That bill was approved by the Senate Judiciary Committee 19-0. In the House of Representatives, Judiciary Committee Chairman Lamar Smith and Ranking Member John Conyers have long recognized the harm from IP theft and supported efforts to address it. We urge you to support bicameral introduction and enactment of carefully balanced rogue sites legislation this year and look forward to working with you in support of that goal.

Sincerely,

1-800-PetMeds
ABRO Industries, Inc.
Acushnet Company
Adidas America
Advanced Medical Technology Association (AdvaMcd)
Alliance of Automobile Manufacturers
Alliance of Visual Artists (AVA)
American Association of Independent Music
American Board of Internal Medicine
American Federation of Musicians
American Made Alliance
American Society of Composers, Authors and Publishers (ASCAP)
American Society of Media Photographers
Anti-Counterfeiting and Piracy Initiative (ACAPI)
Association of American Publishers (AAP)
Association of Equipment Manufacturers
Association of Test Publishers

Autodesk, Inc.
Beachbody, LLC
Beam Global Spirits & Wine
Bose Corporation
Brigid Collins Family Support Center
Broadcast Music, Inc. (BMt)
Cascade Designs Incorporated
Cengage Learning
CFA institute
Chanel USA
Christian Music Publishers Association
Coalition Against Counterfeiting and Piracy (CACP)
Commercial Photographers International
Copyright Clearance Center (CCC)
Country Music Association
Electronic Components Industry Association (ECIA)
Entertainment Software Association (ESA)
ERAI, Inc.
The Estée Lauder Companies
Evidence Photographers International Council
Ex Officio
Exxel Outdoors
Far Bank Enterprises
Fashion Business Incorporated
Federation of State Boards of Physical Therapy
Ford Motor Company
Fortune Brands, Inc.
Gemvision Corporation
Gospel Music Association
Governors America Corp.
Graduate Management Admission Council
Greeting Card Association (GCA)
Harry Fox Agency
Hastings Entertainment, Inc.

IDS Publishing
Imaging Supplies Coalition (ISC)
Independent Distributors of Electronics Association (IDEA)
Innate-gear
Intellectual Property Owners Association
International Trademark Association (INTA)
John Wiley & Sons. Inc.
Kekepana International Services
Leatherman Tool Group, Inc.
Lexmark International, Inc.
LVMH Moot Hennessy Louis Vuitton
Major League Baseball
Marmot
The McGraw-Hill Companies
Messy Face Designs, Inc.
MicroRam Electronics, Inc.
Monster Cable Products, Inc.
Motion Picture Association of America, Inc. (MPAA)
Music Managers Forum-U.S,
Nashville Songwriters Association International
National Association of Broadcasters
National Association of Manufacturers
National Association of Recording Merchandisers
National Association of Theatre Owners (NATO)
National Basketball Association (NBA)
National Football League (NFL)
National Music Publishers' Association (NMPA)
NBCUniversal
Nervous Tattoo Inc., dba Ed Hardy
New Era Cap Co Inc
News Corporation
Nike, Inc.
Nintendo of America Inc.
Oakley, Inc.

OpSec Security, Inc.
Outdoor Industry Association
Outdoor Power Equipment Institute (OPEI)
Outdoor Research, Inc.
Pacific Component Xchange, Inc.
Pearson Education
Personal Care Products Council
Petzl America
Picture Archive Council of America (PACA)
PINO
Professional Photographers of America
Quality Float Works, Inc.
The Recording Academy (National Academy of Recording Arts and Sciences)
Recording Industry Association of America (RIAA)
Reebok International Ltd.
Reed Elsevier Inc.
Romance Writers of America (RWA)
Rosetta Stone Inc.
Schneider Electric
SESAC, Inc.
SG Industries, toe.
Small Business & Entrepreneurship Council
SMT Corp.
Society of Sport & Event Photographers
Software & Information Industry Association (SILA)
Sony Music Entertainment
Sony Pictures Entertainment
SoundExchange
Specialty Equipment Market Association (SEMA)
Sports Rights Owners Coalition
Spyder Active Sports, Inc.
Stock Artist Alliance
Stuart Weitzman Holdings, LLC

Student Photographic Society
SunRise Solar Inc.
Taylor Made Golf Company, Inc.
Tiffany & Co.
The Timberland Company
Time Warner lite.
Toshiba America Business Solutions, Inc.
U.S. Chamber of Commerce
Ultimate Fighting Championship
Underwriters Laboratories Inc.
Universal Music Group
Viacom
Vibram USA, Inc
W.R. Case & Sons Cutlery Co.
The Walt Disney Company
Warner Music Group
Winestem Company
Xerox Corporation
Zippo Manufacturing Company.

The Honorable Ron Wyden

Statement for the Record
U.S. Senate Committee on the Judiciary Hearing:
"Targeting Websites Dedicated to Stealing American Intellectual Property"
February 16, 2011

I would like to take this opportunity to commend Chairman Leahy and Ranking Member Grassley for holding this important hearing and giving others and me the opportunity to share our views about this important subject. I recognize that my stand on this issue has put me in conflict with many of my friends on the committee, so I particularly appreciate the opportunity to have my concerns heard.

Make no mistake, I share the committee's goal of fighting counterfeiting and protecting our creative industries and the good paying jobs they support. The Internet has unquestionably created new opportunities to traffic in counterfeit and illegal goods. The fact that the law has not always kept pace with technology may make it easier for bad actors to exploit new opportunities. Congress is right to want to go after those who are "stealing American intellectual property." However, in writing laws to target the bad actors, Congress cannot afford to forget that the primary uses of the Internet are activities protected by the First Amendment, not civil or criminal violations.

In fact, it is impossible to overestimate the positive effect that the Internet is having on our world. It is revolutionizing the way people engage with one another, the way commerce is conducted and the way citizens organize. Without the Internet, would the democratic uprisings in Tunisia and Egypt have been successful? Would there be real questions about the sustainability of the autocratic regimes in the Middle East and around the world? The Internet has advanced the cause of free speech in ways that I believe would make the nation's Founding Fathers proud. It has made lies harder to sustain, information harder to repress and injustice harder to ignore. Furthermore, I do not believe that twenty years ago, any of us could have foreseen the way in which the Internet has transformed the modern day marketplace for new customers, new audiences and new ideas and I doubt anyone can predict exactly where it will take us twenty years from now.

Yes, the Internet needs reasonable laws and bad actors need to be pursued, but the freedoms of billions of individual Internet users cannot be sacrificed in the interest of easing that pursuit. The decisions we make to police the Internet today will also govern how this relatively new medium will continue to develop and shape our world. I objected to last year's Combating Online Infringement of Copyrights Act not because it might reduce the Internet's ability to facilitate infringement, but because I believe it went about it in a way that would also reduce the Internet's ability to promote democracy, commerce and free speech. We can strike a better balance.

The challenge before us is to develop means to bring bad actors to justice without impinging on the First Amendment and threatening the important architecture and commercial significance of the Internet. Important things to consider:

1. Don't be hasty. Good public policy is not made on the back of a galloping horse. While both Congress and law enforcement are understandably eager to go after bad actors, both must be mindful of the precedents that they are setting in the U.S. and around the world. The law is best applied when the government's assertions can be challenged before its actions are approved.
2. Avoid collateral damage. Granting law enforcement broad authority to censor online content has a chilling effect on free speech. Narrowly focus law enforcement's authority on those who are deliberately breaking the law or infringing on others' property rights for commercial gain.
3. Preserve Fair Use and secondary liability protections. These safeguards are fundamental to Internet commerce and explain why American companies have been so successful in the global marketplace. The network effect is such a powerful driver of commerce on the Internet that any restriction on links and referrals is a serious barrier to economic activity.
4. Be mindful of how remedies can threaten and shape the integrity or architecture of the Internet. Decisions made today can have lasting results.
5. Avoid taking actions that will empower foreign regimes to censor the Internet. The United States has led the world in promoting free speech; our example cannot be allowed to give authoritarian regimes any excuse to go backwards.
6. Recognize the difference between copyright infringement and counterfeits. A one-size-fits-all approach towards trademarks and copyright may not be appropriate.

There is no question that the introduction and development of the Internet is applying pressure to companies of all shapes and sizes to innovate and bring their business into the 21st century. Change is hard and some industries and governments will undoubtedly try to protect what they have by looking for an "Internet Kill Switch." Let us keep that in mind as we steam, drive, fly, or click ahead. Our efforts should be to protect copyrights, not outdated business models.

This is also not the first time that, the content industry has raised concerns about a new technology's threat to their business models. The introduction of recorded music, the photocopier, the VCR, the audio cassette all brought predictions of doom and gloom. Not too long ago, Senator Pete Wilson called his colleagues to join him in fighting the use of Digital Audio Tapes, which he said were "sapping the very life out of the American music industry."

The challenge of adapting to a new technology is one that American entrepreneurs in this country have always succeeded in overcoming. Now, in the digital age, businesses are again faced with a new test. And while Congress should help industries confront these challenges, I have little doubt that we can find a solution that does not jeopardize speech, innovation and an evolving economy.

TESTIMONY OF DENISE YEE, VISA INC.

Visa Inc. welcomes the opportunity to provide its input on targeting websites dedicated to stealing American intellectual property, the challenges of protecting intellectual property online, and proposed legislation for addressing "rogue" websites.

Visa fully appreciates the value of intellectual property. The "VISA" trademark itself is one of our company's most valuable assets, and we expend millions of dollars protecting and enforcing the "VISA" trademark each year.

To promote growth in e-commerce, to protect the Visa brand and because it is the right thing to do, Visa goes beyond any legal requirements to prevent the use of its payment system for illegal electronic commerce transactions. Visa's policy is unequivocal and clear: its system should not be used for illegal transactions. Our rules further state that "[p]articipants in the Visa system agree to take appropriate measures to prevent the Visa system from being used for or associated with illegal activities." The integrity of the Visa brand is critical to the success of the system. The system works because of consumer confidence in its security and reliability. Accordingly, we are committed to ridding our system of merchants that engage in illegal transactions, including transactions involving the sale of counterfeit and copyright infringing goods.

We do, however, recognize that there are some challenges to eliminating had faith infringing merchants from our system. These include chasing merchants who hide in the shadows of the Internet under multiple shell companies, reconciling differences in copyright law in different jurisdictions, an id balancing the competing interests of multiple stakeholders.

Nevertheless, Visa voluntarily and willingly assists intellectual property owners in combating infringement on the Internet, and Visa has spent several years developing and refining its procedures to do so. We believe our current procedures strike a proper balance between taking swift action against clear instances of illegal conduct, and protecting interests of participants in the Visa system when issues of illegality are reasonably disputed.

In this testimony, Visa will provide a brief overview of its operations and structure. It will then discuss the concerns and challenges we face when helping to protect third party intellectual property in the digital environment. We will describe the efforts Visa undertook to prevent the use of its payment system by the Russian website AlloIMP3.com, and the liability and legal costs it and its partner bank incurred as a result. We will also discuss *Perfect 10 v. Visa International Service Association,* where a publisher of an adult magazine sued Visa for copyright infringement, and the Ninth Circuit held that Visa and other payment systems were not secondarily liable for the use of their networks to purchase infringing material from websites. Despite the decision in *Perfect 10* underscoring that Visa is under no legal obligation to take action, Visa does so, because it does not condone illegal activity in its system. Therefore, the testimony will then discuss Visa's current policy for responding to complaints by intellectual property owners concerning websites selling infringing material, and the best practices developed by payment system industry players to address this issue. Next, we will discuss possible unintended consequences to legislative action. And finally, the testimony will provide Visa's views on the Combating Online Infringement and Counterfeiting Act (COICA), including its general support for what this legislation is intended to accomplish.

I. The Visa Network

Visa Inc. is a global company headquartered in San Francisco, California. The company's operating regions include: Asia-Pacific; Canada; Central and Eastern Europe, Middle East and Africa; Latin America and the Caribbean; and USA. Visa Europe is a separate entity that is an exclusive licensee of Visa Inc.'s trademarks and technology in the European region.[68]

Visa operates a global electronic payments network and facilitates global commerce through the transfer of value and information among financial institutions, merchants, consumers, businesses and government entities in more than 200 countries and territories worldwide.

Visa provides its financial institution clients with a broad range of platforms for consumer credit, debit, prepaid and commercial payments. Our network and payment platforms deliver significant value to our clients and their customers in terms of greater efficiency, security, convenience and global reach. We do not issue payment cards, set cardholder fees or interest rates, or sign up merchants to accept Visa cards. These services are

[68] Visa Europe is owned and operated by more than 4,000 European member banks and was incorporated in July 2004. In October 2007, Visa Europe became independent of global Visa Inc., with an exclusive, irrevocable and perpetual license in Europe.

managed by our network of more than 15,700 financial institution clients worldwide.

The typical Visa transaction has four parties:

1. The Merchant is any entity a store, restaurant, online retailer, hotel or airline— that accepts Visa as payment.
2. The Acquirer is a financial institution that enables merchants to accept Visa payments and ensures that the merchant gets paid for each transaction. Acquirers conduct due diligence on potential merchants, accept merchant applications and enter into contract with merchants. Visa generally has no direct contractual relationship with the merchants.
3. The Issuer is a financial institution that provides Visa-branded cards or other Visa-branded payment products to consumers and businesses. When a Visa-branded credit card is used for a transaction, the issuer "lends" the consumer the funds to complete the transaction. When a Visa-branded debit or prepaid card is used for a transaction, the funds are automatically withdrawn from the consumer's account and transferred to the Acquirer.
4. The Account Holder is any consumer or business using a Visa card or other Visa-branded payment product to make purchases.

Visa provides the network that enables these four parties to conduct transactions worldwide within seconds.

In 2010, Visa processed more than S5 trillion worth of transactions comprised of more than 70 billion transactions. The 1.8 billion cards issued by our 15,700 financial institution clients are accepted at millions of merchant outlets and over one million ATMs worldwide.

Maintaining the integrity of the Visa brand in the online environment is a priority for the company, and is demonstrated by Visa's voluntary involvement in this area. For years, our team has worked cooperatively with law enforcement in the United States and around the world. Visa takes special steps in eases of criminal activity and activity that threatens health and safety. For example, Visa voluntarily searches the Internet for merchants selling or advertising child pornography or illegally distributing controlled substances and expels them from our system as soon as they are discovered. Visa works cooperatively with law enforcement, other payment processors and the National Center for Missing and Exploited Children in the Financial Coalition against Child Pornography to share information and take collaborative steps against merchants that sell child pornography.

Visa works with the Secret Service, the Federal Bureau of Investigation, the Federal Trade Commission, and State Attorneys General to assist their efforts to stop fraud, identity theft, and data breaches. We work with the Department of Justice and State Attorneys General to respond to their concerns about illegal online tobacco sales. In response to the Unlawful Internet Gambling Enforcement Act (UIGEA), Visa devised a coding and blocking scheme that prevents U.S. cardholders from engaging in illegal Internet gambling. And most recently, Visa has joined the Center for Safe Internet Pharmacies (CSIP) to combat illegal distribution and counterfeit pharmaceuticals online.

II. Challenges to Protecting Intellectual Property in the Digital Environment

A Payment System's Perspective

The task of preventing the Visa system from being used by merchants to process payments for counterfeit and copyright infringing products is extremely challenging.

First, the Visa system (or any payment system) cannot determine on its own whether a particular transaction involves payment for a counterfeit or copyright infringing product. The billions of payments that Visa processes each year cannot be screened to identify whether an underlying transaction involves the sale of counterfeit and infringing products or not. Instead, we rely on intellectual property owners to notify Visa that a particular merchant may be selling counterfeit and infringing products on the Internet and identify those infringing websites before Visa is able to take any action.

Second, when Visa is alerted to a merchant that may be involved in selling counterfeit and infringing goods, Visa must work through the Acquirer who signed up that entity to be a Visa accepting merchant, as Visa generally has no direct contractual relationship with the merchant. Moreover, nefarious merchants often cover their tracks by creating multiple shell companies under different names and enter into merchant agreements with numerous Acquirers under false pretenses. When an unlawful merchant is identified and expelled from the Visa system, it often changes its name and moves on to another Acquirer under another merchant account name. Ridding our system of these bad faith infringers is like a constant game of "Whack-a-Mole".

Moreover, there are limitations to payment systems' enforcement of third party intellectual property because Visa does not have authority to adjudicate genuine legal disputes between intellectual property owners and merchants. If Visa is forced to make an enforcement decision with which the intellectual property owner or the merchant disagrees, Visa may find itself sued in the jurisdiction of the intellectual property owner or the merchant. In fact, when Visa voluntarily assisted intellectual property owners in a case alleging illegal downloads of music, this assistance proved costly for Visa and the Acquirer.

A. AllofMP3.com

In 2006, Visa received a documented complaint by copyright owners in the recording industry that the AllofMP3.com website based in Russia was allowing downloads of music without authorization. At its own cost, Visa engaged outside legal counsel in Russia to provide an opinion of legality on the matter. Counsel concluded that under Russian law and the law in the vast majority of the jurisdictions in which the merchant's consumers were located (many of whom were located in the United States and the United Kingdom), the merchant's transactions were illegal. In September 2006, after providing appropriate notice to AllofMP3.com, the Russian Acquirer responsible for entering into the merchant contract with

AllofMP3.com stopped processing Visa transactions for the website. When the merchant began routing transactions through an affiliated site called Alltunes, the Russian Acquirer terminated Visa acceptance from that site as well.

The merchant owner of both affiliated sites subsequently sued the Russian Acquirer in a Russian court. Visa intervened in the case as a third party in support of the Acquirer. In June 2007, the Russian court found in favor of the merchant, concluding that by terminating payment processing, the Russian Acquirer was in breach of its contract with the merchant. The court ordered the Acquirer and Visa to resume providing payment processing services to the merchant. The court dismissed the Acquirer's claim that the merchant was acting illegally and in violation of Visa rules. The court found that Visa did not have the authority to determine copyright infringement in Russia; only a Russian court could do this. While some record companies brought a separate copyright infringement action in Russia against the merchant that court had not yet rendered a judgment as of June 2007, when the first court found that the Russian Acquirer had breached its contract with the merchant.

Subsequently, in August 2007, the second court ruled against the record companies in the separate copyright infringement action. Surprisingly, that court held that AllotMP3.com and similar downloading music sites were *legal* in Russia. Even though the copyright owners claimed they had not given permission to the merchant to sell copies of their music, a Russian collective management organization had the right to license use of the sound recordings. The court determined that AlloiMP3.com and its affiliates were in compliance with Russian law to the extent that they paid for rights from this organization.

These court cases created a serious challenge for Visa. Visa had received a fully documented complaint alleging copyright infringement from the copyright owners and an opinion of local counsel that the webs tcs infringed the recording industry's copyrights. The Russian Acquirer and Visa (as a third party intervener) had defended vigorously in court at their own expense. Nonetheless, the Russian courts disagreed with Visa and the copyright owners; they found that there was no infringement and ordered the Russian Acquirer to resume payment processing. Visa had no choice but to allow the Russian Acquirer to resume payment processing for the merchant's domestic transactions.

Visa learned important and costly lessons from this case. First, that there are limitations on private sector enforcement of intellectual property disputes. Visa rules simply cannot override a country's laws, and any attempt by Visa to do so may result in conflicting legal obligations. Intellectual property law (including copyright law) is extremely complex. There are genuine disputes regarding what constitutes infringement and the outcome of such disputes may not he predictable in many cases, particularly when the laws vary from country to country or when we do not have access to all of the relevant evidence. As a payment processor, Visa is not in a position to resolve disputes over allegedly infringing sales, particularly involving cross-border transactions. If Visa takes a position on the dispute and a court later determines that Visa was incorrect, Visa exposes itself to potential claims. Ultimately, resolving these issues requires government-to-government discussions that harmonize local legal structures and lead to predictable and consistent judicial decisions. It is only within these harmonized legal structures that private enforcement efforts can fully succeed.

Second, we recognized that as technology was moving faster and faster, we had to articulate a clear global e-commerce policy for cross-border transactions that accounted for differences in local laws. Accordingly, in 2007, Visa adopted the following global policy: "a transaction must be legal in both the Cardholder's jurisdiction and the Merchant's jurisdiction." This policy is still in effect today.

B. Intellectual Property Owner Attacks Visa in Perfect 10 v. Visa

Despite Visa's voluntary efforts to assist intellectual property owners in combating infringement on the Internet, and although the payment systems are far removed from the infringing activity itself, one intellectual property owner sought to have Visa held liable for secondary infringement based on a merchant's use of the Visa system to process payments for allegedly infringing photographs. In *Perfect 10 v. Visa International*

Service Association, 494 F.3d 788 (9th Cir. 2007), the U.S. Court of Appeals for the Ninth Circuit held that payment systems do not bear secondary copyright liability for the use of their networks by websites selling infringing material. Because *Perfect 10* defines the scope of payments systems' legal liability for third party infringement, it merits attention.

Perfect 10 is a publisher of adult magazines and websites. Perfect 10 believed that operators of other websites had, without authorization, copied images from the Perfect 10 website and then displayed the copied images on their websites. Rather than file suit against the website operators, Perfect 10 initiated a series of suits against a variety of intermediaries, including web hosts, search engines, and payment systems, for facilitating the infringement. The courts rejected Perfect 10's claims.[69]

In its action against Visa, MasterCard, and other providers of payment services, Perfect 10 claimed that by providing payment services to websites selling images that infringed Perfect 10's copyrights, the payment systems were secondarily liable for copyright infringement.[70] The district court granted the payment systems' motion to dismiss Perfect 10's complaint. On appeal, the Ninth Circuit found that Visa and the other defendants were not liable for either contributory infringement or vicarious liability.

Consistent with the Ninth Circuit's finding in *Perfect 10,* Visa continues to believe strongly that payment systems should not be secondarily liable for copyright or trademark infringement committed by merchants, especially in a four-party payment system where the network typically has no contractual relationship with the merchant, and the know-your-merchant duty resides with the Acquirer. Extending liability to payment systems for infringing acts of merchants would shift legal responsibility to parties far removed from the infringing activity that do not have the ability to discover or prevent the infringement. The rights-holders are in the best position to enforce their intellectual property rights, and the

---

[69] See also Perfect 10 v. CCBill, 488 F.3d 1102 (9th Cir. 2007); Perfect 10 v. Amazon.com, 508 F.3d 1146 (9th Cir. 2007).

[70] Perfect 10 also brought claims for trademark infringement and state law claims for false advertising and unfair competition. Perfect 10 lost on these claims as well.

merchants involved in the infringing conduct arc the culpable parties. Payment providers should not be held legally responsible for infringement committed by third parties. Imposing liability on payment providers may discourage Acquirers from signing up innocent, small business merchants in the future. And imposing liability on intermediaries (for instance, shipping companies like the United States Postal Service) may unduly hinder international c-commerce.

III. Joining the Fight to Curb Intellectual Property Infringements

A. Visa's Current Policy

Despite the costly lesson suffered in *A11011/1P3.com,* and the favorable decision finding no secondary liability in *Perfect 10,* Visa continues to believe it is necessary to provide voluntary assistance to rights holders to combat intellectual property infringement on the Internet. We still have deep concerns about cross-border disputes, secondary liability, and the unintended consequences of Visa's efforts to help combat infringement. Foreign courts continue to decline to impose liability on foreign websites considered by U.S. rights-holders to facilitate infringement.[71]

Nevertheless, Visa is committed to protecting the integrity and trust in our payment brand worldwide. As an intellectual property owner who continually plays cat and mouse with phishing sites determined to tarnish our brand, Visa empathizes with other intellectual property owners. It is time consuming, expensive and frustrating to try to stop infringing conduct on the Internet, where the wrongdoers can conceal their identities and make enforcement difficult through the operation of redundant websites on multiple mirrored servers in different locations throughout the world. However, the best course of action is for intellectual property rights

---

[71] For example, Rojadirecta, Rapidshare, and Baidu.

owners, payment providers, and others involved in international commerce to work together to try to stop infringement.

After adopting the cross-border rule in 2007 that the Visa system can only be used to process transactions that are legal in both the cardholder's jurisdiction and the merchant outlet's jurisdiction, Visa formalized procedures to facilitate the enforcement of this rule. Visa has continually reviewed refined and enhanced these procedures resulting in its current anti-counterfeit and piracy policy which is free to the intellectual property owner and made available entirely at Visa's cost. The current policy can be divided into five steps:

1. Report (by intellectual property owner): At no cost, the intellectual property owner may report instances of merchants selling counterfeit or infringing products to Visa at its dedicated c-mail inbox, Inquiries(irvisa.com, attaching any relevant cease and desist letters notifying the merchant of the infringement and a list of the intellectual property owner's rights.
2. Identify: Visa incurs the expense of conducting a test transaction and identifies the Acquirer who has signed up the merchant n the Visa system.
3. Investigate: Visa instructs the Acquirer to conduct an investigation into its merchant's business activities including the alleged infringement.
4. Report (by Acquirer): Visa requests the Acquirer's response within five business days of receiving the inquiry from Visa, including the Acquirer's investigation report into its merchant's business activities.
5. Comply or Terminate: Absent any written documentation proving the legitimacy of the merchant's activity, the Acquirer must require its merchant to comply with Visa rules (namely, ceasing the sale of the infringing goods) or terminate the merchant. If the transaction is clearly illegal and the Acquirer does not take action, Visa can take further enforcement action against the Acquirer.

As mentioned above, Visa Europe operates as a separate entity. Accordingly, if the Acquirer is located in Europe, Visa Europe (which generally has consistent policies with Visa Inc.) has the responsibility for ensuring that the European Acquirer and its merchant are in compliance with Visa rules.

When the Acquirer investigates the merchant's activities, Visa's procedures build in an opportunity for the merchant to prove their lawfulness by providing us with written proof disproving any infringement. In the majority of cases, we believe that it will he clear to the Acquirer and Visa whether the merchant has met its burden. In a minority of cases, however, Visa anticipates that a further inquiry will be warranted to ensure fairness to all parties. For instance, shades of grey in intellectual property law (particularly in copyright), the sale of gray market goods (genuine goods sold in different jurisdictions or through different distribution channels from those authorized by the intellectual property owner), differing opinions among multiple jurisdictions, or the intellectual property owner's dissatisfaction with an Acquirer's conclusion may require further discussion and the intellectual property owner's full involvement. Under these circumstances, if an intellectual property owner continues to allege that a merchant is infringing its rights after completion of Steps I through 5, Visa will work with the intellectual property owner to determine whether a further demand should be made on the Acquirer. If there is a lack of clarity as to whether infringement exists in the relevant jurisdiction, and if undue risk will be shifted to Visa were we to decide in favor of the intellectual property owner, Visa may request indemnity from the intellectual property owner if further steps arc taken by Visa or the Acquirer to force the termination of Visa acceptance by the merchant.

Visa has taken other steps to address the problem of online infringement. We believe that educating Acquirers about the sale of counterfeit and infringing goods is of utmost importance. This past October, Visa circulated a global communication to all Acquirers that specifically highlighted the issue with the sale of counterfeit and infringing goods. Moreover, we are in the process of building a dedicated webpage for intellectual property owners to learn about our policy and report violations. The webpage will go live today and is located at Visa.com/ReportBrandAbusc.

B. Payment Industry's Rest Practices

Visa is not the only payment system that offers voluntary procedures for combating intellectual property infringement. Visa has worked with American Express, Discover, MasterCard and PayPal to develop "Best Practices to Address Copyright Infringement and the Sale of Counterfeit Products on the Internet" for the International Trademark Association (INTA) and developed "Best Practices to Address Copyright Infringement and the Sale of Counterfeit Products on the Internet," at the request of the Intellectual Property Enforcement Coordinator (IPEC), Victoria Espinel. These best practices are consistent with Visa's current policies and demonstrate the payment industry's commitment to work with intellectual property owners to prevent the distribution of sale of counterfeit and infringing products on the Internet.

C. Intellectual Property Owners Must Identify Infringements

Visa believes its voluntary procedures are effective. On the occasions when intellectual property owners provided Visa with documented evidence of websites that were suspected of engaging in illegal activity and accepting Visa as a form of payment, Visa promptly took action under our procedures to address these concerns. Within days of notification, the applicable Acquirers began investigating these websites and, as necessary, terminated payment services to these websites or brought their merchant into compliance. However, few intellectual property owners have availed themselves of Visa's procedures. In the last six months, Visa has received only 30 inquiries. Other payment systems have shared similar experiences. Intellectual property owners have not explained their reluctance to report instances of online infringements to us.

It is imperative to the process that intellectual property owners alert Visa to instances of infringement in the system. Visa is not well positioned to identify counterfeit and copyright infringing material on the Internet. Nor is Visa informed of this activity by anyone else. In many instances, consumers know they are purchasing discounted but infringing products and, therefore, do not complain to Visa about this illegal activity — unlike in cases of fraud, where a consumer will complain and seek a credit for the transaction. Accordingly, Visa must be alerted to cases of online infringement by the intellectual property owners if we are to help expel this illegal activity from our system.

D. Coordinated Enforcement Necessary to Make an Impact

Visa is committed to expelling merchants from the system who are profiting from illegal activities. But, the payment systems can only do so much to disrupt this activity. Because of strong consumer demand for discounted digital content and designer labels, consumers don't report their infringing purchases. And, we cannot permanently eliminate the problem when unlawful merchants hide behind multiple shell companies and enter into contracts with multiple Acquirers under false pretenses. We think a more effective long-term solution would involve government-to-government discussions that harmonize local legal structures, sustained international cooperation among law enforcement agencies, and collaborative action among intellectual property owners, payment processors, website hosting companies, domain name registries and registrars, ad networks, search engines and others involved in international commerce on the Internet. Unless there is a coordinated attack at every layer, the United States cannot be successful in combating online infringement.

IV. Unintended Consequences to Legislative Action

We appreciate the Committee's interest in exploring legal mechanisms to combat rogue websites (particularly websites hosted on foreign servers), in addition to the payment systems' existing voluntary procedures. However, imposing a regulatory framework on top of the existing voluntary procedures may have some unintended negative consequences:

- The extraterritorial application of U.S. law may invite retaliation by other countries' governments. If U.S. law effectively makes payment systems instruments of U.S. intellectual property enforcement actions against foreign websites, foreign governments may well do the same. European countries, for example, believe that many U.S. companies infringe European laws concerning geographical indicators. Under European law, only wineries in the Champagne region of France can call sparkling wine "champagne," and only cheese manufacturers in the Parma region of Italy can use the name "parmesan cheese."

  European countries could require payment systems to stop processing transactions for U.S. merchant websites that sell products that violate European laws concerning geographical indicators. Similarly, repressive governments could force payment systems to stop doing business with legitimate U.S. merchants that sell books critical of their regimes to residents of their countries.
- Legislation might create an unrealistic expectation that payment systems can permanently eliminate online infringement. However, similar to the "Whack-a-Mole" scenario with domain name registrations, merchants engaged in illegal activity often have accounts with multiple financial institutions under several different shell company names. As soon as one Acquirer stops providing payment services to the merchant, the merchant starts using another account under a different name with a different Acquirer. As noted above, there are over 15,700 financial institutions in the Visa network alone, and other payment processing alternatives to the Visa system. This provides the unscrupulous merchant with many alternatives to stay in business, notwithstanding Visa's best efforts. The payment systems should not be perceived as an effective substitute for concerted international cooperation among law enforcement agencies against commercial infringers.
- Placing legal obligations on payment systems to cease providing payment services to infringing websites may increase the likelihood of payment systems being subject to conflicting legal

obligations. Visa has contractual obligations to Acquirers, which in turn have contractual obligations to provide services to merchants that operate websites. If the payment system or Acquirer was legally obligated to cease processing transactions between the website and its customers, the merchant might be inclined to sue the payment system or Acquirer in the country where the website is hosted, and where that activity might be considered legal. In the absence of a finding that the website violates that jurisdiction's laws, foreign courts could very well rule that the payment system or Acquirer breached its contractual obligation to provide payments services to the website operator as they did in AlloP4P3.com. Visa's voluntary process provides us with the flexibility to manage our risk appropriately and respond to issues on a case by case basis.

- Legislation that obligates payment systems to prevent certain transactions could have the long-term effect of eroding *Peiket* 10 v. *Visa.* A private right of action would exacerbate this corrosive effect. Courts could interpret such a private right of action as an indication that payments systems should be secondarily liable for copyright and trademark infringement and result in the reversal of decades of judicial decisions defining the contours of secondary liability. Extending liability to payment systems for infringing acts of merchants would shift legal responsibility to parties far removed from the infringing activity. To protect themselves, Acquirers may become more reluctant to sign innocent, small business merchants, which may unduly hinder international c-commerce.

V. Combating Online Infringement and Counterfeiting Act

Last Congress, Chairman Leahy and other members of the Judiciary Committee introduced the Combating Online Infringement and Counterfeiting Act (COICA), S. 3804. COICA empowers the Department of Justice to pursue *in rein* actions against domain names associated with websites "dedicated to infringing activities." Once the court determines that the website is dedicated to infringing activities, if the domain name has a foreign registry and registrar, the Department of Justice can serve the court's order on a financial transaction provider (FTP). The FTP then would have to take measures designed to "prevent or prohibit its service from completing payment transactions between its customers located within the United States and the Internet site using the domain name....

Visa is supportive of COICA's objectives -- namely, targeting and expelling websites dedicated to infringing activities. Further, we believe that our own voluntary procedures have the same objective and that COICA and Visa's procedures are complementary.

Last Congress, we suggested that the Committee consider a few technical changes to COICA and appreciate the Committee's willingness to address some of those concerns in the bill reported out of the Committee in November, 2010. In particular, the changes to the savings clause and the required actions by FTPs decrease the likelihood of COICA having unintended consequences on payment systems and exposing Visa to conflicting legal obligations. If COICA is reintroduced in substantially the same form, there are some technical concerns that we feel still need to be addressed, and are hopeful we can find common ground.

- An FTP should be permitted to authorize the continued use of its trademark on foreign sites in accordance with its contractual obligations. COICA requires an FTP "to cause notice to be provided to an Internet site using the domain name set forth in the order that the site is not authorized to use the trademark of the financial transaction provider." FTPs would expect that the website would no longer be accessible from the U.S. pursuant to the DNS server operator's obligations under COICA. However, the merchant's website would still be accessible to foreign consumers. In cases where a foreign merchant sufficiently demonstrates that its business is legal in its country of operation, we request the subsection be flexible to permit the continued use of the FTP's logo on the merchant website. Indeed, contracts between Acquirers and merchants allow for merchants to display an FTP's logo if the merchant is engaged in legal activity in its jurisdiction. The subsection as written would create conflicting legal obligations for FTPs and would require Acquirers to breach their contracts with merchants outside of the U.S.

- A financial transaction provider (FTP) should not he required to modify its systems to comply with an order issued under COCIA. COICA provides that an operator of a domain name system server shall not be required "to modify its network or other facilities to comply with" an order under this section. This provision clarifies that a DNS server operator's obligation to "take technically feasible and reasonable steps" does not include the modification of its network or facilities. FTPs would like the same protection. An FTP is required to take "reasonable measures" to prevent its service from completing certain payment transactions. We would request that the provision make clear that "reasonable measures" do not include an FTP modifying its service or systems. This clarification is particularly necessary in light of the language provided for DNS server operators.

With the two technical amendments we propose above, Visa would be supportive of COICA as currently structured.

VI. Conclusion

Visa prohibits the use of its network for the online purchase of counterfeit and copyright infringing goods. To promote growth in e-commerce, to protect the Visa brand and because it is the right thing to do, Visa goes far beyond any legal requirement to prevent the use of its payment system to sell infringing material.

Visa works with Acquirers and intellectual property owners to ensure that rogue merchants are expelled from the system. Visa offers a simple, fair and expeditious procedure to address intellectual property owner's complaints about merchants engaged in the sale of counterfeit and copyright infringing products. We think payment systems' voluntary efforts can help to disrupt online infringement, but are not well positioned to identify online infringement, nor eliminate the problem completely. Visa continues to believe that cooperation among governments (including harmonization of intellectual property laws), law enforcement agencies, intellectual property owners, payment systems and others involved in international electronic commerce is the only way to respond effectively to the constantly changing tactics of these rogue merchants.

We understand the Committee's interest in exploring legal mechanisms to combat rogue websites in addition to the payment systems' existing voluntary procedures. Imposing a regulatory framework on top of the existing voluntary procedures may have some unintended negative consequences, and some additional risk to the payment systems. Nonetheless, Visa is supportive of COICA's objectives and believes that COICA and Visa's procedures are complementary.

Visa is committed to continuing to work with the Committee to protect American intellectual property and to help fight this global menace.

February 16, 2011

INDEX

A

B

C

D

J

L

M

N

O

P

R

S

T

U

V

W

Y